Advances in Distributed Computing and Intelligent Data Analytics

nova
science publishers
www.novapublishers.com

Advances in Distributed Computing and Intelligent Data Analytics

Industry 4.0 and Intelligent Business Analytics for Healthcare
M. Niranjanamurthy, PhD, Shruti Nagpal, PhD,
Soumi Dutta, PhD, Vinod Kumar Shukla, PhD
2022. ISBN: 978-1-68507-602-3 (Hardcover)
2022. ISBN: 978-1-68507-718-1 (eBook)

More information about this series can be found at
https://novapublishers.com/product-category/series/advances-in-distributed-computing-and-intelligent-data-analytics-edited-series/

Basetty Mallikarjuna,
Niranjanamurthy M,
Sheng-Lung Peng and Amulya MP
Editors

Blockchain Technology Based Big Data for Healthcare

Concept and Paradigm

nova
science publishers

www.novapublishers.com

Library of Congress Cataloging-in-Publication Data

ISBN: 978-1-68507-968-0

Published by Nova Science Publishers, Inc. † New York

Contents

Preface

Blockchain is an open-source technology that offers an alternative to the traditional intermediary for transfers of the crypto-currency Bitcoin. The term "Blockchain Technology" is familiar to everyone because of its current trend. This book discusses concepts of existing research on Blockchain and big data. The book would provide its readers with state-of-the-art in Blockchain based on big data for healthcare. The book will include all the prerequisite methodologies so that new researchers and practitioners will find it very useful.

Chapter 1 deals with the evolution of Blockchain technology with big data in health care and its fundamental characteristics. Blockchain technology is one of the most recent breakthroughs and creative improvements that is now playing a significant role in the professional world. The world continues to be revolutionised and changed by Blockchain technology. It's a set of blocks that protect data and bring people together, no matter how far apart they are. Blockchain technology's rapid development has opened up a plethora of new application possibilities, including healthcare.

Chapter 2 reveals the algorithms of Blockchain technology with big data, multi-dimensional, data transmission, challenges, and scenarios in healthcare. Algorithms of Blockchain technology can process the distributed ledger that everyone can access but it is not controlled by a central authority that may be utilized to decrease time when logging transactions between parties, remove costs associated with middlemen, and reduce chances of fraud and manipulation. Individuals and corporations may work with confidence and transparency owing to this technology.

Chapter 3 reports the architectural framework of Blockchain technology with big data in healthcare, smart contract, and distributed ledger for healthcare informatics. This chapter present some of the leading business framework for implementing Blockchain solutions. This chapter examines and proposes a solution for managing and sharing individual health information among institutions. The solution increases clinical efficiency and explore when the information are shared with investigators. Blockchain technology is proposed as a solution for providers, hospitals, clinics, insurers and patients. The data would belong in the whole process to the individual or the patient.

Chapter 4 depicts the healthcare data management and remote monitoring using big data analytics and Blockchain technology, Blockchain powered EHR in the pharmaceutical industry. In this chapter, data management and remote monitoring of the healthcare data by using big data analytics and Blockchain technology is discussed. It deals with big data analytics and how Blockchain amalgamation is done to implement Blockchain in healthcare systems. Blockchain validates the integrity of the healthcare data and any modification done is identified and gets registered. Big data analytics in healthcare makes the system more accurate that provides suggestion up to larger precessions.

Chapter 5 addresses on framework for approaching big data with Blockchain, big data algorithms, gathering data, data preparation, choosing a model and evaluation. This chapter provides a comprehensive survey of Blockchain-based big data applications, focusing on the most recent approaches, opportunities, and future directions. This chapter also deals with the overview of Blockchain and big data, followed by integration Blockchain with big data. It also followed by the Blockchain-based big data services, including collection of data, storage of data, and transmitting data securely.

Chapter 6 presents on big data with Blockchain support inpatient management and medical history management data advancement of deep learning and Blockchain technology in healthcare. This chapter also provides an in-depth assessment of the development of Blockchain-based healthcare technology and its applications, as well as the consequences of these developments. This inquiry calls attention to the unsolved research challenges in this rapidly developing field, and we go into further detail about them in this report. The potential of digital currency in the transformation of the healthcare sector is also demonstrated.

Chapter 7 delineates the Blockchain with big data and machine learning in healthcare. The important data received from sensors used for monitoring the health of a patient, is collected, cleaned, transformed, visualized and analyzed for the purpose of diagnosis. Machine learning models can be prepared for analyzing this data and making suitable decisions for prescribing medicines and then monitoring the progress of the patient's health. The visualization techniques so designed could provide an enhanced tool both for the patient and the doctor.

Chapter 8 narrates the research challenges, opportunities and future directions in applying big data technology in healthcare sector. Close by different innovations, big information is assuming a fundamental part in opening new entryways of conceivable outcomes. Clinical information is touchy and can cause extreme issues whenever controlled. Information science in medical care can secure this information and concentrate on numerous significant highlights to bring progressive changes. The new advancement of AI, picture handling, and information mining procedures are additionally accessible to discover examples and make representable visuals utilizing big data in medical services. The motivation behind this chapter was to sum up the highlights, applications, examination approaches, and difficulties of big data in medical services.

Acknowledgments

We thank our family and the following institutions: Galgotias University, Ramaiah Institute of Technology, National Taipei University of Business, and BGSIT/Adichunchanagiri University (ACU) for their continuous support and encouragement for completion of this book. We would also like to thank the authors of these chapters and our friends for their contributions to this book.

Introduction

Blockchain technology with big data can mitigate issues such as effective access of medical data system interoperability, patient agency, improved data quality and quantity for medical research. Blockchain has the mechanism to store information and big data is a decentralized ledger of transactions, where every network participant validates the transaction so that the data stored is immutable and cannot be forged.

Using Blockchain adds another data layer to the big data analytics process. Most importantly in health care, this book provides the big data layer in healthcare analysis. Blockchain-generated big data is secure, as it cannot be forged due to the network architecture in health care. Blockchain-based big data in health care is valuable, meaning it is structured, abundant and complete, making it a perfect source for further analysis. The big data's ledger in Blockchain transmits huge amounts of data transmissions such as audio data, video data, image data, and so on. It is a dynamic exchange of data in Blockchain technology and maintains the electronic health records (EHR). There are multiple big data analytic improvements stemming from this fact. For instance, peer to peer data transmission and fraud prevention, as Blockchain technology allows financial institutions to check every transaction in real-time.

This book provides the analysis of health care records, transmission of data and big data analytics with Blockchain. The banks and hospitals are able to identify risky or fraudulent transactions on the fly and prevent the fraud entirely. This book represents the evolution of Blockchain technology with big data in health care and its fundamental characteristics.

Chapter 1

Evolution of Blockchain Technology with Big Data in Health Care and Its Fundamental Characteristics

R. Srinivasan[*], R. Kavitha and M. Kavitha
Department of CSE, Vel Tech, Tamil Nadu, India

Abstract

Blockchain technology is one of the most recent breakthroughs and creative improvements that is now playing a significant role in the professional world. The world continues to be revolutionised and changed by Blockchain technology. It's a set of blocks that protect data and bring people together, no matter how far apart they are. Blockchain technology's rapid development has opened up a plethora of new application possibilities, including healthcare. This research examines emerging Blockchain-based healthcare technology and applications in depth. In this inquiry, we call attention to the open research concerns in this fast-growing topic and examine them in depth. We also show how Blockchain technology has the potential to revolutionise the healthcare sector. In this research, we review and propose a system for dealing with individual health information just as cross-institutional distribution. The purpose of this study is to analyze and propose a framework for handling individual wellbeing information just as cross-institutional exchange. In this paper, we analyze and propose a framework for taking care of individual wellbeing information just as cross-institutional information exchange. The arrangement will support clinical adequacy and examination when the information is imparted to scientists. The proposed framework arrangement, which depends on Blockchain innovation,

[*] Corresponding Author's Email: rsrinivasan@veltech.edu.in.

In: Blockchain Technology Based Big Data for Healthcare
Editors: Basetty Mallikarjuna, Niranjanamurthy M, Sheng-Lung Peng et al.
ISBN: 978-1-68507-968-0

incorporates suppliers, emergency clinics and centres, insurance agencies, and patients. At all times, the data would be owned by the individual or patient. In order to ensure data privacy and security, we advocate adopting a private Blockchain system in which all participants are known and trusted. We advocate adopting a private Blockchain system with known and trustworthy members to ensure data privacy and security. The basic features of Blockchain technology are discussed in the context of big data in health care in this research.

Keywords: Blockchain, big data, health care, data processing

Introduction

A collection of values for a specific variable, either qualitative or quantitative, is referred to as data (Rod Pierce, S., 2017). Quantitative data emphasises quantity and statistics, but qualitative data is more categorical and can be represented by categories like height, colour, race, gender, and so on. Every research project necessitates the use of data. Primary data sources have delivered stable and relatively small amounts of data over time when compared to secondary data sources. The worldwide web has made data collecting for research initiatives easier in recent years. Big data is defined as the massive volumes of data generated each second by numerous social media platforms, internet marketing platforms, and commercial websites, among others generally defines big data (X. Wu, Q., et al., 2014).

The type of data obtained, as well as the pre-processing procedures employed, has a significant role in achieving exceptional research results. Data is primarily gathered by direct observations and the performance of surveys (Mallikarjuna, B., et al., 2021a), and it is obtained through primary and secondary sources. Second, data can be gained through thorough market research or information generated electronically or downloaded from the internet.

Blockchain is a distributed database system that stores and manages transactions as a "open ledger." A block is a database record that contains information such as the transaction timestamp and a link to the preceding block. Anyone attempting to change information about the records in the future will be unable to do so (Mallikarjuna, B., et al., 2020a). The technology is also safe by design because the identical transaction is logged across numerous, dispersed database servers. With the foregoing in mind, Blockchain is immutable - information remains in the same state for the duration of the network.

Big data is a term that refers to vast amounts of structured and unstructured data that are challenging to handle using typical database or software procedures. The healthcare industry continuously generates data every time the chief doctor or an expert is consulted, whenever an emergency room (ER) is visited, or whenever several medical treatments are undergone.

Furthermore, with the proliferation of wearable and more IoT methods, the quantity of information created is rapidly increasing. Firstly are the insurance companies that pay healthcare providers based on the information provided by them (Mallikarjuna, B., et al., 2020a). This information arrives in a variety of formats. More than basic patient information, every physician gets a complete report of data regarding their patients, as we've all personally experienced. As patients, we are required to sign a piece of paper by our physicians. Recognising that we are aware of their privacy policies, yet they still aren't up to par when it comes to protecting our information. There has been a number of well-publicized breaches in which patients' personal information has been compromised. Theft or loss of information has occurred (J. Son, J., et al., 2017).

Why Security Is Important in Healthcare

Healthcare providers have been increasingly reliant on smart technologies since the advent of the Healthcare 4.0 era. Since technologies aid around the care and analysis of patient diseases, as well as the transmission, reception, and collection of patient data for health record management. The quality of information maintained upon Electronic Healthcare Record (EHR) techniques is important for a healthcare provider's success (W. Meng, E., et al., 2018).

As a result, data must always be secure and free of risks. But these prerequisites aren't encountered, the knowledges deployed cannot work well before remaining considered trustworthy. The size and complexity of healthcare records are growing as a result of big data, and they are even not optimal. Data have been frequently reproduced, uneven utilizing various characters / specifying standards, been offered across several healthcare systems and files. Health care record security is developing progressively crucial in order to protect data from protection violations and illegal action. But unauthorised clients obtain access to patient information, it can be sold or released to the market, exposing patients' sensitive information to anybody who has read. This data could contain things like addresses, phone numbers, complete names, and so on. In order to run a successful health care organisation, patients' data must be kept private (X. Wu, Q., et al., 2014).

Considering these issues, various countries have recommended or set up administrative rules intended for medical services frameworks to forestall cyber-threats, which assists with securing patient protection and confidence in the supplier patient relationship (Mallikarjuna, B., et al., 2020b). Most medical care frameworks as of now utilize brought together customer worker plans, in which a focal authority has full oversight over the framework. For this situation, an absence of protection or security shortcomings could cause framework breakdowns, permitting digital lawbreakers to gain admittance to patient information.

Blockchain and Big Data in Healthcare

Blockchain Technology

The interconnection of decentralised chunks of information is known as Blockchain. In order to accomplish decentralisation, the technology relies on peer-to-peer networks. Each peer writes an entry into a record in a Blockchain (Athmaja, M., et al., 2017). Figure 1 shows a sample Blockchain with blocks.

A block is made up of a number of records of in- formation from a single peer. Within the network, each peer has their own block. These blocks are linked together to form a chain of information-containing blocks (Bhuiyan, M., et al., 2017). Within these connected blocks, water flows freely. However, group must agree to entries published into a record by each peer within the network of users. Information is made freely available to all peers within a group or network using Blockchain technology. A number of protocols are used to determine whether or not the information should be updated or altered.

Three different technologies contribute to the technology's strength. Peer to Peer Networking, Public Key Cryptography, and the Blockchain Protocol are the three (Suthar, S R., et al., 2017).

The recommended system solution, which is based on Blockchain technology, includes providers, hospitals and clinics, insurance companies, and patients. At all times, the individual or patient would be the exclusive owner of the data. In the solution, we advocate adopting a private Blockchain system with known and trustworthy participants to ensure data privacy and security. Data privacy and security can be ensured by adopting a private Blockchain system with known and trustworthy users.

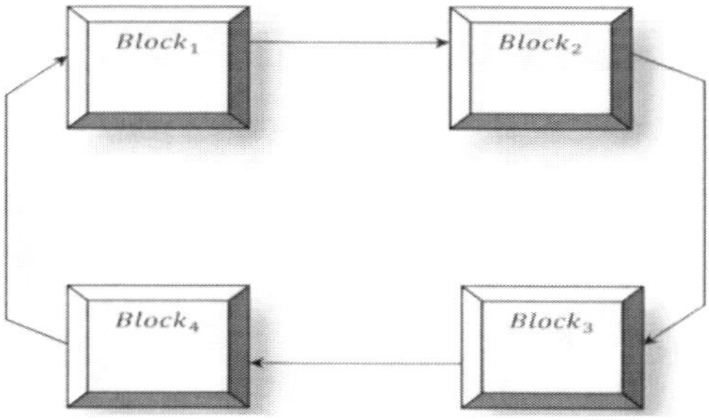

Figure 1. A sample Blockchain.

In the context of big data in health care, this article explores the underlying features of Blockchain technology.

The previous block's hash is also included. The main block without a reference to the past block is the beginning block, be validated, indicating that data has been tampered with. This tamper-proofing is what gives Blockchain data immutability, or the ability to never change data within a block (Mallikarjuna, B., et al., 2020b).

Big data refers to vast amounts of data that are challenging to manage with traditional software or web-based solutions, as the term implies. By 2020, Google will have collected 44 trillion gigabytes of data and will be processing 40,000 search queries each second. Every day, 3.46 million searches are made, totaling 1.2 trillion every year. There is currently more storage space, processing power, and analytical power available than ever before (Mallikarjuna, B., et al., 2020b).

Despite the fact that there are a number of different definitions for big data, Douglas Laney's is the most widely used. Laney emphasised that (big) data was growing in three dimensions: volume, velocity, and variety (the three "V's"). The 'large' component of big data refers to its size. Big data encompasses not only volume but also velocity and variety (Xiang, Li., & Yian-fang, Qi., 2012).

Patients can use Blockchain technology to restrict access to their medical data, such as granting specific researchers' temporary access to portions of their data. Patients can link to other hospitals using Blockchain technology and have their medical data collected automatically. Because of its transparency, it provides a secure method for storing and sending data (Athmaja, M., et al., 2017).

Medical record proprietorship and information exchange is another delicate topic. Medical records can be structured or unstructured and come in a variety of formats, including reports, pictures, videos, and data. They could be in an alternate configuration relying upon the framework utilized by a particular provider, which could cause similarity issues. All patient records are the doctors' property, and they have the right to keep them private and not share them with anybody else, even the patient. It is important to know that the data entered into the file has not been edited, erased, or otherwise destroyed.

A specialist's access to a patient's medical records may be required on occasion. Having quick and efficient access to such information could make the difference between life and death. Patient records ought to be predictable and accessible across institutions, and the patient should have control over who has access to them. In this paper, we review and study about Blockchain technology with big data in health care and its fundamental characteristics (Mallikarjuna, B., et al., 2021b).

The purpose of this paper is to study the evolution of Blockchain technology and its applications, and also the integration of Blockchain with big data in health care. Furthermore the different types of characteristics of Blockchain technology are examined. (Luo, E., et al., 2018).

Portable health applications, monitoring gadgets, sharing and putting away electronic medical records, medical preliminary information, and distributed storage of protection data are only a couple of the medical care applications conceivable on the Blockchain (Mallikarjuna, B., et al., 2021b).

Because anyone wishing to change a block after it has been added to the chain would have to rearrange the altered block as well as all following blocks, which would require an impossibly large amount of computational power, the Blockchain is stable.

Blockchain Architecture

Blockchain types:

- Node
- Consensus algorithm

- Block
- Header
- Transaction counter
- Transaction data

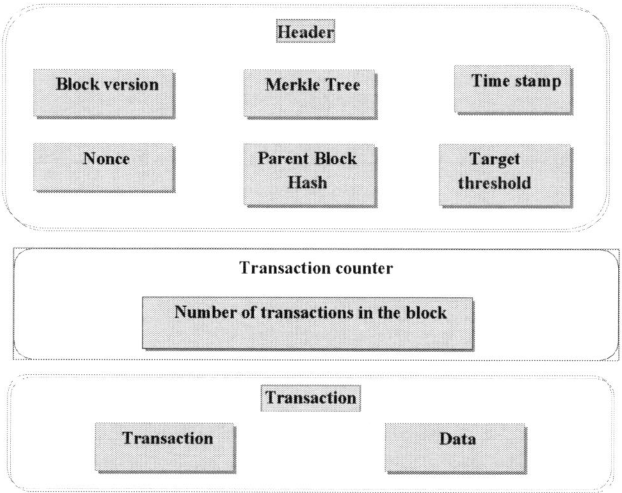

Figure 2. Blockchain architecture.

Blockchain Types

Blockchain is classified into three forms based on the operation: public Blockchain, private Blockchain, and consortium Blockchain. Both private and consortium Blockchain are employed at the organisational level. On the other hand, in the case of public Blockchain, security is claimed to be on the rise, while privacy is supposed to be on the decline (Mallikarjuna, B., 2022a).

Node

Node can also be referred to as a computer. It is claimed to be possessed by a Blockchain network participating organization. This is also referred to as a user. In Blockchains, the node acts as the central authority. The purpose of this network is to double-check transactions with other computers or nodes.

The node in the Blockchain framework serves as a link between the Blockchain technology and the user.

Consensus Algorithm

The agreement between the Blockchain and the user is often referred to as the consensus algorithm. It is used in the framework to give nodes or computers permission to make choices. Proof of work (PoW), proof of stake (PoS), and proof of burn (PoB) are some of the most well-known consensus algorithms.

Block

The transaction decision included in the current chain following successful consent is referred to as a block.

Header

The current block version in a block-chain network is referred to as block version. In addition to the predecessor block hash, the header also contains the successor blockhash. To change the block hash output, a nonce is used.

Transaction Counter

A transaction counter is used to represent the serial number of the current and previous blocks.

Transaction Data

This field's meaning, i.e., transaction data, changes depending on usability. It could be a Bitcoin transaction, records, user personal information, healthcare information, or something else (OMallikarjuna, B., 2020c).

Features of the Blockchain

There are several features from the Blockchain technologies.

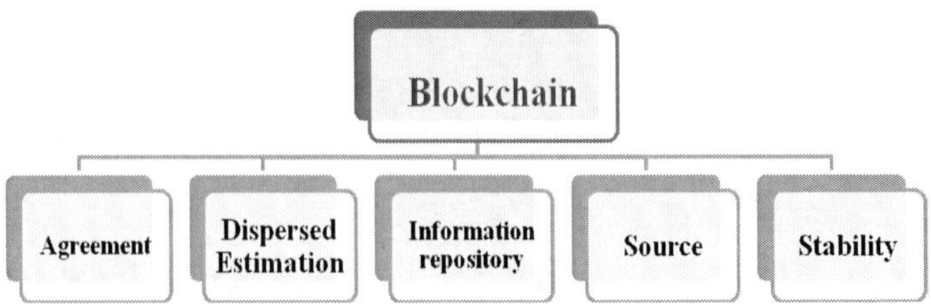

Figure 3. Blockchain features.

Agreement

The agreement is the first and most important characteristic of Blockchain. The term "agreement" defines the ability of all anonymous network users to agree on the network's rules and regulations. In addition, whether network members are obeying the laws and regulations is reviewed on a regular basis in the Blockchain architecture. The agreement in Blockchain is stated to be reached by a variety of methods, including the PoW algorithm or the PoS algorithm, among others. Crypto currency miners solve complex mathematical equations in order to implement the PoW algorithm. The block reward, a fraction of digital Bitcoin, was awarded to the competing crypto miner who solved these complicated calculations. The PoS algorithm, on the other hand, is deterministic in its validation. In this case, the more coins a crypto miner possesses, the more likely he or she is to be chosen to validate blocks and add to the Blockchain.

Dispersed Estimation

The dispersed estimation of Blockchain is the second key aspect. In the case of the Bitcoin Blockchain, any user that is running a full node will have an exact copy of the whole Blockchain. The replica is made up of all of the data from the Bitcoin Blockchain's transactions. The replica is made up of all of the data from the Bitcoin Blockchain's transactions. The node is supposed to be run in a separate manner after the download is completed and the transactions are processed. They are subsequently transferred across the network via various nodes. One of the most fundamental elements of the Blockchain's dispersed estimation is that there is no single node processing and distributing the data. Every node that makes up a block in the Blockchain, on the other hand, is considered to be executed independently.

Information Repository

The information repository is the third most important characteristic of Blockchain. The information repository refers to the data storage area in this case. For instance, on the Bitcoin Blockchain, the information repository refers to data relevant to Bitcoin transactions.

Source

In a pre-programmed manner, Blockchains verify source. The customer knows that the money deposited or the jewels kept in the locker are safe in the bank when they use traditional banking. Blockchain transactions, on the other hand, are completely traceable, documented, and recognizable without the need for third parties to attest to a specific action's completion.

Stability

Because of the reason that it is highly claimed to be steady, Blockchain transactions are said to be stable. As a result, once a transaction is recorded on the Blockchain, it cannot be modified. Even in the case of an incorrect record, the record cannot be erased because it is claimed to be noticeable. Furthermore, a new transaction is said to be generated in order to correct errors in previously recorded transactions. The erroneous record is then referred to by the produced transaction.

Shared Ledger

A ledger's reason for existing is to make an unchanging record of all exchanges that can be analyzed by anyone. The sole believable wellspring of data is the common record. Because of replication, every member has a duplicate of the record. The record can be set up so every client can just see the substance that they've been allowed to see.

Permission

It is possible to assign permissions to a Blockchain. With permission Blockchains, each user has a digital identity with policies that provide selective access to transaction information based on their permissions. This enables businesses to adhere to data protection standards such as HIPAA. In a counterparty exchange, for example, both parties approach the exchange's subtleties. A free substance can see that the exchange has occurred, yet it can't see the subtleties. Upon joining the organization, an examiner can be given a computerized declaration so they can see information exchanged. A digital certificate can be used to authenticate the users or party's identification, and the Blockchain network can be arranged to help out a certification authority that can check the certificate.

Consensus

A consensus method guarantees that the following square in the chain is the main genuine variant of reality, just as keeping other amazing gatherings from forking the chain and modifying with information. To set up whether an exchange is forever included into the Blockchain, agreement is required.

There are four consensus algorithms:

- Practical Byzantine Fault Tolerance
- Proof of Work
- Proof of Stake
- Delegated Proof of Stake

Smart Contracts

A smart contract is an agreement or set of decides that administers a business transaction and it is kept on the square chain and performed naturally as a component of the transaction. Take, for example, a pizza delivery firm that promises to bring our pizza in 30 minutes. If the delivery does not occur within 30 minutes, a smart system contract can be put up to provide a partial refund over the Blockchain. These types of contracts are particularly useful in situations when payments must be made by a given date, such as financial contracts, or for automatic reimbursements of travel insurance, such as when a flight is delayed for longer than the maximum allowable delay period.

The Various Types of Blockchain

While the Blockchain model was established for the bitcoin currency, various new and unforeseen businesses have begun to grasp Blockchain's potential. The limits imposed by the public bitcoin model used by bitcoin may not be required or in some ways hinder adoption in a variety of industries. There are various sorts of Blockchains that could be employed depending on the necessity and business model.

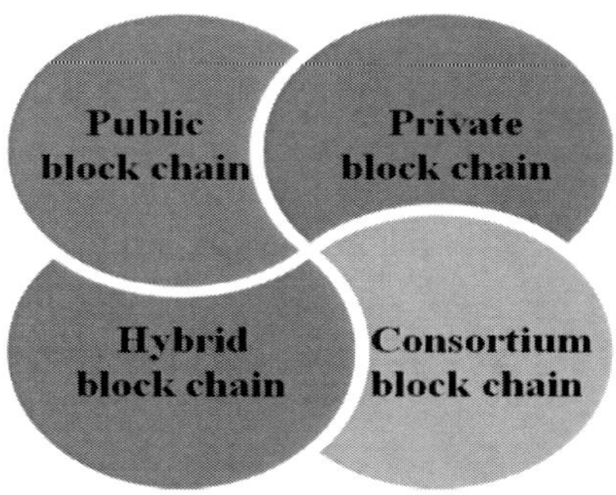

Figure 4. Types of Blockchain.

There are four main types of Blockchain:

- Public Blockchains
- Private Blockchains
- Hybrid Blockchain
- Consortium Blockchains

Public Blockchains

The public Blockchain is the first type of Blockchain technology. This is the place where Bitcoin and other digital forms of money like it were conceived, and where they assisted with advancing appropriated record innovation (DLT). As a result, there are no safety and straightforwardness issues that characterize centralization. DLT disperses information all through a shared organization as opposed to putting away it in a solitary area. Due to its decentralized nature, it requires some strategy for information validation. That approach is a consensus algorithm that allows Blockchain participants to agree on the present state of the ledger. Two common consensus approaches are proof of work (PoW) and proof of stake (PoS). Anyone with internet connectivity can join on to a Blockchain platform and become an authorised node, making public Blockchain non-restrictive and permission less. This user has access to current and historical records, as well as the ability to perform mining operations, which are sophisticated calculations required to verify transactions and add them to the ledger. On the network, no valid record or transaction may be modified, and because the source code is usually open source, anybody can verify the transactions, uncover errors, and offer fixes.

Private Blockchains

Private Blockchains, also known as managed Blockchains, are permissioned Blockchains that are administered by a single entity. The central authority in a private Blockchain decides who can be a node. In addition, the central authority does not always grant each node identical rights to execute functions. Because public access to private Blockchains is restricted, they are only partially decentralised. Ripple, a business-to-business virtual currency exchange network, and Hyperledger, an umbrella project for open-source Blockchain applications, are two instances of private Blockchains.

Hybrid Blockchains

Hybrid Blockchains are those that are managed by a single entity but have some oversight from the public Blockchain, which is necessary to conduct certain transaction validations. IBM Food Trust is an example of a hybrid Blockchain, which was created to improve efficiency across the whole food supply chain. This series will continue with a deeper look at IBM Food Trust.

Consortium Blockchains

A consortium Blockchain is a kind of hybrid between entirely private and completely public Blockchains. This is a hybrid system that does not have the same level of trust as a public chain or as high as the highly trusted entity paradigm of a private chain. A consortium platform offers some of the advantages of private Blockchains, such as anonymity and efficiency, without handing power over to a single business. A consortium platform offers some of the advantages of private Blockchains, such as anonymity and efficiency, without entrusting control to a single entity. A consortium is usually governed by a body that supervises it.

Advantages of Blockchain Technology

Blockchain technology is based on a decentralised network that stores data in tamper-proof formats. Existing transactions cannot be amended because Blockchain transactions can only be updated or added by creating new hash values. To grasp this, all features that distinguish the Blockchain from others must be described against the prospective usage of Blockchain technology:

- *Distributed ledger:* Transactions are added on the organization in an appropriated framework, which takes into account framework recuperation by eliminating a weak link or unified substance.

- *Consensus mechanism:* Just when all checked clients in the organization concur on the exchange's condition are exchanges refreshed.
- *Provenance:* On the Blockchain network, you can see the entire history of your data or asset.
- *Immutability:* Records on the network can't be changed or tampered with, therefore all data is safe and secure.
- *Finality:* On a Blockchain, once a transaction is committed, it cannot be changed or reversed.
- *Smart contract:* The programmes are produced on a Blockchain network, and they are executed by the computer and nodes in response to a triggered event. As a result, the programmes are performed automatically inside the time range.

Big Data

Big data is described as a large amount of structured, semi structured, or unstructured data acquired from several or a single source (Bhuiyan, M., et al., 2017). Big data is critical for drawing useful findings, generalisations, and inferences from research. Big data may be effectively mined to identify hidden patterns and gain deeper understanding about events, which is particularly important. The 4Vs (Volume, Variety, Velocity, and Veracity) are frequently used to describe big data (Kenneth, M., et al., 2011).

Volume

A large amount of data is collected on a daily basis from health, business, transportation, entertainment, and other key aspects of our lives. The magnitude of the data defines whether it is big data or not (Mallikarjuna, B., et al., 2022b).

Variety

Data is generated at the speed of light from various sources. These data from various sources are clearly of various categories. The variety qualities of big data are defined by the various sorts of data produced in the blink of an eye from various sources (Mallikarjuna, B., et al., 2022c).

Velocity

In the past, researchers had difficulty obtaining data for their studies. However, with contemporary technological improvements, data is being generated at an alarming rate these days through advertising sites, marketing sites, social networking platforms, and company websites, to name a few. The Velocity of Data refers to the rate at which data is added at a rapid rate. Given that data collecting is no longer as time-consuming as it was a few years ago; this function has proven to be quite beneficial to researchers (Michael, C., et al., 2016).

Veracity

This feature specifies what constitutes high-quality data. Making an analysis with high-quality data can help you draw appropriate conclusions. It's worth noting that all big data, whether organised, semi-structured, or unstructured, must be pre-processed before being used. This helps to clean up the gathered data by removing unclean, irrelevant, redundant, and noisy data. Data must be pre-processed in order to achieve correct findings for a certain system/model.

Peer to Peer Network

The potential of Blockchain Technology to authorise and decentralise is driven by Peer to Peer Technology. Peers come to an agreement and decide on specific data changes or amendments. Without the consent of others, no one peer can make changes to information (Suthar, S R., et al., 2017).

Public Key Cryptography (PuKC)

PuKC's participation in Blockchain technology ensures a safe digital identification. A digital signature with a strong sense of ownership and thus a secure digital identity might be established using the related private and public keys. A user who wishes to communicate sends a message to a peer along with their public key in public key cryptography. The receiving peer receives the message and decrypts and retrieves it using their private key (Bhuiyan, M., et al., 2017). This method of information security allows for a high level of authentication. Blockchain has a built-in feature. Blockchain's authorisation and authentication process has made it a force to be reckoned with in recent years.

Blockchain Protocol

This protocol sets the ground rules for how Blockchain works, such as broadcasting digitally signed information to all nodes/peers in a network at the same time. There is no single point of failure because the nodes involved agree on the information update and each node/block receives a copy of the new information. Decentralization/shared controls are the main aspect of Blockchain that ensures security and general efficacy of the system.

Healthcare and Big Data

When it comes to big data, there have been significant changes in healthcare over the last few years, as the amount of data collected has expanded. Furthermore, technological advancements have made it a lot simpler to secure and assess information from an assortment of sources, including protection suppliers, emergency clinics, labs, and doctors ‘workplaces. Doctors have generally depended on their judgment when settling on treatment choices, yet this has moved as of late to a more proof based methodology.

This new technique involves dissecting clinical information and putting together treatment suggestions with respect to the best data accessible. When it comes to the utilisation of big data, the healthcare industry has fallen behind other industries such as finance and retail.

In medical services, enormous information is being used to expect pestilences, fix sicknesses, work on personal satisfaction, and forestall avoidable passings. Fit piece, Samsung Gear Fit, and Jawbone are only a couple of the wearable gadgets that have as of late arrived at the market and permit us to keep tabs on our development.

When we consult with our primary care physician about an issue, we will be able to gradually impart this information, which he/she will be able to utilize as part of their diagnosis process. Specialists will actually want to offer treatment options dependent on information from different patients with practically identical infections, genetic variables, and way of life decisions as more information is gathered.

Huge information is at present held in storehouses inside different specialist's PC frameworks, emergency clinics, and centers. To utilize this information later on, it should be imparted to other people (Dash, S., et al., 2019).

Healthcare and Blockchain Technology

The utilization of Blockchain innovation in the medical services industry is going through an applied shift. It has altogether worked on the productivity, access control, specialized development, security assurance, and security of information the board tasks. The discoveries uncover that current requirements are for the most part associated with model execution, just as execution limitations and expenses.

Security and Privacy of Healthcare Data

A patient's clinical records belong to the doctor or the patient. Specialists contend that clinical records address their clinical feelings on a patient and subsequently are not the patient's property.

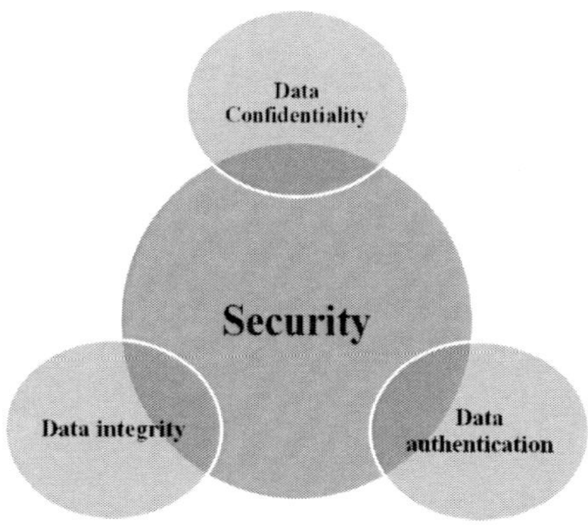

Figure 5. Conceptual diagram of security for Blockchain.

The record, then again, is about the patient, and the lab work is pivotal data about the patient; for what reason would it be a good idea for someone to else have it? Is it the specialist or the patient who possesses a patient's clinical record? Specialists contend that clinical records address their clinical sentiments on a patient and consequently are not the patient's property. Nonetheless, the record is about the patient, and the lab work is crucial data about the patient; why should it be owned by someone else?

Data confidentiality, data integrity, and data authentication are investigated as security challenges in Blockchain for big data management. The conceptual diagram of security considerations in Blockchain is shown in Figure 5.

Data Confidentiality

This is the process of concealing information. It is done with the goal of disguising information so that only the intended receivers can see the data or information that the source provides. Data secrecy is believed to be achieved using a variety of industry-standard data encryption technologies as well as key pair models.

Data Integrity

This is the process of guaranteeing that data sent from a source machine or user to a destination machine or user is invariable in every way. During the transfer of data from the source machine or user to the destination machine or user, the data can be paused and edited. Nowadays, data integrity is claimed to be achieved by the use of a fingerprinting technique, which allows the destination computer or user to verify that the data or information has not been tampered with.

Data Authentication

This is the process of ensuring that the data supplier is clearly the data provider. As a result, the data provider should be authenticated in such a way that the source machine or the sender pretending to be the source machine cannot deceive the system.

Every year, as a vast amount of data is generated, the amount of information stored in healthcare systems grows exponentially. All of this information has the potential to attract unwelcome attention. Cybercrime is a major social and political issue, with fresh breaches being found or publicised on a daily basis. The government, healthcare companies, and patients all bear significant financial and reputational expenses as a result of these breaches. Data security is a concern for both the corporate and public sectors.

Hyper Ledger Frameworks

The Hyper Ledger Framework is an open-source collective effort hosted by the Linux Foundation to enable cross-industry Blockchain solutions. Hyper ledger is a form of software that is stated to be used by everyone with the goal of constructing their own personalised Blockchain. The hyper ledger structure is depicted in metaphorical form in Figure 6.

Figure 6. Hyper ledger framework for healthcare industry.

Blockchain and Bitcoin Transactions

Bitcoin on the other hand is a cryptocurrency. As far as Bitcoin is concerned, it is a decentralised kind of digital currency that does not require the involvement of a third party or bank. Transactions are considered to be carried out between users without the involvement of third parties or intermediaries. The verification procedure is carried out using encryption and maintained in a public distributed ledger known as a Blockchain.

Blockchain-Based Healthcare Applications

The stakeholder layer, which includes parties who benefit from Blockchain-based healthcare applications such as business users, researchers, and patients, is at the top of the structure. Data sharing, processing, and management at this level are primarily concerned with maintaining security and privacy. Figure 7 depicts Blockchain-based healthcare applications.

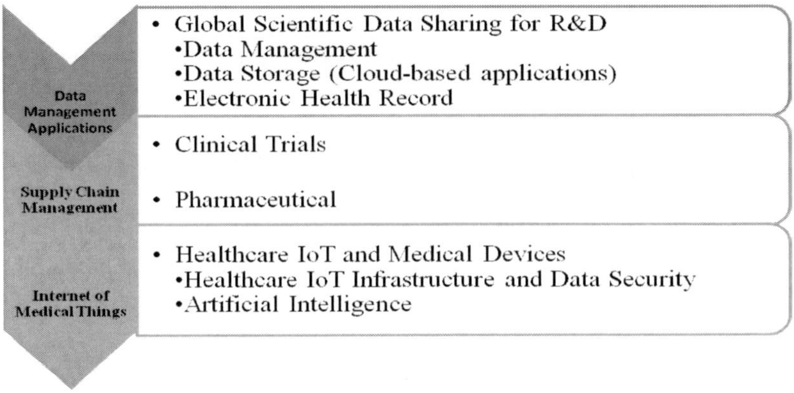

Figure 7. Blockchain-based healthcare applications.

Blockchain-Based Healthcare Management Applications

New options for health information the executives, just as understanding straightforwardness in getting to and sharing their wellbeing information, are opening up as electronic wellbeing related information, cloud medical services information stockpiling, and patient information security insurance strategies advance. Getting information, stockpiling, exchanges, and dealing with their consistent combination are significant to any information driven organization, especially in medical care, where Blockchain innovation can address these basic worries in a vigorous and successful way. Information sharing, information the executives, information stockpiling (e.g., cloud-based applications), and EHR are instances of Blockchain-based applications in this class, which are canvassed in more detail underneath.

- *Step 1:* Primary data is created when a patient interacts with their primary care physicians and subject matter experts. This data incorporates clinical history, present manifestations, and other physiological information.
- *Step 2:* Using the primary data acquired in the first step, an EHR is constructed for each patient. Other medical data, such as that

generated by nursing care, medical imaging, and prescription history, is also stored in the EHR.

- *Step 3:* Each patient has ownership of sensitive EHR, and only the owner of this property is granted personalised access control. Access to such sensitive information must be requested by parties, which is then approved by the EHR owner.
- *Steps 4, 5, and 6:* Database, Blockchain, and cloud storage are at the core of the entire process. Databases and cloud storage store records in a dispersed fashion, but a Blockchain ensures extreme privacy and customizable authentic user access.
- *Step-7:* Healthcare providers, such as ad hoc clinics, community care centres, and hospitals, are end users who seek to gain access to a secure and reliable care delivery system that is permitted by the owner. For example, your health record will be open and accessible on your phone, and authenticated through a distributed ledger such as Blockchain, which healthcare professionals will continue to contribute to over time.

Conclusion

Blockchain has become a key component of today's healthcare systems. It can lead to automated data collecting and verification processes, as well as correct and aggregated data from a variety of sources that is immutable, tamper-resistant, and safe, with a lower risk of cybercrime. It also allows distributed data, as well as system redundancy and failure tolerance. The present issues facing the health-care industry are highlighted in this study. This study examines and discusses recent research on big data analytics and Blockchain technology applications in various health issues, surveillance, and epidemic management using medical data. Medical data research is still in its infancy, and there are numerous hurdles to overcome. Because public health encompasses many dimensions of individual, environmental, and societal issues, big data storage, mining, analysis, and related research are required to adequately harness the intense patterns in vast data.

References

Athmaja, S., M. Hanumanthappa, and V. Kavitha (2017). A survey of machine learning algorithms for big data analytics. In *2017 International Conference on Innovations in Information, Embedded and Communication Systems* (ICIIECS), pages 1–4.

Bhuiyan, M., G. Wang, W. Tian, M. Rahman, and J. Wu (2017). Content-centric event-insensitive big data reduction in internet of things, *IEEE GLOBECOM* 2017, Singapore, December 4-8, 2017.

Bhuiyan, M., M. Zaman, G. Wang, T. Wang, and J. Wu (2017). Privacy-protected data collection in wireless medical sensor networks, *The 12th International Conference on Networking, Architect and Storage* (NAS 2017), August 7- 8, Shenzhen, China.

Cachin, C. Blockchains and consensus protocols: Snake oil warning (2017). In *2017 13th European Dependable Computing Conference* (EDCC), pages 1–2.

Crosby, Michael, Pradan Pattanayak, Sanjeev Verma, and Vignesh Kalyanaraman (2016). *Blockchain Technology: Beyond Bitcoin Applied Innovation*, 2:6–10.

Dash, S., Shakyawar, S. K., Sharma, M., Sandeep K. (2019) Big data in healthcare: Management, analysis and future prospects. *J. Big Data,* 6, 1–25.

Dimitrov, D. V. (2019). Blockchain applications for healthcare data management. *Healthc. Inform. Res.* 25, 51–56.

George Washington University Hirsh Health Law and Policy Program. Who owns medical records: 50 state comparison. (2015). *Health Information and the Law*. Aug. 20.

Hathaliya, J. J., Tanwar S., Tyagi S., Kumar N. (2019). Securing electronics healthcare records in healthcare 4.0: a biometric-based approach. *Comput Electric Eng,* 76:398–410.

Kenneth, M., D. Markwell, R. MacDonald, P. Szolovits, and I. Kohane (2011). Public standards and patients' control: how to keep electronic medical records accessible but private. *BMJ* 322, no. 7281: 283-287.

Luo, E., M. A. Bhuiyan, G. Wang, M. Rahman, J. Wu, and M. Atiquzzaman, Privacy Protector (2018). Privacy-protected patient data collection in IoT-based healthcare systems, *IEEE Communication Magazine* (COMMAG), 56(2): 163-168.

Mallikarjuna, B. (2020c). Feedback-based resource utilization for smart home automation in fog assistance IoT-Based cloud. *International Journal of Fog Computing* (IJFC), 3(1), 41-63.

Mallikarjuna, B., Addanke, S., & Anusha, D. J. (2022a). An improved deep learning algorithm for diabetes prediction. In *Handbook of Research on Advances in Data Analytics and Complex Communication Networks* (pp. 103-119). IGI Global.

Mallikarjuna, B., Addanke, S., & Sabharwal, M. (2022c). An improved model for house price/land price prediction using deep learning. In *Handbook of Research on Advances in Data Analytics and Complex Communication Networks* (pp. 76-87). IGI Global.

Mallikarjuna, B., Anusha, D. J., & Sabharwal, M. (2022b). An effective video surveillance system by using CNN for COVID-19. In *Handbook of Research on Advances in Data Analytics and Complex Communication Networks* (pp. 88-102). IGI Global.

Mallikarjuna, B., Kiranmayee, D., Saritha, V., & Krishna, P. V. (2021b, June). Development of efficient e-health records using IoT and Blockchain technology. In *ICC 2021-IEEE International Conference on Communications* (pp. 1-7). IEEE.

Mallikarjuna, B., Sathish, K., Krishna, P. V., & Viswanathan, R. (2020a). The effective SVM-based binary prediction of ground water table. *Evolutionary Intelligence*, 1-9.

Mallikarjuna, B., Shrivastava, G., & Sharma, M. (2021a). *Blockchain Technology: A DNN Token-Based Approach in Healthcare and COVID-19 to Generate Extracted Data.* Expert Systems, e12778.

Mallikarjuna, B., Viswanathan, R., & Naib, B. B. (2020b). Feedback-based gait identification using deep neural network classification. *Journal of Critical Reviews,* 7(4), 661-667.

Meng, W., E. Tischhauser, Q. Wang, Y. Wang, and J. Han (2018). When intrusion detection meets Blockchain technology: A review. *IEEE Access,* PP (99):1–1.

Pierce, Rod. What is data? (2018). *Math is fun*, Available at http://www.mathsisfun.com/data/data.html, 2017.

Rahman, F., M. Bhuiyan, and S. Ahamed (2018). A privacy preserving framework for RFID based healthcare systems, *Future Generation Computer Systems,* 72: 339-352.

Shae, Z., Tsai J.J. (2017). On the design of a Blockchain platform for clinical trial and Precision medicine. In: *2017 IEEE 37th International Conference on Distributed Computing Systems (ICDCS)*; p. 1972–80.

Son, J., J. Park, H. Oh, M. Bhuiyan, J. Hur, and K. Kang (2017). *Privacy-Preserving Electrocardiogram Monitoring for Intelligent Arrhythmia Detection, Sensors,* 17(6):1-22, 1360, doi:10.3390/s17061360.

Suthar, S. R., V. K. Dabhi, and H. B. Prajapati. Machine learning techniques in hadoop environment (2017): A survey. In *2017 Innovations in Power and Advanced Computing Technologies* (i-PACT), pages 1–8.

Tandon, A. Dhir, A., Islam, N., Mäntymäki (2020). M. Blockchain in healthcare: A systematic literature review, synthesizing framework and future research agenda. *Computer. Ind.,* 122, 103290.

Tanwar, Sudeep, Karan Parekh, Richard Evans (2020). Blockchain-based electronic healthcare record system for healthcare 4.0 applications, *Journal of Information Security and Applications*, pp 1-13.

Wang, T., M. A. Bhuiyan, G. Wang, M. Rahman, J. Wu, and J. Cao (2012). Big data reduction for Smart City's critical infrastructural health monitoring, *IEEE Communication Magazine (COMMAG)*, 56(3): 128 – 133.

Wst, Karl and Arthur Gervais. *Do you need a Blockchain?* (2017). Cryptology ePrint Archive, Report 2017/375, https: //eprint.iacr.org/2017/375.

Wu, X., X. Zhu, G. Q. Wu, and W. Ding (2014). Data mining with big data. *IEEE Transactions on Knowledge and Data Engineering,* 26(1):97–107.

Xiang-wei Li, and Qi Yian-fang (2012). A data pre-processing algorithm for classification model based on rough sets. *Physics Procedia*, 25:2025–2029.

Yoon, H.-J. Blockchain technology and healthcare (2019). *Health Inform. Res.,* 25, 59–60.

Chapter 2

Algorithms of Blockchain Technology with Big Data, Data Transmission, Challenges, and Scenarios in Healthcare

Himani Sharma* **and Basetty Mallikarjuna**
School of Computing Science and Engineering,
Galgotias University, Uttar Pradesh, India

Abstract

Blockchain Technology with big data is an emerging technology that can significantly enhance transaction security at banking, supply chain, and other transaction networks. It's multidimensional and data transmission, that Blockchain would produce $3.1 trillion in new company value by 2030. Algorithms of Blockchain technology can process the distributed ledger that everyone can access but it is not controlled by a central authority that may be utilised to decrease time when logging transactions between parties, remove costs associated with middlemen, and reduce chances of fraud and manipulation. Individuals and corporations may work with confidence and transparency owing to this technology. There are huge challenges in cryptographic currencies, such as Bitcoin and others, are among the most well-known applications in health care of Blockchain, although there are many others. Next major revolution in information technology is predicted to be fueled by Blockchain technology. Today, several Blockchain applications are widely accessible, with their own set of strengths for a particular application area. Readers will grasp the inner workings and uses of this revolutionary technology and its potential influence on all sectors of the corporate world and society.

* Corresponding Author's Email: himani.sharma2483@gmail.com.

In: Blockchain Technology Based Big Data for Healthcare
Editors: Basetty Mallikarjuna, Niranjanamurthy M, Sheng-Lung Peng et al.
ISBN: 978-1-68507-968-0

Keywords: Blockchain technology with big data, bitcoin, cryptographic currency, Blockchain applications in health care

Introduction

Bitcoin was the first application of Blockchain technology. It was a type of cryptocurrency created by Satoshi Nakamoto in order to provide a fast, affordable, and transparent peer-to-peer money transaction (Kim, S. K., et al., 2020). With the rapid advancement of the internet era, the future industrial revolution needed that data-driven enterprise architecture be improved in terms of privacy, including but not limited to decentralisation, persistence, anonymity, and auditability.

A Blockchain (Stavrou et al., 2018), which is made up of the words block and chain, is a continuously expanding list of computerised records within the shape of bundles, or pieces, that are connected and secured utilising cryptographic mechanisms. The Blockchain, too known as digitally recorded squares of information, may be a straight chain that's shielded and kept Lu, Y. (2019). Each square within the linear chain contains various pieces of data, such as a Bitcoin transaction. This Bitcoin exchange, on the other hand, is secured by cryptographically hashed technology that's time stamped. A hash of the going before square will be included in each modern square (Kumari, A., et al., 2020). These squares are requested chronologically, beginning with the primary square since the Blockchain's initiation and finishing with the foremost as of late created square (Lu, Y., 2019). It is rehashed until the arrangement has developed and is stable.

Simple Blockchain Algorithm

The chain of blocks in an advanced arrangement is alluded to as a Blockchain. It's also known as the decentralised record, which keeps track of all exchanges (Kumari, A., et al., 2020). A few analysts within the field of think about have as of now begun utilising the Blockchain to handle person characters (Kumari, A., et al., 2020). Be that as it may, various analysts have proposed a unused set of rules for managing with users' individual data within the setting of Blockchain (Mallikarjuna, B., et al., 2021a).

Each time a client buys, offers, or exchanges advanced money through a decentralised trade, an advanced record records the exchange in an scrambled arrangement that no one can decipher (Kumari, A., et al., 2020). The exchange put away in a computerised organisation is accepted to be secure against cybercriminals in this way, without the prerequisite for a third party. Figure 1 portrays an allegorical outline of Blockchain (Mallikarjuna, B., et al., 2021a).

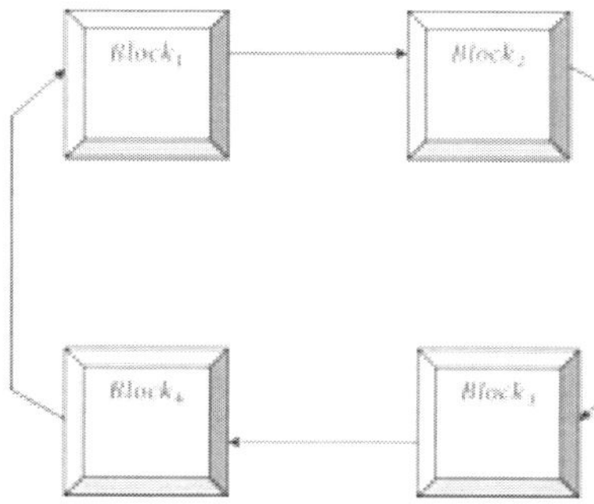

Figure 1. Simple Blockchain algorithm (Kumari, A., et al., 2020).

Four pieces are included, as shown in Figure 1, with each square connected to the others in a chain. Piece 1 is associated with piece 2, which is associated with piece 3, which is associated with piece 4, which is associated with square 1, building up a chain. The piece, in other words, is considered to be the holder of a square, as seen in this chart.

Each piece within the Bitcoin Blockchain is made up of information related to Bitcoin exchanges, Square Header, Piece Distinguishes, and Merkle Trees. The piece structure (Table 1.) (Kim et al., 2019) is portrayed in detail in this area. Figure 2 delineates and depicts a few of the frequently utilised expressions of Blockchain innovation including the creation of Blockchain engineering.

Table 1. Blockchain structure (Otoum, S., et al., 2021)

Block Structure Field	Description	Size
Block size	Size of block in bytes	
Block Header	Several fields comprises of block header and frequency of transactions	80 bytes in transaction counters and frequency 1-9 bytes
Transaction	Actual transactions recorded	Variable

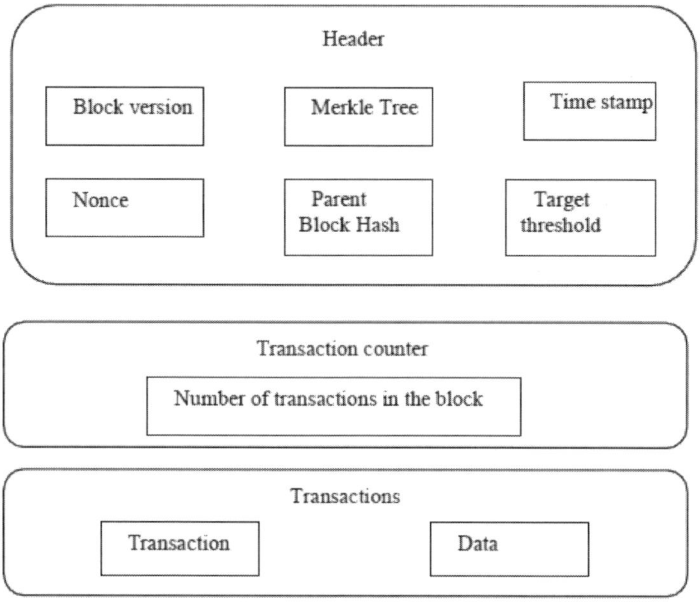

Figure 2. Blockchain architecture (Otoum, S., et al., 2021).

Components of Blockchain Architecture

Blockchain types:

- Node
- Consensus algorithm
- Block
- Header
- Transaction counter
- Transaction data

Blockchain Types

Blockchain is categorised into three kinds based on the operation: public Blockchain, private Blockchain, and consortium Blockchain. Both private and consortium Blockchain are utilised at the organisational level (Mallikarjuna,

B., et al., 2020a). In the case of public Blockchain, on the other hand, security is said to be on the rise, while privacy is believed to be on the fall.

Node

Node can then again be alluded to as a computer. An association that takes part within the Blockchain arrange is considered to have it (Miao, Y., et al., 2020). A client is another word for it. Any Blockchain's central proprietor remains the Node. Its work is to double-check exchanges with other nodes or computers. Within the Blockchain system, the Node acts as an interfacing point between the Blockchain innovation and the client.

Consensus Algorithm

The assertion between the Blockchain and the client is additionally known as the consensus calculation (Miao, Y., et al., 2020). It's within the system to endorse node or machine choices. Verification of work (PoW), confirmation of stake (PoS), confirmation of burn (PoB), and other well-known agreement calculations are cases (Miao, Y., et al., 2020).

Block

The exchange choice included within the current chain taking after fruitful assent is alluded to as a block (Mohsin, A. H., et al., 2021).

Header

The current block version in a block-chain organise is alluded to as block version In expansion to the forerunner block hash, the header moreover contains the successor block hash. To alter the block hash yield, a nonce is utilised (Mohsin, A. H., et al., 2021).

Transaction Counter

It is a serial number of the current and previous blocks (Mohsin, A. H., et al., 2021).

Transaction Data

This field's meaning, i.e., exchange information, changes depending on ease of use. It can be a Bitcoin exchange, records, client individual data, health-related data, and so on (Mohsin, A. H., et al., 2021).

Step by Step Procedure of Blockchain Algorithm

Step 1. Block Header

The block header is made of data with respect to that specific piece. A block header is used to recognize a certain piece inside a Blockchain (Mallikarjuna, B., et al., 2020a). It is hashed numerous times in order to produce verification of work for mining motivating forces. Since the Blockchain is made up of arrangements of various blocks that are utilised to hold data, square headers are utilised to recognize between the blocks.

The Blockchain arrange incorporates a distinct header. The block header hash is used to distinguish each block. The header's necessities incorporate an 80-byte string containing a 4-byte Bitcoin version number and a 32-byte earlier block hash (Nguyen, D. C., et al., 2020). It moreover highlights a 32-byte Merkle root that bolsters a 4-byte timestamp and a 4-byte nonce for cryptography diggers to utilise.

The block header moreover carries the taking after data in expansion to the above depiction:

- Cryptographic hash
- Mining competition
- Data structure to summarise the transactions in the block

Step 2. Block Identifiers

The cryptographic hash is used as the block identifier. The particular block is claimed to be recognized in a unique manner using these block IDs. Block header hash and block height are believed to be the two block IDs in most instances. When it comes to block header hashes, each node assesses the block's hash as soon as it is received from the network (Nguyen, D. C., et al., 2020). The second method to acquire a block is to know where it is in the Blockchain, which is known as the block height.

Step 3. Merkle Trees

The Merkle tree is the structure of exchanges in a single block of a Blockchain. The Merkle tree is a data structure that's used to summarise and confirm the dataset's keenness using cryptographic hashes (Mallikarjuna, B., et al., 2020b). It is used to record the outline of all exchanges in a block. It's moreover a way to summarise all of the exchanges in a block, guaranteeing a speedy preparation for deciding whether or not a transaction has a place in that block. An ordinary Blockchain Merkle tree appears in Figure 3 underneath.

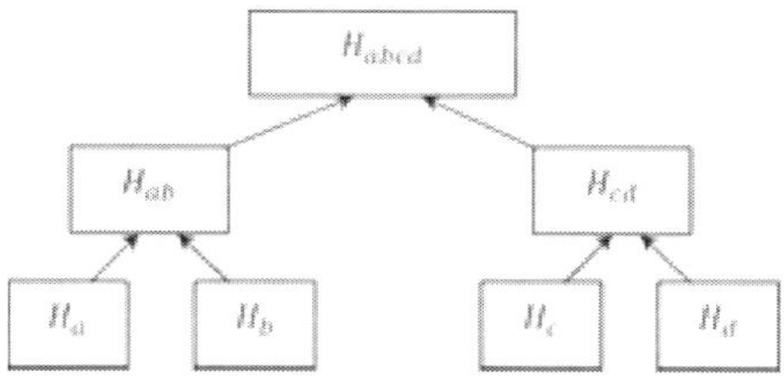

Figure 3. Calculating the blocks using Merkle tree (Nguyen, D. C., et al., 2020).

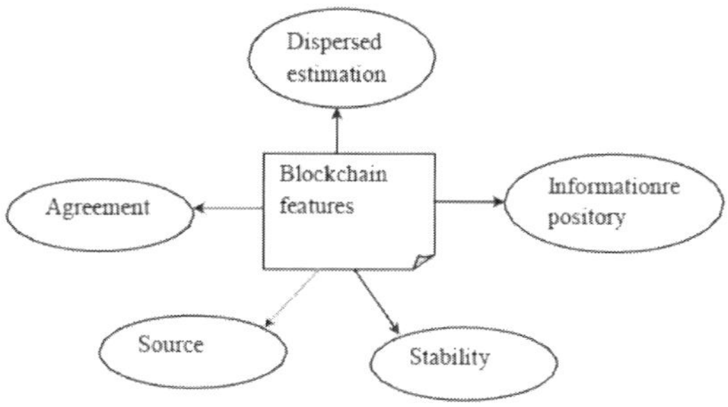

Figure 4. Features of Blockchain (Nguyen, D. C., et al., 2020).

Step 4. Creating the Transaction and Features of Blockchain

The features of Blockchain should be understood in order to grasp how a Blockchain operates (Nguyen, D. C., et al., 2020) from a technological viewpoint. The block-chain is prepared to modify a number of things. It is realistic to assume that the Blockchain will cause considerable harm to many institutions and organisations while simultaneously making operations more representative, safe, clear, and efficient. In a number of sectors and characteristics, Blockchain is a required and unexpected trend. As the development continues, the number of intermediates reduces, and the whole system decentralises, giving security and transparency (Mallikarjuna, B., et al., 2020b).

Some of the fundamental features of Blockchain are described here. It is versatile, in the sense that it may be modified to meet particular demands. The Blockchain features are illustrated in Figure 4, which is followed by a description of the features (Nguyen, D. C., et al., 2020).

Some of the Blockchain's features, as seen in above figure are:

- Agreement
- Dispersed estimation
- Information repository
- Source
- Stability

Step 4.1. Agreement

The agreement is the primary and most vital characteristic of Blockchain. As the state infers, agreement alludes to all mysterious arrange clients consenting to the network's rules and controls. In expansion, whether network individuals are complying with the laws and controls is surveyed on a normal premise within the Blockchain engineering (Mallikarjuna, B., et al., 2020b). The agreement in Blockchain is expressed to be come to by an assortment of strategies, counting the PoW or PoS calculations.

Crypto currency miners perform difficult mathematical calculations in order to implement the PoW algorithm. The block reward, a portion of digital Bitcoin, was paid to the competing crypto miner who performed these difficult computations. The PoS algorithm, on the other hand, is deterministic in its validation. In this instance, the more coins a crypto miner owns, the more likely he or she is to be picked to validate blocks and add to the Blockchain.

Step 4.2. Dispersed Estimation

The distributed estimate of Blockchain is the second essential component. In the case of the Bitcoin Blockchain, each user that is running a full node will have an exact copy of the complete Blockchain. The copy is made up of all of the data from the Bitcoin Blockchain's transactions.

Following the successful completion of the download, the node is said to be performed in an independent way, in which the transactions are processed and then sent across the network via many nodes. One of the most fundamental elements of the Blockchain's dispersed estimation is that there is no single node processing and distributing the data. Every node that makes up a block in the Blockchain, on the other hand, is considered to run independently.

Step 4.3. Information Repository
The third crucial aspect of Blockchain is the information repository. Here, the information repository refers to the information storage space. For instance, in Bitcoin Blockchain, the information repository here refers to the information connected to the Bitcoin transactional data.

Step 4.4. Source
Blockchains guarantee source in a preprogrammed way. In conventional banking, the client is mindful that the money deposited or the gems kept within the locker are secure within the bank. Be that as it may, in case of Blockchain transaction, each movement performed by the client is followed, documented and completely identifiable without the help of third-party required to validate for a particular activity to be taken (Mallikarjuna, B., et al., 2021b).

Step 4.5. Stability
The Blockchain transaction is believed to be stable because of the reason that it is highly said to be stable. In that respect, the transaction pertaining to Blockchain cannot be altered as soon as the transaction is registered. Even in the case of an incorrect record, the record cannot be removed and is considered to be visible cannot be deleted (Mallikarjuna, B., et al., 2021b). Moreover, in order to create corrections in the recorded transactions, a new transaction is said to be generated. That created transaction then refers to the incorrect record.

Step 5. Blockchain and Bitcoin Transactions

Bitcoin on the other hand is a cryptocurrency. As far as Bitcoin is concerned, it is a type of digital currency in a decentralised form without the necessity of the third party or bank. Transactions are stated to be done between the users without the third parties or the middlemen. The verification procedure is conducted using cryptography technology and kept in a public distributed ledger called a Blockchain.

Step 6. Hyperledger Frameworks

The Hyperledger framework alludes to an open source collaborative attempt to deliver cross industry Blockchain technology, hosted by Linux Foundation.

Hyperledger refers to the sort of software that everybody is stated to utilise with the objective of creating one's own customised Blockchain. Figure 5 depicts the figurative representation of Hyperledger structure.

Figure 5. Hyperledger framework for healthcare industry (Otoum, S., et al., 2021).

As illustrated in Figure 5, utilising tailored software with the help of specialist developers, software is built for healthcare business

Smart Contract Algorithm and Its Working

The architecture of smart contract is created in such a fashion that it allows to digitally permit, crosscheck, or authenticate the negotiation or contrast performance. The objective of employing smart contracts is that it permits the completion of credible transactions without the participation of third parties or banks. The operation of smart contracts is demonstrated with the assistance of Figure 1.6.

As indicated in Figure 6, the smart contract working is separated into three phases and they are as follows:

Step 1: Smart contracts are written in the form of code. With the written code, it is sent to the Blockchain. Both the code and the rules and regulations relating to the usage of the contract are published on the digital ledger in a public way (Otoum, S., et al., 2021).

Step 2: Whenever an event given in the contract is triggered, to name a few are, expiry date or arrival of goal price for acquiring a product, the event of code is considered to be performed.

Step 3: The regulators have the ability to check into the contract activity on the Blockchain. This is conducted with the goal of gaining an understanding of the market. This is believed to be accomplished with a better degree of privacy for the individual users (Otoum, S., et al., 2021).

Some of the uses of smart contract working are:

- Blockchain healthcare

- Blockchain music
- Blockchain government

Blockchain Healthcare

With the specialisation of smart contracts, one of the sectors of interest is healthcare, where the personal health records of the individuals are claimed to be encoded and kept on the Blockchain. Then, with the assistance of just a private key, access to information is supplied to particular persons. Besides, the surgery that has to be conducted with specific patients are first saved on a Blockchain and are then further delivered to insurance companies as proof-of-delivery. The digital ledger has proven to be beneficial for controlling the healthcare of patients, especially for drug supervision, keeping norms and regulations, testing, and combining with the healthcare supplies (Santa-Clara, P. and Valkanov, R., 2003).

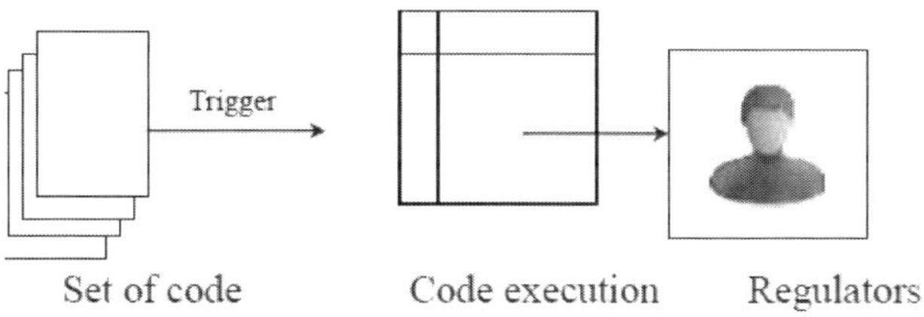

Figure 6. Smart contract working (Santa-Clara, P. and Valkanov, R., 2003).

Blockchain Music

Certain significant concerns in the case of music business are the property rights, distribution of royalties in a fair way and guaranteeing transparency (Kim, S. K., et al., 2020). Industry concerned digital music emphasises on producing monetization, although the rights related to ownership are often disregarded. The tech of Blockchain and smart contracts technology cut away this problem by establishing a comprehensive and exact fragmented database of streaming rights. Besides, the digital ledger and transparent transmission of artist royalties and real-time disbursements to those connected with the labels are also being given. In turn, the music musicians or vocalist are compensated with digital money based on the performances being conducted by them or terms of the contract (Santa-Clara, P. and Valkanov, R., 2003).

Blockchain Government

Digital analysis of data indicates hackers misuse the electronic system to affect voting. The digital ledger in Blockchain technology will prevent this as the votes are claimed to be in the form of encrypted form. In this manner, the private persons may verify that their precious and sensitive ballots were included and ensure who they chose for. In this approach, by employing the Blockchains, the entire system will result in reducing the money for the government too (Santa-Clara, P. and Valkanov, R., 2003). Also, based on the research of McKinsey and Company made in 2013 report that open data that are publicly accessible from freely accessible government-sourced data being available on the internet to all residents of the nation. Even companies have started employing this Blockchain technology to combat fraud schemes; farmers may utilise precision farm-cropping; and etc.

Algorithms of Blockchain Technology with Big Data

As stated above in depth about the Blockchain, to offer a precise definition, Blockchain refers to a time-stamped set of data that is monitored by a collection of computers and specifically not held by any single organisation. As far as security is concerned, each block of data is considered to be protected using cryptographic mechanisms. On the other hand, large data refers to the data sets that are likely to be difficult for traditional kinds of data processing software (Santa-Clara, P. and Valkanov, R., 2003). Although data with multiple rows assure more statistical significance, nevertheless, data with higher complexity, i.e., incorporating more columns leads to a larger quantity of false discovery rate. Figure 1.7 depicts the conceptual diagram of big data and Blockchain.

As illustrated in Figure 7, the rationale for the effective interaction between big data and Blockchain is that the Blockchain readily solves the disadvantages of big data. A few of the reasons are:

- Decentralisation

- Transparency
- Immutability

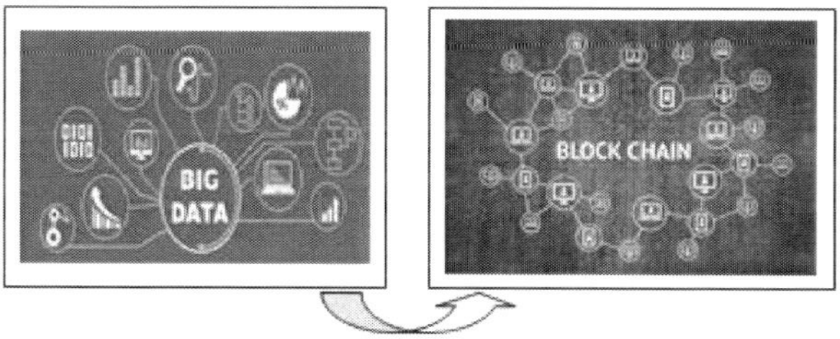

Figure 7. Conceptual diagram of big data and Blockchain (Santa-Clara, P. and Valkanov, R., 2003).

Step 1. Decentralisation

The data recorded in a Blockchain is not stated to be owned by one entity. Therefore, there is no possibility of data or information becoming lose if that entity is deemed to be hacked. The usual manner of data storage before the emergence of Bitcoin was discovered to be centralised services. Thus, the entity was discovered to be centralised that kept all the information relating to all the network users. Alternatively, while retrieving the information, this entity was claimed to be called whenever necessary with information, i.e., traditional banking system. In the case of the decentralised system, the information is not maintained at a single entity; on the other hand, every user in the network (Santa-Clara, P. and Valkanov, R., 2003). To communicate with another user, it can be done directly, without a third party or another entity.

Step 2. Transparency

The transparency of the Blockchain aids in tracking the data back to its place of origination. Yet another intriguing feature regarding the big data and Blockchain convergence is transparency. The person or the users' identity is stated to be disguised by employing the complex cryptographic process and described solely via public address. Hence, while the users' true identity is safeguarded, the transactions that were performed via the public address are only stated to be observed.

Step 3. Immutability

Ultimately, immutability refers to that after certain transactions have been placed into the Blockchain framework, the transactions are not stated to be damaged or destroyed with. The reason behind immutability is because of the application [Casino et al. (2019)] of cryptographic hash algorithms. By using this function, an input string of arbitrary length is acquired as input and creates an output of a definite length. In cryptocurrencies like Bitcoin are concerned, the transactions through digital ledger are treated as input, processed via a hashing algorithm, resulting in a set length output.

Blockchain and Big Data to Secure Data

The technology combining Blockchain and big data assists in safeguarding the data from possible data leaks. With the information being stored on the channel, or blocks, even the most senior executives do not have the access to retrieve the information given numerous permissions are requested from the network to access the big data. Therefore, it becomes very sophisticated and complicated from a cybercriminal point of view to capture it.

It is because of the reason that instead of uploading the huge data to a database server or to a cloud server, Blockchain divides into a finite number of chunks and distributes them throughout the whole network of computers. In this approach, the involvement of intermediary or third party is avoided for executing a transaction. Thus, instead of resting the confidence on a service provider, decentralisation is stated to be established via immutable ledger. Moreover, the big data in Blockchain is supposed to be in the encrypted form. Hence, it is termed to be extremely secure.

Step 1. Blockchain and Big Data Technologies for Data Analysis

Blockchain is alluded to above as a digital and decentralised public ledger that records transactions across many machines in a peer-to-peer network. Though it was initially built for cryptocurrency assets involving Bitcoin; however, in the present years it has been used for many reasons. Besides the above stated uses, Blockchain also holds a huge amount of potentiality in analytics.

Some commercial establishments have started benefiting from data analytics. Predictive analytics is one form of data analytics that is certain to revolutionise and metamorphose the business. Predictive analytics is centred on performing the predictions about the future course of activities on the basis of an incredible amount of previous data as well as methods employing machine learning methods.

Moreover, with data analytics concern, the computing power of Blockchain is held from collective associated computers. Thus it is stated to be powerful enough to accurately build the model to be tested on the basis of larger and massive quantities of information, stored across the computers and hence the network and bring up the ones that can offer the response. Blockchain analytics are discovered to be of heavily useful in the domain of marketing, i.e., digital marketing. In this approach, even digital marketers may be able to plan for future marketing advertising with the help of data gathered from market demands.

Step 2. Blockchain for Private Big Data Management

Blockchain for private big data management is one of the key ways wherein block- chain sets itself from the standard models of mechanisms that are widely employed today. No identities are stated to be necessary in the network layer for Blockchain. This implies that no name, email id, address, or other information relating to the user is necessary to download the information and the technology is started for usage (Mallikarjuna, B., et al., 2021a).

In other terms it implies that it requires no third party of central server to keep the users' information, making Blockchain technology much more secure than a centralised server. The latter can be readily hacked, putting its users' highly sensitive data at danger. However, Blockchain especially enhances the data analysis transparency. This is built in such a way that if an entry or transaction is not said to be verified, it is rejected in an automatic manner. Thus, the big data stored in Blockchain is highly transparent

Step 3. Confidentiality, Data Integrity, and Authentication

Security problems in Blockchain for large data management are investigated from the data confidentiality, data integrity and data authentication perspective (Farhin, F., et al., 2021). Figure 8 depicts the conceptual structure of security problems in Blockchain.

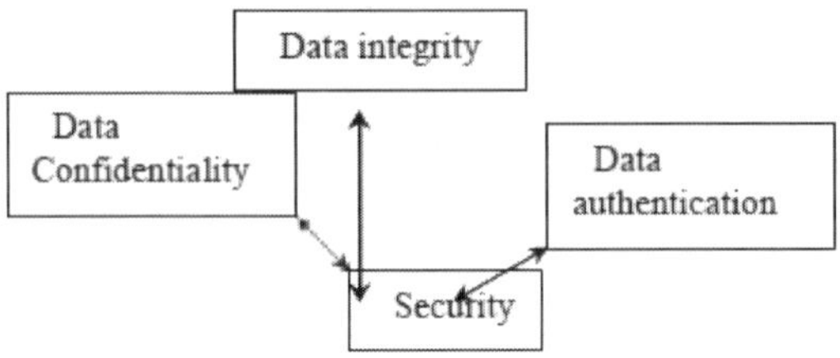

Figure 8. Conceptual diagram of security for Blockchain (Mallikarjuna, B., et al., 2021a).

Step 3.1. Data Confidentiality

It refers to the process of hiding information. It is conducted with the goal of concealing information in such a way that only the intended receivers view the data or information given by the source (Farhin, F., et al., 2021). Data secrecy is claimed to be obtained by employing numerous data encryption techniques available in the market and via key pair models.

Step 3.2. Data Integrity

It is the process of guaranteeing that the data transferred from the source computer/user to the destination machine/user is invariable by all methods (Farhin, F., et al., 2021). Data could be stopped or changed during the transit from the source machine to the destination machine or user (Farhin, F., et al., 2021). Nowadays, data integrity is stated to be accomplished by fingerprinting technique so that the destination machine or user may confim that the data or information is not altered.

Step 3.3. Data Authentication

This refers to the process of ensuring that the data provider is obviously the provider of data. Therefore, the data provider should be authenticated in such a manner that the source machine or the sender bluffing to be the source machine would not be able to fake the communication.

Step 3.3.1. Security Management Scenario for User Big Data in Blockchain

In this part a security management scenario for user big data in the Blockchain environment is given. The scenario given in Figure 9 combines multiple users controlled by Bigchain, the third parties inclined to access the information pertaining to private provided by Blockchain users, around the Blockchain infrastructure which is going to provide secure access to the data controlled by end users.

As stated in the above scenario, end users of the Blockchain ecosystem administer their own security key (Farhin, F., et al., 2021). The security keys are produced using multiple cryptographic techniques to be supplied to the Blockchain users. Besides producing security keys for Blockchain users, credentials are also stated to be produced for the third parties so that the data is supposed to be accessible under rigorous access control (Farhin, F., et al., 2021). Both credentials and security keys are then translated to the Blockchain environment such that rules specified by the end user with respect to storage of data and accessing of data is stated to be ensured in a seamless way.

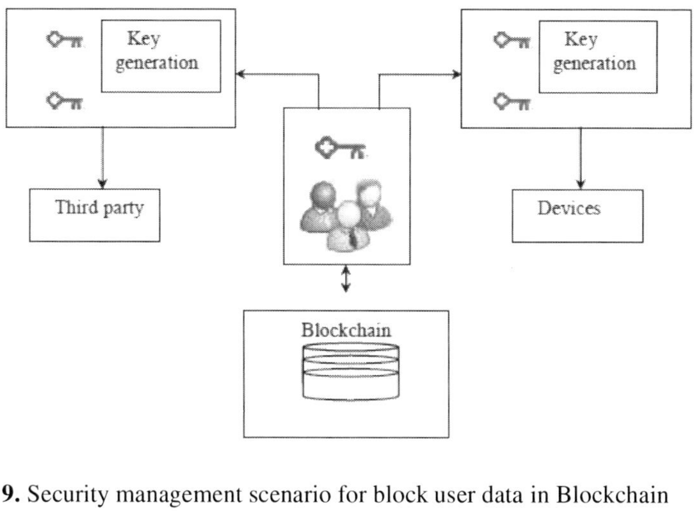

Figure 9. Security management scenario for block user data in Blockchain (Mallikarjuna, B., et al., 2021a).

The devices in Blockchain employing the security keys in turn store the information into the Blockchain. Finally, the end users feed the Blockchain with specific and relevant information, whereby the smart contract are then implemented by applying limitations based on the security factor for each Blockchain user to store and retrieve data. Besides, the third party on the other hand asking authorization to corresponding end user for using private data might in turn access those data stored on the Blockchain.

Multi-Dimensional, Data Transmission and Blockchain Use Cases in Big Data

With rising need for data analytics, where who can allocate more intuitions with data and aid in addressing more difficult challenges, the necessity of Blockchain in data came into existence. It is far more complex and proven to be more problematic when big data is concerned, a developed feature of data science that bestows with enormous data, which cannot be handled by traditional data processing techniques (Farhin, F., et al., 2021).

As far as Blockchain and big data are concerned, data science analyses data for analyses data for actionable views, whereas Blockchain documents and per- forms data validation. In other words, data science is utilised for prediction, whereas Blockchain is employed in data integrity. As per Maria Weinberger of Janexter, "if large is the number, Blockchain is the quality." Therefore, Blockchain is centred on data validation while big data is centred on generating predictions from huge volumes of data. In this way, Blockchain has established a new kind of approach in data administration and operation, without depending on the central angle where the complete data should be merged but in the form of decentralisation.

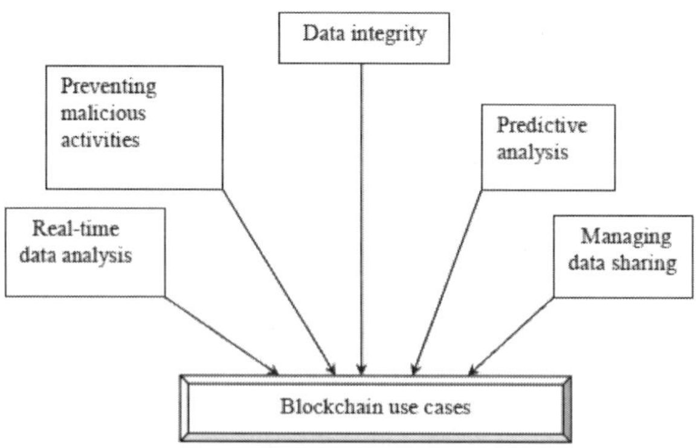

Figure 10. Conceptual diagram of Blockchain use cases in big data (Tang, M., et al., 2020).

In addition, authenticated data created using Blockchain technology takes the form of structured way and exactness. Also, the other key element where the data created by Blockchain has become a boost for big data is the data integrity since Blockchain validates the source where the data came from its connected chains without the help of a third party (Figure 10).

Figure 10 shows the conceptual format of Blockchain use cases in big data and involves:

- Ensuring data integrity
- Preventing malicious activities
- Predictive analysis
- Real-time data analysis
- Managing data sharing

The above said use cases in big data are described in the following sections.

Step 1. Ensuring Data Integrity

The first feature making the Blockchain usable in big data is that the data stored on the Blockchain are reliable. It is because of the process including verification, especially designed for assuring quality (Bazel, M. A., et al., 2021). Hence, the Blockchain is claimed to give transparency as well. Though block- chain technology was created and handled with the aim of enhancing the integrity of Bitcoin, with the success of Bitcoin, the technology involved behind the design of Blockchain has begun getting its acceptance in other segments as well. Figure 11 demonstrates the data integrity for large data Blockchain.

The digital signatures in turn were controlled using the computers comprising the net- Perhaps the most remarkable movement in the area of IT industry over the past several years (Bazel, M. A., et al., 2021), the Blockchain framework has the potential in terms to transform the way the big data is conceived with greater degree of both security and data quality. This is because the actions and transactions occurring on the Blockchain architecture cannot be traced easily.

For instance, Lenovo studied a use case of Blockchain architecture to identify unlawful papers and forms. Lenovo employed Blockchain architecture for certifying papers that were encoded using digital signatures. Work and the validity of the document was cross verified using a Blockchain record. Blockchain, which was launched and built with the objective of authenticating and tracking the Bitcoin transactions is claimed to be employed for many reasons (Tang, M., et al., 2020).

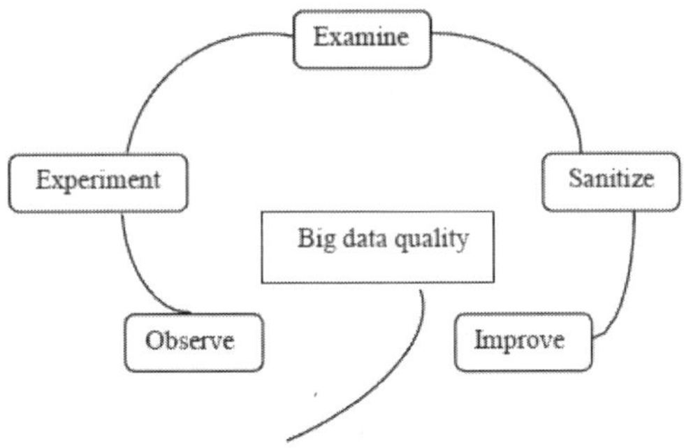

Figure 11. Big data Blockchain data integrity (Tang, M., et al., 2020).

Many companies and establishments have started utilising block- chain for the goal of verifying their firm data. The major impetus for the application of Blockchain is its security. In some situations, data integrity was said to be assured when information related to the originality of the transaction and interlinks about a data block were recorded on the Blockchain and checked in an automated way.

Step 2. Preventing Malicious Activities

As Blockchain utilises a concurrency method for validating the transactions, it is extremely impossible for a single user to generate a warning to the whole data network (Bazel, M. A., et al., 2021). A node or device that starts to perform anomalously is said to be straightforwardly identified and removed from the network. It is because of the fact that the complete network is widely spread in nature, making it extremely impracticable for an one user to begin adequate computational power to modify the acceptance factor and therefore allowing undesirable data in the network. Hence, to alter the block- chain rules, a huge number of nodes or devices must be grouped together to establish an agreement. This is not said to occur with a single individual or equipment (Tang, M., et al., 2020).

Step 3. Predictive Analysis

Blockchain data, like other kinds of data, are also employed to gain helpful and beneficial insight into the behavioural patterns related to big data, various trends present in the market and thus are stated to be utilised in forecasting future outcomes (Ejaz, W., & Anpalagan, A., 2019). Hence, Blockchain ensures organised form of data collected from multiple or individual machines. With predictive analysis, data analysts discover consumer preferences of specific goods above other, lifetime value of a product, pricing trends and churn variables linked to companies. Figure 12 depicts the process flow of Blockchain Predictive Big Data analysis.

The predictive analysis therefore is not restricted in business analysis, but also effective in forecasting the emotive elements linked to online social networks, investment analysis, stock markets and so on. Moreover, due to its distributed feature of Blockchain and the vast amount of processing capacity through it, with the presence of data scientists in smaller businesses may even do predictive analysis in an extended way (Bazel, M. A., et al., 2021). These data scientists connected on a Blockchain framework employ the computing capability of several thousand computers for evaluating the social results on a large scale.

The first use of predictive analytics using Blockchain is believed to be autologous. The predictive analyses are claimed to be of highly value in anticipating pricing patterns for cryptocurrencies and other economic categories. This is because predictive analysis is at the centre of numerous marketing applications (Ejaz, W., & Anpalagan, A., 2019). To quote for example, consumer segmentation consider just preferences and rating coordinates in online social networks, however in the current scenario, new sort of classifications can be created using market actualities.

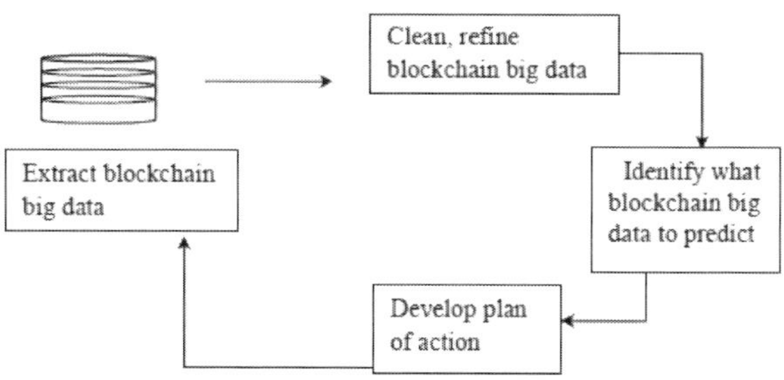

Figure 12. Blockchain predictive big data analysis (Tang, M., et al., 2020).

Moreover, employing predictive analytics, recommendation techniques for systems for the hitherto defined classes also results in the growth of sales, customer preferences and satisfaction with a certain brand. Through this way, the predictive analysis not only create a model to sell or purchase product but also regulate the price in a more progressive way with the aim of maintaining the price in a more competitive and comparative manner, and thus resulting in the increase of profitability.

Step 4. Real-Time Data Analysis

As has been demonstrated in various banking and payment systems, with the help of Blockchain, real-time cross-border transactions have come into reality. Various banking businesses and financial firms have recently started to study block- chain (Bazel, M. A., et al., 2021). This is because it usually gives fast, settlement of big volume of money assuring both affordability and real-time clearing the barriers. In a same way, organisation that needs real-time analysis of large data in a broad manner also employs Blockchain-enabled system. Using Blockchain, even online stores and other commercial establishments started detecting changes in large data in real-time analysis making it possible for rapid decision making, ranging from banning suspicious activities to tracking out the participation of abnormal occurrences (Ejaz, W., & Anpalagan, A., 2019).

Step 5. Managing Data Sharing

With management of data getting shared, data gathered from research investigations are believed to be kept in a Blockchain network. In this approach, software developers do not conduct data analysis which has been already done or erroneously replicate the data that's been previously utilised. However, the Blockchain framework aids data scientists in monitoring the activity, by evaluating the consequences of trade on the Blockchain ecosystem.

Management of data sharing in Blockchain is made of two categories as illustrated in Figure 13. They are data Blockchain (DBC) and trade Blockchain (TBC).

The data Blockchain holds the real user data and the trading block chain maintains just the information that is of high esteem for the goal of trading and performing the transaction.

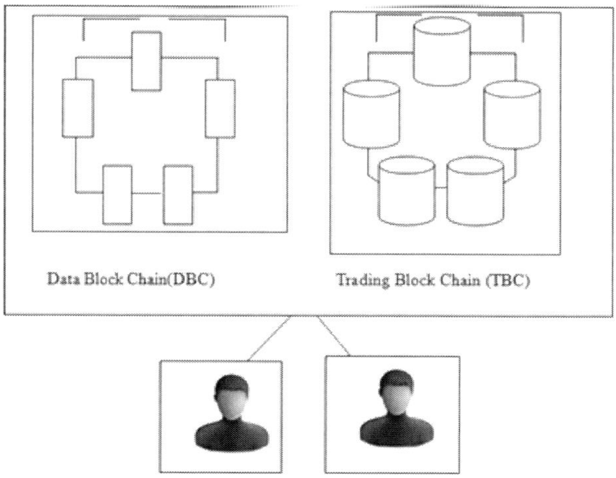

Figure 13. Structure of managing data sharing (Tang, M., et al., 2020).

Every block as indicated in the picture contains a timestamp. The block in turn has hashed the preceding block information (Bazel, M. A., et al., 2021). Moreover, the transaction in each block is stated to be confirmed. The Blockchains, DBC and TBC, are claimed to function in an independent way. Besides, both the Blockchains exchange information related to big data and authenticity is stated to be obtained using cryptographic procedures.

The key to handling data exchange via a tiny case includes:

- Personal data sharing
- Smart contract
- Block creation

Step 5.1. Personal Data Sharing

A controller distributes a user's private data via DBC and TBC. It also notifies about this personal data exchange to the intended user. The processor engaged in the data sharing mechanism again isolates the private information (Bazel, M. A., et al., 2021).

Step 5.2. Smart Contract

All the network nodes establish a newsmart contract, accountable for containing terms, conditions, rules, and regulations for utilising the personal info for data sharing. Once all the processors or the users agree upon the terms and conditions, processors or users then are authorised to access the personal information through data sharing (Ejaz, W., & Anpalagan, A., 2019).

Step 5.3. Block Creation

Finally, a new block is created. The block contains a smart contract and hash of the user's local database.

Challenges and Scenarios in Healthcare

Blockchain as stated in the previous section as one of the type of digital, distributed, and decentralised ledger based on virtual currency is very beneficial for the purpose of monitoring all the transactions without the necessity of a third party Ejaz, W., & Anpalagan, A. (2019), like a bank. In other words, in the modern technology, Blockchain provides the modern means for sending the cash or gaining log into the information immediately. The Blockchain has been designed in the new era of modern computers owing to some amount of faults being identified in the conventional banking system (Amalina, F., et al., 2019). To recapitulate, the essential properties of Blockchain are presented, before detailing the applications (Mallikarjuna, B., et al., 2022a). Decentralised technology provides a way to store the created assets in a Blockchain network accessed through the Internet. The asset to mention a few includes a token, a smart contract, evidential documents, property registration documents, and etc. (Bazel, M. A., et al., 2021).

By adopting a decentralised technology, the owner of the organisation using Blockchain has direct control through cryptographic technique, following a private key directly connected to the asset (Mallikarjuna, B., et al., 2022b). The owner of the organisation with the decentralised technology followed with Blockchain transfer the asset whenever needed to anyone.

Specific reasons for decentralisation include:

- Authorised users
- Fault tolerance
- Scam-free mechanism

- Third party removal
- Lower transaction cost and time

Moreover, Blockchain being a public digital ledge gives method for delivering the valuable and most sensitive data of all users and digital transactions involved by the users that's ever been completed. This Blockchain technology in turn aids in recording each transaction transmitted across the network around the globe (Bazel, M. A., et al., 2021). With this, every person in the company has the capacity to validate the transactions and keep an identical digital ledger copy. Some enticing features include:

- Privacy preservation
- Stopping of fraudulent activities
- Removal of mediator
- Cut costing speed

Next, a vital feature of Blockchain stays in the authentication supplied since several institutions hold sensitive records, and contracts have to be secured from hostile actions or organisations. To preserve the most sensitive records, a hash is stated to be produced in Blockchain for each file, unique for each single transaction.

- Header part
- Transaction part

Particularly, the community modern period is seeing the financial institutions as third parties and stealing the fees in the name of transaction (Farhin, F., et al., 2021). However, in the case of Blockchain, real-time transactions probably lower transaction fees as illustrated in Figure 14.

Blockchain technology provides an absolute engine to give a fresh concept for the future linked world in the era of the internet. While digital ledgers and identities on the one hand give a huge and inescapable means of the linked world, the technique and mechanism through which online information in Blockchain technology is safeguarded is under severe examination. As shown in Figure 14, some of the applications of Blockchain technology with big data analytics include:

- Anti-money laundering

- Cyber security
- Supply chain monitoring
- Financial AI systems
- Medical records

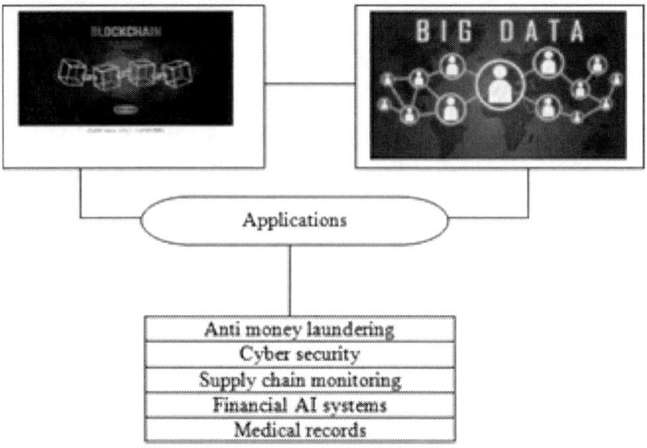

Figure 14. Applications of Blockchain with big data analytics (Tang, M., et al., 2020).

Anti-Money Laundering

Blockchain technology and its digital ledger enables larger quantity of transparency with smart contractors or regulators revamping the reporting procedure. Moreover, the distributed and immutable digital ledge enables permanent transaction history. Additionally, the digital ledger also functions as a crucial centre for keeping the huge data with the aim of processing massive transactions. By conducting anti money laundering, it can operate with the undertaking beyond with the risk officers inside the banking organisations (Mallikarjuna, B., et al., 2022c).

Cryptocurrencies provide the user across the world with quick, secure, and money where the Blockchains provide both dynamic and static storage of record for their associated transactions (Farhin, F., et al., 2021). Traditional system simply needed the usage of central authority wherever the money supply and payment transfer were claimed to be accomplished without the altering possibilities. On the other hand, Blockchain mechanisms restrict this kind of money transfer by offering a third party environment for assuring payment transfers, thereby establishing a peer to peer environment.

To attain anti money laundering, currently in every company establishments, refined identity management employing encryption-based techniques is being structured in a decentralised way. In fact, identity management based on digital signatures also aids the financial and banking sectors to fulfil the needs of the ever-changing know your customer (KYC) and customer due diligence (CDD) regulations. With all this, the expenses involved in robust KYC are also discovered to be minimised and eventually, crimes connected to money and breaches related to consent may be minimised in the long run (Amalina, F., et al., 2019).

Smart contracts in the present years with the usage of Blockchain for big data have begun metamorphosing the traditional lending system. For instance, traditional money lenders provide the borrowers with the needed loans, while simultaneously applying a higher interest rate for the borrowed loan amount and attesting their property in the collateral (Bazel, M. A., et al., 2021). Due to this, a higher number of debtors have slipped into bankruptcy and also began losing their house or property. With the growth of Blockchain technology, this is undermined by removing a stranger to loan the needed money or property as security. In this approach, there is no requirement of presenting the credit history by using Blockchain. No need at all to demonstrate the lender credit or job history and also laborious processing of numerous papers has been likewise cut short.

Cyber Security

The Blockchain mechanism in the present era is found or stated to be employed in a broader way in every area of our life, spanning from banking to healthcare and beyond. Moreover, cybersecurity is an area that has gotten broader attention with the debut of this Blockchain technology Chen, X., et al., (2019) with an ability for more in the recent future. Thus, by removing most of the human effort made from the viewpoint of data storage, Blockchain technology significantly reduces the danger of error involving humans that represents the major source of data breaches. The reason behind the success of this Blockchain technology is that any kind of digital transactions are stated to be put into the Blockchain and the specifications of the industry do not stay the primary concern. Also, using Blockchain technology in any sorts of sectors may reduce the risk involving data theft to a great extent; hence, the nature and size of data remains private and secure.

Supply Chain Monitoring

Blockchain additionally comes in especially simple when it seems to monitor the supplier chains connected in the company. By removing paper-based trails, institutions and businesses should be in a position to point out the flaws within their supply chains Chen, X., et al., (2019) in a quick method and also to locate things in real time. Moreover, Blockchain technology would let institutions and organisations to observe how items or services are executed from the viewpoint of quality control from the point of origin to destination.

The possibilities for implementation of the Blockchain technology in big-data supply chain solutions are that it examines products' status while they are in transportation. Here, the data related to all the consumers or users is discovered to be available with all the users in real time. A few of the benefits for supply chain monitoring Chen, X., et al., (2019) remained in the verification of product labelling claims as well as that of product origins. Also, one of the most crucial and paramount stays in the likelihood of supplying human rights together with decent wages.

For instance, Blockchain allows banks, financial firms, and companies in a long-run have started end-to-end visibility of their supply chain by providing larger amount of data in millions or trillions relating to several location and condition of the supplies by transporting them all across globe. As per the state of 2016, a Deloitte and MHI Mallikarjuna, B., et al., (2021a) research examined 99 top supply chain businesses and determined that the sensors were employed by almost 44 percent of these respondents. Among them, almost 87 percent of these institutions indicated they are required to implement this technology by 2020. Besides, the Blockchain technology also stores, supervises, protects, and transfers this smart information.

Financial AI Systems

As far as financial transactions are concerned, Blockchain technology with big data is likely becoming an extensive component involving financial transactions. Moreover, financial transactions, big data, and Blockchain are discovered to be in sync with each other in delivering the products and services connected to the financial services Chen, X., et al., (2019) industry. This is because standard type of financial systems are proven to be both difficult in terms of time and cost involved, consequently resulting in incorrect information. Besides, mediators or the third party are also necessary to conduct or perform the process so that in case of disagreements, it may be addressed in a seamless manner. This in turn leads to larger amount of expense, stress, time stamp, money depending on the kind and magnitude of data involved (Bialkowski, J., et al., 2008). Due to this numerous banks and financial industries have begun adopting this Blockchain technology with the goal of bringing innovations like smart contracts, smart bonds, and so on.

Medical Records

Medical records (Mallikarjuna, B., et al., 2021b) are considered to be an area where records are deemed to be very critical and so have to be reviewed on a continuous basis. When the big-data systems that enter into this data-oriented industry are developed with the help of Blockchain technology, all records are then claimed to be concealed with a clear track record and also preserved with greater transparency rate.

Conclusion

This chapter examined algorithms of Blockchain technology with big data, multi-dimensional, data transmission, challenges, and scenarios in healthcare. A Blockchain is a distributed ledger that everyone can access but it is not controlled by a central authority that may be utilised to decrease time when logging transactions between parties, remove costs associated with middlemen, and reduce chances of fraud and manipulation. Individuals and corporations may work with confidence and transparency owing to this technology. Cryptographic currencies, such as Bitcoin and others, are among the most well-known applications of Blockchains, although there are many others. And described the huge challenges in cryptographic currencies, such as Bitcoin and others, are various well-known applications in health care of Blockchain. In the healthcare industry Blockchain technology with big data plays a revolution in information technology. Today, several Blockchain real time applications are widely accessible.

References

Amalina, F., Hashem, I. A. T., Azizul, Z. H., Fong, A. T., Firdaus, A., Imran, M., & Anuar, N. B. (2019). Blending big data analytics: Review on challenges and a recent study. *Ieee Access*, 8, 3629-3645.

Bazel, M. A., Mohammed, F., & Ahmed, M. (2021, August). Blockchain technology in healthcare big data management: benefits, applications and challenges. *In 2021 1st International Conference on Emerging Smart Technologies and Applications* (eSmarTA) (pp. 1-8). IEEE.

Chen, X., Wang, X., & Yang, K. (2019, December). Asynchronous Blockchain-based privacy-preserving training framework for disease diagnosis. *In 2019 IEEE International Conference on Big Data* (Big Data) (pp. 5469-5473). IEEE.

Ejaz, W., & Anpalagan, A. (2019). Internet of things for smart cities: technologies, big data and security (pp. 1-15). *Springer International* Publishing.

Farhin, F., Kaiser, M. S., & Mahmud, M. (2021). Secured smart healthcare system: Blockchain and Bayesian inference based approach. *In Proceedings of International Conference on Trends in Computational and Cognitive Engineering* (pp. 455-465). Springer, Singapore.

Kim, S. K., & Huh, J. H. (2020). Artificial neural network Blockchain techniques for healthcare system: Focusing on the personal health records. *Electronics,* 9(5), 763.

Kumari, A., Gupta, R., Tanwar, S., & Kumar, N. (2020). A taxonomy of Blockchain-enabled softwarization for secure UAV networks. *Computer Communications*, 161, 304-323.

Lu, Y. (2019). Artificial intelligence: a survey on evolution, models, applications and future trends. *Journal of Management Analytics*, 6(1), 1-29.

Mallikarjuna, B., Sathish, K., Krishna, P. V., & Viswanathan, R. (2020a). The effective SVM-based binary prediction of ground water table. *Evolutionary Intelligence*, 1-9.

Mallikarjuna, B., Viswanathan, R., & Naib, B. B. (2020b). Feedback-based gait identification using deep neural network classification. *Journal of Critical Reviews*, *7*(4), 661-667.

Mallikarjuna, B. (2020c). Feedback-Based Resource Utilizations for Smart Home Automation in Fog Assistance IoT-Based Cloud. *International Journal of Fog Computing* (IJFC), 3(1), 41-63.

Mallikarjuna, B., Shrivastava, G., & Sharma, M. (2021a). Blockchain technology: A DNN token-based approach in healthcare and COVID-19 to generate extracted data. *Expert Systems*, e12778.

Mallikarjuna, B., Kiranmayee, D., Saritha, V., & Krishna, P. V. (2021b, June). Development of efficient e-health records using IoT and Blockchain technology. In *ICC 2021-IEEE International Conference on Communications* (pp. 1-7). IEEE.

Mallikarjuna, B., Addanke, S., & Anusha, D. J. (2022a). An improved deep learning algorithm for diabetes prediction. In *Handbook of Research on Advances in Data Analytics and Complex Communication Networks* (pp. 103-119). IGI Global.

Mallikarjuna, B., Anusha, D. J., & Sabharwal, M. (2022b). An effective video surveillance system by using CNN for COVID-19. In *Handbook of Research on Advances in Data Analytics and Complex Communication Networks* (pp. 88-102). IGI Global.

Mallikarjuna, B., Addanke, S., & Sabharwal, M. (2022c). An improved model for house price/land price prediction using deep learning. In *Handbook of Research on Advances in Data Analytics and Complex Communication Networks* (pp. 76-87). IGI Global.

Miao, Y., Zhou, M., & Ghoneim, A. (2020). Blockchain and AI-based natural gas industrial IoT system: Architecture and design issues. *IEEE Network*, 34(5), 84-90.

Mohsin, A. H., Zaidan, A. A., Zaidan, B. B., Mohammed, K. I., Albahri, O. S., Albahri, A. S., & Alsalem, M. A. (2021). PSO–Blockchain-based image steganography: towards a new method to secure updating and sharing COVID-19 data in decentralised hospitals intelligence architecture. *Multimedia Tools and Applications*, 80(9), 14137-14161.

Nguyen, D. C., Pathirana, P. N., Ding, M., & Seneviratne, A. (2020). Blockchain for 5G and beyond networks: A state of the art survey. *Journal of Network and Computer Applications*, 166, 102693.

Otoum, S., Al Ridhawi, I., & Mouftah, H. T. (2021). Preventing and controlling epidemics through Blockchain-assisted AI-enabled networks. *IEEE Network*, 35(3), 34-41.

Santa-Clara, P. and Valkanov, R. (2003). The presidential puzzle: Political cycles and the stock market. *The Journal of Finance*, 1841-1872.

Tang, M., Gao, L., & Huang, J. (2020). Communication, computation, and caching resource sharing for the internet of things. *IEEE Communications Magazine*, 58(4), 75-80.

Chapter 3

Comprehensivc Review on Architectural Framework of Blockchain Technology with Big Data in Healthcare

R. Kavitha, R. Srinivasan and M. Kavitha
Department of CSE, Vel Tech, Chennai, Tamil Nadu, India

Abstract

The Blockchain is fascinating in many fields, including financial, health, government, security and much more. The basic principle of Blockchain is based on distributed booklets, which solve many existing issues. Every Blockchain framework has a different purpose and application. Many important criteria have to be taken into account in selecting the Blockchain framework. The advantage and disadvantages of every Blockchain structure and platform. In this section, we present some of the leading business framework for implementing Blockchain solutions. This paper examines and proposes a solution for managing and sharing individual health information among institutions. The solution increases clinical efficiency and explore when the information is shared with investigators. Blockchain technology is proposed as a solution for providers, hospitals, clinics, insurers and patients. The data would belong in the whole process to the individual or the patient. This solution proposes an isolated Blockchain framework which allows all users to know and trust the privacy and security of the data.

Keywords: Blockchain, big data, framework, EHR

In: Blockchain Technology Based Big Data for Healthcare
Editors: Basetty Mallikarjuna, Niranjanamurthy M, Sheng-Lung Peng et al.
ISBN: 978-1-68507-968-0

Introduction

A traditional database is an information storage structure. A database stores information in the form of tables. An information component called a table is used for a regular database. It contains fields that define attributes that store data. A single user named as an administrator may modify, manage and control a database. The database always features a user who works as a Database Administrator and who controls the database completely. Any record stored in a database can be created, removed, and modified by that user. Administration in the database can also perform, such as performance optimization and size management. A large database tends to slow performance, allowing administrators to use performance optimization methods.

The Blockchain framework enables developers to build, deploy, and maintain technically complex products more easily. Developers apply the Blockchain framework and its basic modules to create all the specific components. An essential part of the Blockchain architecture is a node, a computer or user that has a full copy of the ledger, and a block, a data structure used to maintain an array of transactions (records, information, etc.).

Blockchain Architecture

Blockchain is an electronic network that stores specific information of the database (peer-to-peer), and it is securely and authenticated into one network. The Blockchain is not a central server, but a collection of interconnected computers, thus decentralizing the entire network shown in Figure 1 (Mallikarjuna, B., et al., 2021a).

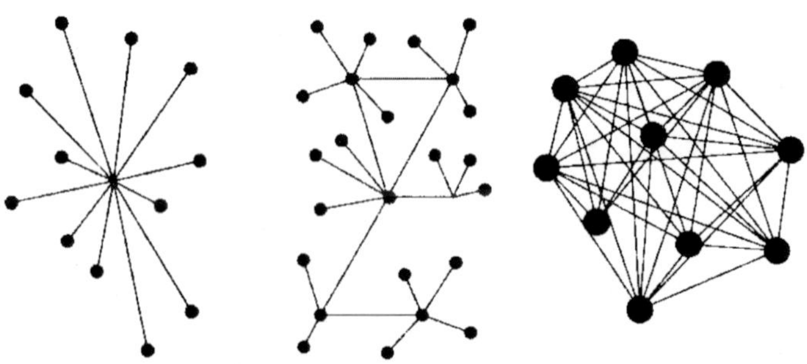

Figure 1. a) Centralized b) Decentralized c) Distributed ledger.

The WWW uses a client-server architecture. As a central database is measured by several authorized admins, all information is kept in one place, so updating is easy in the server machine. Every partner in a distributed Blockchain network keeps, approves, and updates new entries. A distributed network is measured by everyone, not just individual users. In this system, each member is responsible for ensuring the validity and security of data by ordering and reviewing records shown in Figure 2 (Mallikarjuna, B., et al., 2020a).

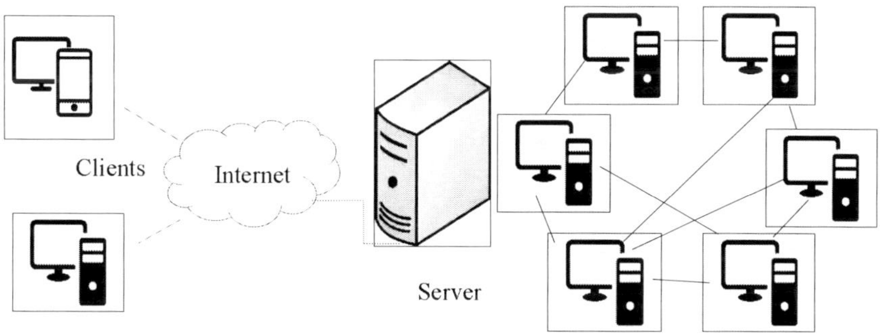

Figure 2. Blockchain architecture.

Structure of Blockchain

A Blockchain stores information on blocks of a uniform size; each structure includes the hashed data for cryptographic safety from the earlier block. The hash function used is SHA256, which is one-way. In addition to the data and digital signatures from the previous block, this hashed information represents the chain hash going all the way back to the first block called the starting block. The data is then processed using a hash function based on the position of the previous block at that point. For example, Merkle tree is a Blockchain data structure used to verify data effectively.

Two important Blockchain data structures include:

- Pointers - variables that contain information about another variable's location. This indicates the position of a different variable in particular.
- Linked lists - a block sequence with the support of a pointer to provide a specific data for each block and links to the next block.

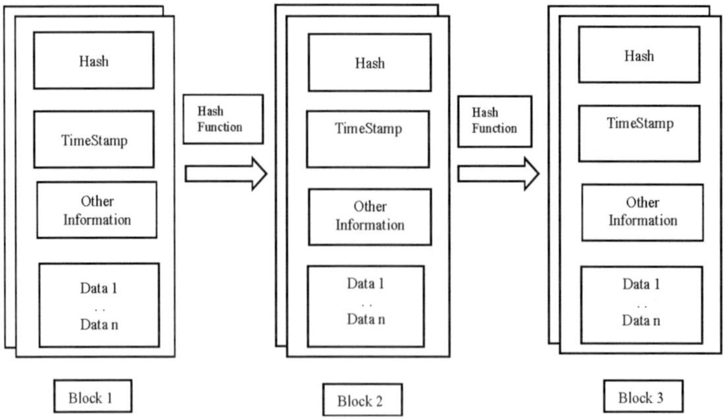

Figure 3. Structure of Blockchain.

Motivation Behind Blockchain

The motivation behind why Blockchain innovation changes the way we interact with each other includes:

1. The method by which information is tracked and stored: In clusters, Blockchain stores data that are considered blockages, which are sequentially linked. Should the data in a specific block be improved, you will not revamp the data; instead, the change is inserted into a new block that shows that x has been changed to y at a given time and date. This is because Blockchain depends on the technique for hundreds of years.
2. It trusts the information: Few things must happen before a block can be added to a chain. The cryptographic riddle must be initially solved, which makes the block along these lines. Secondly, the puzzle-solving computer shares the solution on the network with all other computers. This is known as work proof. Thirdly, the network checks work evidence. The block is added to the chain if it is true.

Blockchain Features

a) Shared ledger: It is designed to generate undisputable information about all transactions, which can be accessed by all participants. The only source of truth is the common ledger. Every user has a copy of the shared ledger through replication. The directory may be allowed to allow every user to only view the content they have access to (Mallikarjuna, B., et al., 2020b).

b) Permission: Each user has a digital identity with authorized Blockchains which allows selective access to transaction details by means of policies around his/her permission. This enables companies to comply with regulations on data protection, for example, HIPAA. For instance, both users can see the details of the transaction in a counterparty transaction. The transaction is seen by an independent entity but cannot see details. When an assessor joins the system, they can set up the transaction using digital certificates (Mallikarjuna, B., et al., 2021b).

c) Consensus: An algorithm of consensus ensure that the only truth is the next block in the chain and prevents the forging and manipulation of data by other powerful parties. It is needed to regulate whether the transaction is permanent or not.

d) Smart agreements: It is a contract or set of instructions with commercial transaction. It is stored and automatically executed during a transaction.

Big Data

The volume of big data makes it difficult to use traditional databases or software techniques. Unstructured and structured data generate a large amount of information. During every appointment with our family doctors or specialists, every trip to the ER or any surgical procedure, data is continuously collected in healthcare. Wearables and other IoT devices are making it possible to generate more data faster now than ever before. Healthcare providers provide information to insurance companies that insurers use.

Smart Contract

Smart contracts can make compromise or concert of an agreement with the Blockchain framework easier, more effective and efficient. The whole process is robotic and can complement or replace an agreement on a legal paper. This idea uses Blockchain technology in order to develop a reliable distributed system that can safely store the health information of an individual. The individual user may manage his or her data permission through a web portal and other key features like checking logs to see who has retrieved their information. This gives the user security and privacy control over their important data. They can also give third parties access if required.

If a healthcare provider or medical centre creates a medical record, all the medical data should be stored in an encrypted database. Each time the information is stored in the database, a pointer to that record and unique user identifier are registered in the Blockchain. A new record will be notified to the patient who owns this information. This is not only true for a third person, but also for wearable sensors and other devices the patient can add.

In order to decrypt data in the storage, the database decrypts the data with the public key of the requester to keep the data in movement. The requester may encrypt the data via his or her private key. In order for healthcare providers, laboratories, and hospitals to share information with each other or to provide it to visitors, we are using a private Blockchain solution for them. Throughout the patient's lifetime, the Blockchain will contain all medical records and data that they have collected, including various kinds of data as well as the locations of the data.

The technology of Blockchain is constantly improving, not complete, and it has several potential challenges to be addressed in biomedical and healthcare applications. Openness and confidentiality are the first challenge. On a Blockchain network, everyone can see everything. Many believe medical information is stored off-chain, and only the hash is stored in a Blockchain. Speed and scalability are the second challenge. Transaction processing speeds are only expected to be several hundredths as standard, such as credit cards, in a proof-of-concept study.

Applications of Blockchain

Billing Management

Health services cost themselves a trillion dollars' worth of the whole industry and are rapidly growing. The medical billing process is a major component of medical services. Because a proper service can't be guaranteed without billing. This procedure begins when the patient is admitted to the hospital until the check-out takes place. It includes several steps, including check-in, financial accountability, compliance with the coding and billing procedure, transmission and payment by assurance companies (Mallikarjuna, B., et al., 2022a).

Quality Management

The study revealed that the detection of active elements and the composition of the sample image is effective with techniques such as spectroscopy and chromatograph. But they have limits because they rely on electromechanical devices, which increase the costs. One way of overcoming the problems is to get information from pharmaceutical producers including product serial numbers and package numbers to check the authenticity of data through the Blockchain. This process ensures cheap quality management, product registration, and drug tracking (Mallikarjuna, B., et al., 2022b).

IoMT

A crucial role is played by IoMT systems in the development of health information systems. IoMT technology can be used to collect, process, and share data from medical devices such as cardiac monitors and body scanners. With AI, for example, providers can capture imaging-intensive images, categorize suspected cells or malignant components and share their findings with those authorized to see them (Mallikarjuna, B., et al., 2022c).

Education

The Blockchain is used primarily as a mechanism for recording the digital currency transaction of Bitcoin. The basis of education is knowledge exchange and multi-source skills. It assumes the confidence of all involved parties. As online learning proliferates, regulatory agencies are challenged to control the alteration of medical learning knowledge. The Blockchain technology of health care providers could potentially improve education quality and impact education in several generations of learners, according to Fuk et al.

Security

Due to its importance to overwhelm the EHR safety problems, Blockchain technologies have reached a major boom in the health sector. It is possible for EHRs to improve health care delivery. It is produced by admitting the patient to a hospital and diagnosing the patient or by saving diagnosis results such as the EHR scan. The safety of this digital information, therefore, takes precedence and currently uses Blockchain for safe and secure healthcare data.

Literature

Ossipova et al. (2018) implemented the integration of wireless networks with smart Blockchain contracts to secure patient and medical monitoring systems in real time. The study proposes the integration of Blockchain in intelligent contracts to evaluate the data gathered on the basis of customized thresholds by patient IoMT medical equipment. The problem of data transmission logging in an IoT healthcare system is solved. The smart dyslexia analytic solution was introduced by Hassanain et al. (2018) where a decentralized big data repository is stored and then shared with healthcare groups, groups and people using Blockchain.

The Healthcare Data Gateway (HGD), which is based on the Blockchain architecture, was developed by Wang et al. (2016). The solution provided facilitates the control and sharing of customer data without compromising confidentiality. It is a good way to increase the intelligence of medical systems while retaining patient information in private. Furthermore, Patal (2018) presented a cross-domain image sharing framework, using the distributed Blockchain technology.

Zhang et al. (2018) proposed a multi-level Blockchain technology location sharing scheme. The objective was to achieve the protection of the information system's privacy through Blockchains. They define the main requirements for location sharing by using Merkle Tree and order preservation. The experimental results show that the scheme for patients and medical personnel is practical and feasible and can be used in the protection of information in telecom systems (Mallikarjuna, B., 2020c).

MedRec is a decentralized EMR management system that records data authorization and operation on the Blockchain and concludes smart contracts with its performance. MedRec collaborates with providers on the complete authentication, confidentiality, reviewing and distribution of data and provides patients with comprehensive and unalterable medical information and service. In additional research, Zhang et al. (2018) proposed an approach in the cloud environment to achieve controllable data management by the Blockchain to address users' concerns about the lack of control over published books.

Bhuiyan et al. (2019) proposed a cloud cloud-based patient-centered data management system using Blockchain technology to help privacy. The main purpose of the work was to maintain sensitive health data on the Blockchain by defining a number of safety and confidentiality requirements for accountability. Alam et al. (2018) introduced a new term, however, Block Cloud, which is, in fact, a cloud-based blend of Blockchains. The idea behind the cloud implementation is to keep the data under the same roof without third parties. Blockchain technology, healthcare applications, and different levels of stakeholders all play a role in emerging Blockchain innovations in healthcare. In her healthcare review, Banerjee (2018) wrapped up her discussion of ways in which Blockchain technology could be used to enable patient control of data sharing via the institutional monitoring system. Using Blockchain technology, the research team demonstrated how healthcare could be transformed through digital access and network identity.

Yang et al. (2019) proposed to use Blockchains and peer-to-peer networks, which are called MedChains, to share medical data. A system designed for medical data and patient data generation has been designed using IoT sensors and mobile applications. Moniruzzaman et al. (2019) discussed various health management system issues and how Blockchain technology could be used to solve them. Current health research using distributed ledger technology has been presented with a number of possible clinical applications that can make the process more efficient through Blockchain technology. They also proposed the IoMT networking system protocols.

Jamil et al. discussed drug regulatory issues and how to use Blockchain to standardize drugs. They stressed the difficulties of detecting falsified drugs and proposed Blockchain to detect falsified medication in their work. Lee and Yang have worked with Blockchain and microscopy sensors on the fingernail analysis management system. Human clots are very special and reflect the human being's physiological nature. In their work, microscopic sensors have been used to capture nail pictures and to obtain clear images using image preprocessing methods. For the performance surveillance of an extraction algorithm, a deep neural network was used.

The inefficiencies and heavy regulations have slowed down innovation in health care. These regulatory problems causing inefficiencies in the EMR system were discussed by Vieira et al. (2016). They proposed a Blockchain-based medical data management solution known as MedRec in the EMR system. Using an audit access log system, they engaged in unique and innovative ways to access health records. The distributed ledger technology employed by MedRec enables the sharing of medical data among patients, doctors, and other parties. They give people such as researchers and other health professionals incentives to take part in the mining process.

Philip et al. (2018) presented e-health management as a safe and consistent solution for managing the information in healthcare. Digital security has become a major concern because of hacking and privacy abuses in this digital age. This is especially true in the eHealth sector, where health record systems are hackable. eHealth provides this opportunity, and it is important to note that the health information management systems of patients must comply with most of the laws while also being accessible to the proper health care professionals. Blockchains are most familiar to those in the payment region due to Bitcoin's most popular use.

The Media Lab report highlights all Blockchain technology deployments on data and personal information management security and privacy. It is the value of safe data processing – it cannot be manipulated. Data protection and privacy are another aspect of data security. Enigma, for example, is a decentralized, private computer platform and a Blockchain technology in advance. Block Verify is a start-up that uses Blockchain to claim intellectual property by checks on the origins of physical objects, and by verifying the legal status of pharmaceutical products, diamonds and electronic products to tackle the problem of counterfeit goods. This kind of security is due to the decentralization of Blockchain, so that it does not depend on one authority for maintenance and therefore one case of malpractice causing a failure does not affect record consistency.

Blockchain is described as a decentralized system that is suitable for handling sensitive data. Encryption is key to securing the records of a Blockchain transaction, and every Blockchain activity is protected by encryption. Each transaction on a Blockchain is protected by encryption, and each of these transactions is linked with previous transactions or records. Blockchain transactions are verified at nodes equipped with algorithms. Transparency allows everyone to see transactions in real time. Intelligent contracts ensure that third parties do not interfere with the transaction. Blockchains eventually allow everyone to track transactions.

Healthcare Framework

Using the Ethereum platform, smart representations of current medical records can be produced that can be stored within individual network nodes. Contract ownership and permissions are outlined in addition to securing data integrity. To manage these properties, we have signed instructions for encrypting the Blockchain transactions.

A smart contract, which could be stored on Blockchain technology, could be designed that could cover all the necessary terms and conditions for managing different data authorizations, as shown in Figure 2. This contributes to better doctor-patient interaction. In smart contracts the rules for data authorization are embedded. It also can help to track all activities from their origin to surrender by means of a unique id. In addition to all functions and processes, different scenarios have been developed and explained well integrated in intelligent contracts. Providers can add a new patient record and patients can allow a record sharing between providers. The new information received by the party receives an automated notification and, before the data is accepted or rejected, can verify the proposed record. This informs and engages participants in the development of their records. This system prioritizes usability by also providing a designated contract which includes references to all user relationships between patients and providers, provides a single reference point for verifying updates of medical history.

Blockchain technology allows us to structure data to verify and record transactions while at the same time achieving consensus among all involved parties. The technology uses a concept of a leading authority that monitors all events. Current leader systems contain data at a single centralized location, an electronic health record system, a database, or a repository operated through an exchange of health information. Often, they are individually developed and can generate and store data in their own proprietary formats, resulting in data siloes and interoperability problems that frustrate providers, patients, and researchers.

Blockchain will provide the validation needed by the healthcare industry and this is something that all parties can trust. One entity is responsible for maintaining the data as part of the process; however, everyone who participates in the Blockchain is responsible for ensuring integrity. Unlike a public Blockchain financial facility, the Blockchain healthcare system should be limited to a patient, healthcare provider, and the family, if needed, by the number of authorized patients.

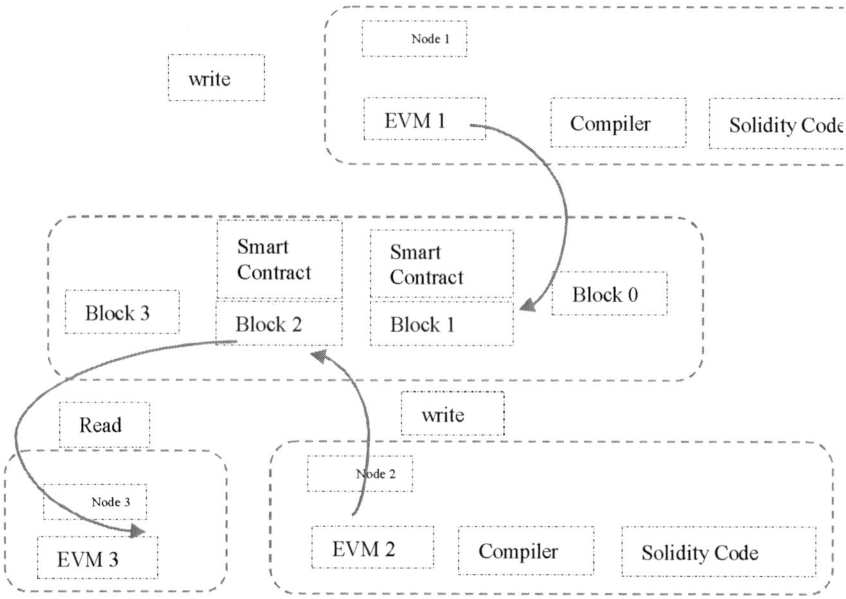

Figure 4. Healthcare framework.

In terms of safety and privacy, the health care system faces fundamental problems. Data about your health are personal and private, and they are currently stored centrally. A bank vault would be similar to this where access is limited to authorized individuals and the key is available to all. In addition, patients do not have to assemble their own data from various providers when they see a new specialist. Blockchain provides access to the chain. A participant can then access the same data as everyone else involved. The ultimate benefit for patients is that information can be readily shared between stakeholders instantly, saving time on manual reconciliation.

Blockchain technology facilitates the creation of an affordable, reliable, and secure way to store healthcare records on individuals. A web portal enables users to manage their data access permissions, as well as view logs to determine who has accessed their information. By self-managing their data, the individual can safeguard their privacy and ensure its security, rather than allowing a third party to do so. The individual can also permit third parties' access if necessary.

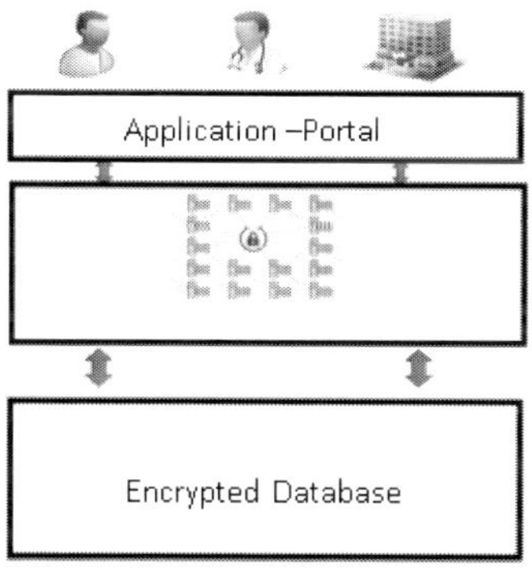

Figure 5. Proposed framework.

A Blockchain platform can be difficult to choose when there are so many options available. We propose to build the application on the Hyperledger platform developed by the Linux Foundation or the Ethereum Blockchain application platform. As part of the application layer, a portal is used to connect users to resources, generate reports, etc. As part of the application layer, a Blockchain implementation is displayed. As a second layer, we would have the Blockchain layer, which is comprised of only the Blockchain node network, other nodes, a key creator, and a database. The author is responsible for creating public/private key pairs that are used in the Blockchain.

If a health care provider or healthcare center creates a medical record, all medical data would be stored in an encrypted database and encrypted and sent to the database to be stored. Whenever information is saved into the database, a sign for this health record and a specific user identifier are registered in the Blockchain. The patient who is the owner will be informed of the addition of a new record. In order to decrypt data in the storage, the database encrypts the data by using the public key requesters to protect the data in transit. The requester can encrypt the data using his or her personal key. There are several key elements related to identification information and a list of transactions stored in one single block in the Blockchain. The block content represents data ownership and the rights of private Blockchain network members shared.

Medical Prescriptions

The main goal of this work is to reduce the amount of time spent waiting for a prescription to be written. Fraud will also be removed from the system, as well as the miscommunication rate between doctors and patients. Physicians write prescriptions on behalf of patients and place them in health records via intelligent contracts. A smart contract on the Ethereum Blockchain will give the pharmacy access to this prescription via the permission of the primary physician and a patient. As soon as the prescription is received, a smart contract releases the medication for usage and expiration.

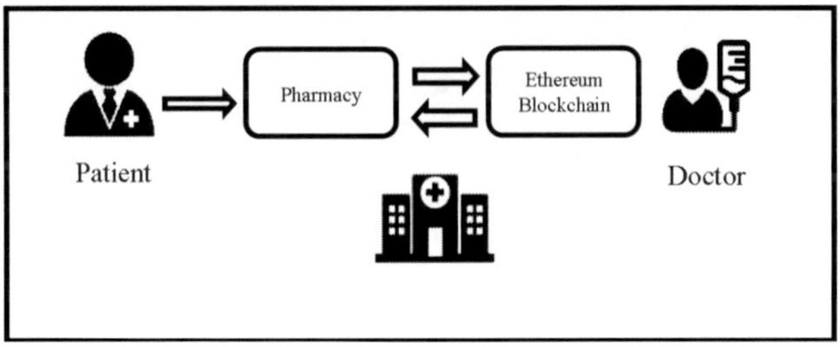

Figure 6. Medical prescription.

Medical Laboratories

In order to access and share therapeutic data among different stakeholders effectively, laboratories, doctors, emergency clinics, and various partners will access and share information via the Blockchain of intelligent contracts, as shown in Figure 4.

Consider a case in which a patient is visiting a blood test laboratory. The patient will be notified via Ethereum Blockchain, notifying the patient that the processed test results are accessible and may decide whether to enroll the information and put it on the Ethereum Blockchain by the laboratory.

A patient does not need to carry laboratory results and provide records to different healthcare professionals in order for medical records to be posted on the healthcare Blockchain. Also, he makes sure that all of his medical providers are given up-to-date information. For printing and mailing or faxing regulatory costs, laboratories reduce each test result to the individual supplier. The payment from security firms that receive the transferred information can be received to process claim payments by laboratories and pharmaceutical organizations, depending on the information used.

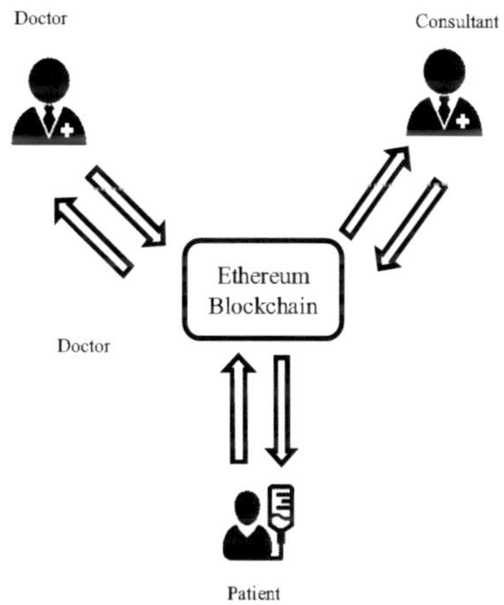

Figure 7. Medical laboratory.

The patient's request is sent automatically by an intelligent contract system to the primary physician. Any request and response must be considered by a doctor, and the patients referred to a specialist if appropriate for further treatment. EHR should provide any patient information about therapy history. A database holds patient records, where there are specific rules that allow access to a record of the extent and regulations governed by Ethereum Blockchain smart contracts.

Personalized recommendations are given to patients seeking health information on a particular topic, rather than results from a web search. While senior physicians gain the ability to monetize their expertise without overscheduling, junior physicians gain the opportunity to build a brand and gain access to new markets within their specialty. By offering payments, young physicians encourage their patients to recommend them.

Advantages

The healthcare industry has several advantages based on our solution. The use of Blockchain will make it possible to access accurate information quickly to patients, health workers, researchers and others. At present, there are centralized electronic medical record systems, or the data are stored in the doctor's office in paper files. It may take several days, if not weeks, for access to this information. This solution has many advantages in the healthcare industry for clinicians, users and investigators involved. Blockchain can provide real-time data access, which could enhance the coordination of health care and expand emergency clinical care considerably. This will enable scientists and public health professionals to quickly detect conditions that may have an impact on public health. The detection and containment of epidemics is faster.

Results and Discussions

One of the fields in which Blockchain has great potential is healthcare. In 2016, the National Coordinating Office for Health Information Technology (ONC), which understood the relevance and importance of Blockchain in health services, compiled a challenge for asking the white papers on Blockchain use in health services. This challenge has led to several proposed Blockchain medical applications.

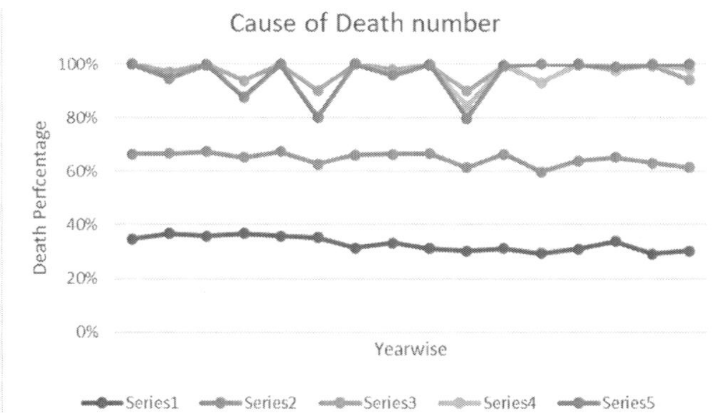

Figure 8. Cause of death percentages.

Public health and social services are provided by the Health Service Executive, which is a government organization in India. It depends on the hospital how many patients are waiting for each specialty, according to each report. We aggregated the numbers under the Small Volume heading where there are more than five patients waiting in one specialty or hospital. Monthly data for the entire year is presented with each report. The costs associated with integrating smart contracts in healthcare Blockchain need to be accounted for. Our ultimate goal is to integrate Blockchain into the medical health system. All programming calculations on the Ethereum Blockchain are subject to a fee to ensure network security. As a result, smart contracts with greater complexity have higher fees. From the standpoint of feasibility, smart contracts can be deployed with relatively low deployment costs for healthcare management systems. According to the medical system, this cost is quite reasonable, and everyone would be happy to pay it to gain control over their EHR and to keep their medical records forever.

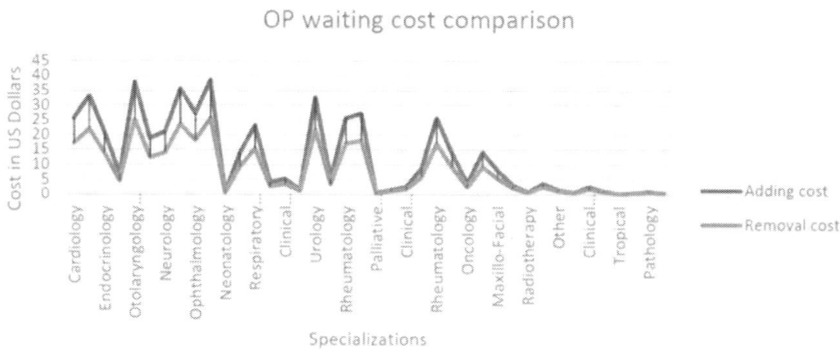

Figure 9. OP waiting cost comparison.

For different categories of patients, we have estimated the costs. This figure shows how many transactions and how much they cost for each of these instances based on our system's calculations.

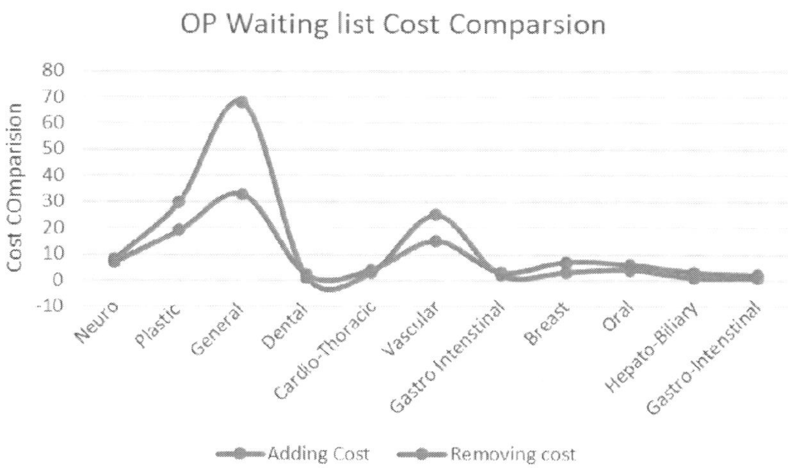

Figure 10. OP waiting list cost comparison.

Conclusion

Blockchain technology has demonstrated how decentralization policies are applied to large-scale data management in the medical ecosystem and to simplify complex medical procedures. Healthcare Big Data that is growing exponentially every year among providers, researchers, and patients can now be used in a way that prevents many issues. The health industry may be able to solve many of its problems more quickly if it can integrate this approach. To exchange information or to send visit information to hospitals, health care providers, labs, etc., use a private Blockchain. Each patient's entire health records and data, as well as the type of information and where it is stored, is recorded on the Blockchain. An encrypted link to store the user's health record is linked to a transaction in the block that contains a unique identifier for the individual.

References

Ahram, T., Sargolzaei, A., Sargolzaei, S., Daniels, J., Amaba, B. (2017). Blockchain technology innovations. In *Proceedings of the 2017 IEEE Technology and Engineering Management Conference (TEMSCON),* Santa Clara, CA, USA.

Andrade, M. (2016*). Systems and Methods for Personal Identification and Verification.* U.S. Patent Appilication No. 14/940,142, 29 September 2016.

Beck, R., Avital, M., Rossi, M., Thatcher, J.B. (2017). Blockchain technology in business and information systems research. *Bus. Inf. Syst. Eng,* 59, 381–384. [CrossRef]

Bhuiyan, M., Wang, G., Tian, W., Rahman, M. and Wu, J. (2017). Content-centric event-insensitive big data reduction in internet of things, *IEEE GLOBECOM* 2017, Singapore, December 4-8.

Bhuiyan, M., M. Zaman, G. Wang, T. Wang, and J. Wu, (2017). Privacy-protected data collection in wireless medical sensor networks," *The 12th International Conference on Networking, Architect and Storage (NAS 2017),* August 7- 8, Shenzhen, China

Buterin, V. (2014). *A Next-Generation Smart Contract and Decentralized Application Platform*; White Paper; 2014. Available online: ethereum.org (accessed on 10 September 2020).

Chris, J. (2019). *Blockchain: Background and Policy Issues;* Congressional Research Service.

Crosby, M., Pattanayak, P., Verma, S., Kalyanaraman, V. (2016). Blockchain technology: Beyond bitcoin. *Appl. Innov,* 2, 71.

Curran, B. (2018). *What Are the Trustless Environments and How Cryptocurrencies Create Them?* Blockonomi.com.

Dorri, A., Kanhere, S.S., Jurdak, R., Gauravaram, P (2017). Blockchain for IoT security and privacy: The case study of a smart home. In *Proceedings of the 2017 IEEE*

International Conference on Pervasive Computing and Communications Workshops (PerCom Workshops), Seattle, WA, USA, 21–25, pp. 618–623.

Dovey, (2020). M. Love on the block. In *Artists Re:Thinking the Blockchain*. Liverpool University Press.

Engelhardt, M.A. (2017). Hitching healthcare to the chain: An introduction to Blockchain technology in the healthcare sector. *Technol. Innov. Manag. Rev,* 7, 22–34.

Erik, H., Strewe, U.M., Bosia, N. (2018). Background III—What is Blockchain technology? In *Supply Chain Finance and Blockchain Technology*; Springer: Cham, Switzerland, pp. 35–49.

Ernest, A., Hourt, N., Larimer, D. (2016). *Blockchain Electronic Voting System and Method.* U.S. Patent Appilication No. 15/298,177, 20 April 2016.

Esposito, C., De Santis, A., Tortora, G., Chang, H., Choo, K.K.R. (2019). Blockchain: A panacea for healthcare cloud-based data security and privacy*? IEEE Cloud Comput,* 5, 31–37. [CrossRef]

Florian, G. (2019). Pervasive Decentralisation of digital infrastructures: a framework for Blockchain enabled system and use case analysis. In *Proceedings of the Hawaii International Conference on System Sciences,* Puako, HI, USA.

Gipp, B., Kosti, J., Breitinger, C. (2016). Securing video integrity using decentralized trusted timestamping on the Bitcoin Blockchain. In *Proceedings of the Mediterranean Conference on Information Systems (MCIS),* Paphos, Cyprus; p. 51.

Hölbl, M., Kompara, M., Kamisalic, A., Zlatolas, L.N. (2018). A systematic review of the use of Blockchain in healthcare. *Symmetry,* 10, 470. [CrossRef]

Jacobovitz, O. (2016). Blockchain for identity management. In *The Lynne and William Frankel Center for Computer Science Department of Computer Science.* Ben-Gurion University, Beer Sheva; Ben-Gurion University: Beersheba, Israel, 2016.

Kenneth, M., D. Markwell, R. MacDonald, P. Szolovits, and I. Kohane, (2001). Public standards and patients' control: how to keep electronic medical records accessible but private. *BMJ* 322, no. 7281: 283-28.

Khatoon, A., Verma, P., Southernwood, J., Massey, B., Corcoran, P. (2019). Blockchain in energy efficiency: potential applications and benefits. *Energies*, 12, 3317.

Korpela, K., Hallikas, J., Dahlberg, T. (2017). Digital supply chain transformation toward Blockchain integration In *Proceedings of the 50th Hawaii International Conference on System Sciences,* Waikoloa Village, HI, USA

Liang, X., Shetty, S., Tosh, D., Kamhoua, C., Kwiat, K., Njilla, L. Provchain: (2017). A Blockchain-based data provenance architecture in cloud environment with enhanced privacy and availability. In *Proceedings of the 17th IEEE/ACM International Symposium on Cluster, Cloud and Grid Computing,* Madrid, Spain, 14–17 May 2017; pp. 468–477.

Liu, S. (2017). *Medical Record System Using Blockchain, Big Data and Tokenization,* https://hbr.org/2014/12/why-health-care-may-finally-be- ready-for-big-data.

Luo, E., Bhuiyan, M.A., Wang, G., Rahman, M., Wu, J. and Atiquzzaman, M. (2018), Protector: Privacy-protected patient data collection in IoT-based healthcare systems, *IEEE Communication Magazine* (COMMAG), 56(2): 163-168, 2018.

Mallikarjuna, B., Sathish, K., Krishna, P.V., & Viswanathan, R. (2020a). The effective SVM-based binary prediction of ground water table. *Evolutionary Intelligence,* 1-9.

Mallikarjuna, B., Viswanathan, R., & Naib, B.B. (2020b). Feedback-based gait identification using deep neural network classification. *Journal of Critical Reviews,* 7(4), 661-667.

Mallikarjuna, B. (2020c). Feedback-based resource utilization for smart home automation in fog assistance IoT-based cloud. *International Journal of Fog Computing (IJFC),* 3(1), 41-63.

Mallikarjuna, B., Shrivastava, G., & Sharma, M. (2021a). Blockchain technology: A DNN Mallikarjuna, B., Kiranmayee, D., Saritha, V., & Krishna, P.V. (2021b, June). Development of efficient e-health records using IoT and Blockchain technology. In *ICC 2021-IEEE International Conference on Communications* (pp. 1-7). IEEE.

Mallikarjuna, B., Addanke, S., & Anusha, D.J. (2022a). An improved deep learning algorithm for diabetes prediction. In *Handbook of Research on Advances in Data Analytics and Complex Communication Networks* (pp. 103-119). IGI Global.

Mallikarjuna, B., Anusha, D.J., & Sabharwal, M. (2022b). An effective video surveillance system by using CNN for COVID-19. In *Handbook of Research on Advances in Data Analytics and Complex Communication Networks* (pp. 88-102). IGI Global.

Martin, Z. Digital art as 'monetised graphics': Enforcing intellectual property on the Blockchain. *Philos. Technol.* 2018, 31, 15–41.

McGhin, T., Choo, K.-K.R., Liu, C.Z., He, D. (2019). Blockchain in healthcare applications: Research challenges and opportunities. *J. Netw. Comput. Appl,* 135, 62–75. [CrossRef]

Mehdi, B., Ravaud, (2017). P. Blockchain technology for improving clinical research quality. *Trials,* 18, 335.

Meng, W., Tischhauser, E.W., Wang, Q., Wang, Y., Han, J. (2018). When intrusion detection meets Blockchain technology: A review. *IEEE Access,* 6, 10179–10188. [CrossRef]

Mettler, M. (2016). Blockchain technology in healthcare: The revolution starts here. In *Proceedings of the 2016 IEEE 18th International Conference on e-Health Networking, Applications and Services (Healthcom),* Munich, Germany, 14–16 September 2016; pp. 1–3.

MrChrisJ. *World Citizenship—Creating Affordable Decentralised Passport Services Using Available Cryptographic Tools.* Available online: https://github.com/MrChrisJ/World-Citizenship (accessed on 10 September 2020).

Nakamoto, S. (2008). *Bitcoin: A Peer-to-Peer Electronic Cash System;* Available online: ww.bitcoin.org (accessed on 31 December 2019).

Nofer, M., Gomber, P., Hinz, O., Schiereck, D. (2017). *Blockchain. Bus. Inf. Syst. Eng.* 2017, 59, 183–187. [CrossRef]

Notheisen, B., Cholewa, J.B., Shanmugam, A.P. (2017). Trading real-world assets on Blockchain. *Bus. Inf. Syst. Eng*. 59, 425–440. [CrossRef]

Osgood, R. (2016). The future of democracy: Blockchain voting. In *COMP116: Information Security;* Tuft University: Boston, MA, USA, 2016. Available online: http://www.cs.tufts.edu/comp/116/archive/fall2016/rosgood.pdf (accessed on 20 September 2020).

Ovais, A. (2019). *Blockchain Technology: Concept of Digital Economics;* University Library of Munich, Germany: Munich, Germany.

Price, M. (2017). *Blockchain: The Complete Guide to Understanding Blockchain Technology,* CreateSpace Independent Publishing Platform Fast Healthcare Interoperability Resources (FHIR) https://www.hl7.org/fhir/overview.html

Rabah, K.V.O. (2017). Challenges & opportunities for Blockchain powered healthcare systems: A review. *Mara Res. J. Med. Health Sci.* 1, 45–52.

Rahman, F., M. Bhuiyan, and S. Ahamed, (2017). A privacy preserving framework for RFID based healthcare systems, *Future Generation Computer Systems,* 72: 339-352.

Rawat, D.B., Parwez, M.S., Alshammari, (2017). A. Edge computing enabled resilient wireless network virtualization for Internet of Things. In *Proceedings of the 2017 IEEE 3rd International Conference on Collaboration and Internet Computing (CIC),* San Jose, CA, USA, 15–17 October 2017; pp. 155–162.

Rawat, D.B., Song, M., Shetty, S. *Dynamic Spectrum Access for Wireless Networks*; Springer: Berlin/Heidelberg, Germany, 2015.

Saberi, S., Kouhizadeh, M., Sarkis, J., Shen, L. (2019). Blockchain technology and its relationships to sustainable supply chain management. *Int. J. Prod* 57, 2117–2135. [CrossRef]

Son, J., Park, J., Oh, H., Bhuiyan, M., Hur, J. and Kang, K. (2017). Privacy-preserving electrocardiogram monitoring for intelligent arrhythmia detection, *Sensors,* 17(6):1-22, 136, doi:10.3390/s17061360.

Spielman, A. (2016). A. *Blockchain: Digitally Rebuilding the Real Estate Industry.* Ph.D. Thesis, Massachusetts Institute of Technology, Cambridge, MA, USA, 2016.

Sullivan, C., Burger, E. (2017). E-residency and Blockchain. *Comput. Law Secur. Rev.* 2017, 33, 470–481. [CrossRef]

Suveen, A., Krumholz, H.M., Schulz, W.L. (2017). Blockchain technology: Applications in health care. *Circ. Cardiovasc. Qual. Outcomes 10,* e003800.

Tosh, D.K., Shetty, S., Foytik, P., Njilla, L., Kamhoua, C.A. (2018). Blockchain-empowered secure Internet-of Battlefield Things (IoBT) architecture. In *Proceedings of the MILCOM 2018-2018 IEEE Military Communications Conference (MILCOM),* Los Angeles, CA, USA, 29–31, pp. 593–598.

Tran, T., M. Rahman, M. Bhuiyan, A. Kubota, S. Kiyomoto, and K. Omote, (2017). Optimizing share size in efficient and robust secret sharing scheme for big data, *IEEE Transactions on Big Data,* DOI: ttps://doi.org/10.1109/TBDATA.2017.27080.

Wang, T., Bhuiyan, M.A., Wang, G., Rahman, M., Wu, J. and Cao, J. (2017). Big data reduction for Smart City's critical infrastructural health monitoring, *IEEE Communication Magazine (COMMAG),* 56(3): 128 – 133.

Witchey, N.J. (2019). *Healthcare Transaction Validation via Blockchain, Systems and Methods.* U.S. Patent No. 10,340,038.

Zhu, H., Zhou, Z.Z. (2016). Analysis and outlook of applications of Blockchain technology to equity crowdfunding in China. *Financ. Innov.* 2016, 2, 29. [CrossRef]

Zillner, S. and Neururer, S. (2019). Big data in the health sector, In: Cavanillas J., Curry E., Wahlster W. (eds) *New Horizons for a Data-Driven Economy.* Springer, Cham

Zyskind, G., Nathan, O. (2015). Decentralizing privacy: Using Blockchain to protect personal data. In *Proceedings of the 2015 IEEE Security and Privacy Workshops,* San Jose, CA, USA, 21–22.

Chapter 4

Healthcarc Data Management and Remote Monitoring Using Big Data Analytics, Blockchain Technology, and Blockchain Powered HER in the Pharmaceutical Industry

Nutan Gusain*, Himanshu Sharma and Basetty Mallikarjuna
School of Computing Science and Engineering,
Galgotias University, Uttar Pradesh, India

Abstract

In this chapter, data management and remote monitoring of the healthcare data by using big data analytics and Blockchain technology is discussed. A discussion on big data analytics and Blockchain amalgamation is done to implement Blockchain in healthcare systems. Blockchain validates the integrity of the healthcare data and any modification done is identified and gets registered. Big data analytics in healthcare makes the system more accurate. Blockchain and big data support one another to implement healthcare monitoring and data accumulation in a more secure way.

Keywords: healthcare, Blockchain, big data, public key infrastructure (PKI)

---

* Corresponding Author's Email: nautan.gusain@galgotiasuniversity.edu.in.

In: Blockchain Technology Based Big Data for Healthcare
Editors: Basetty Mallikarjuna, Niranjanamurthy M, Sheng-Lung Peng et al.
ISBN: 978-1-68507-968-0

Introduction

In the field of academics and industries, Blockchain technology in big data is very effective and evolving automation and business process management. Transparency and privacy of data get enhanced when Blockchain technology along with big data are used together. In Blockchain technology, blocks are used to store data that holds the hash value of the previous block and the current block. SHA256 is used to execute the hash value. To store and transfer information, a Blockchain is a decentralized system (Siyal, A. A., et al., 2019). The efficiency is high since Blockchain technology uses cryptographic distributed database technology to enhance the security and quality of data. Hackers can't modify the data since it requires permission on many levels. The application area of Blockchain technology is vast like social media, banking, smart contracts, medical record system, etc. (Durneva, P., et al., 2020). Researchers are finding ways to use Blockchain technology in space missions to make them more powerful. In addition, Blockchain technology is suitable for storing data online and, using this technology with big data, various banks can improve the privacy and security of customers' digital currency. Blockchain in big data surely increases the efficiency of data sharing (Saif, S., et al., 2020).

Blockchain checks the integrity of the data and any modification done is registered.

Since the number of users who are using Blockchain services is increasing, high quality data is generating efficiently. These analytics are making great advancements in the field of big data analytics (Al Omar, A., et al., 2019).

An Overview of Blockchain Technology and Management

For the last two decades, Blockchain gained popularity as it is a foundation of the digital currency Bitcoin. Decentralized transactions are maintained in the Blockchain. In the field of banking, financial services, social media, the Internet of Things, etc. Blockchain applications are everywhere (Yaqoob, I., et al., 2021). Scalability and security are two major concerns. Researchers are facing issues in Blockchain technology.

Figure 1 explains how blocks are linked together within Blockchain technology. The first block is known as the genesis block, which doesn't have a parent block (Dubovitskaya, A., et al., 2020). Every block holds the hash value of the previous block as well as the hash of the current block. This sequence of blocks stores the transaction information just like the traditional record of the transactions.

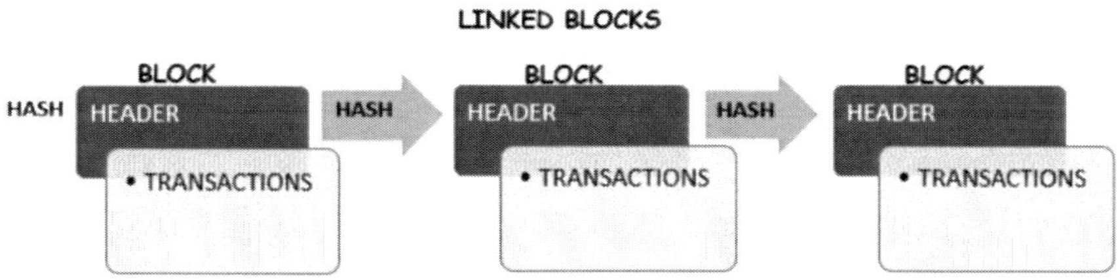

Figure 1. Blockchain technology.

Each block comprises two things: header and body. The block header stores 256 bits hash-value which points to the parent block, the hash value of all the transactions, and validation rules which need to be followed. The block body holds the transactions and counter for transactions (Dagher, G. G., et al., 2018). The size of every transaction and block decides the maximum number of transactions that any block can hold. The asymmetric cryptographic mechanism, which is a digital signature-based technology, is used for the validation process for the authentication of all the transactions. Decentralization, anonymity, and persistence are the best features of Blockchain that can transform the traditional industry (Girardi, F., et al., 2020).

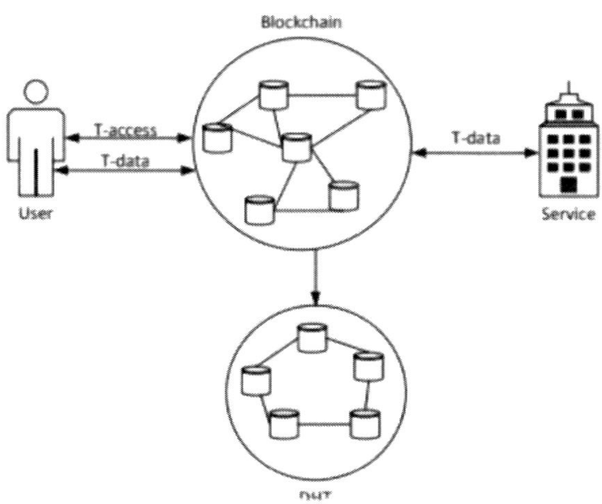

Figure 2. Decentralized system (Chattu, V. K., 2021).

The best features of Blockchain are as follows:

- Decentralization: Central banks validate each transaction in a centralized transaction system which needs cost and central server powers. As shown in Figure 2, in Blockchain technology, a third party is not required. Distributed networks in Blockchain use a consensus algorithm to maintain the data persistency.
- Persistency: Any block in Blockchain doesn't contain invalid transactions as only validated transactions are accepted. Any modification or alteration in the transaction is not possible.
- Anonymity: A unique address is provided to each user, which is best for not revealing the real identity of the user for security purpose. However, Blockchain has some constraints due to which full privacy can't be attained.
- Auditability: User's balance information is stored on the Unspent Transaction Output (UTXO) model. Once the transaction is registered in the Blockchain, the unspent transaction is converted to spent, then the server verifies the transaction and tracking can also be done easily.

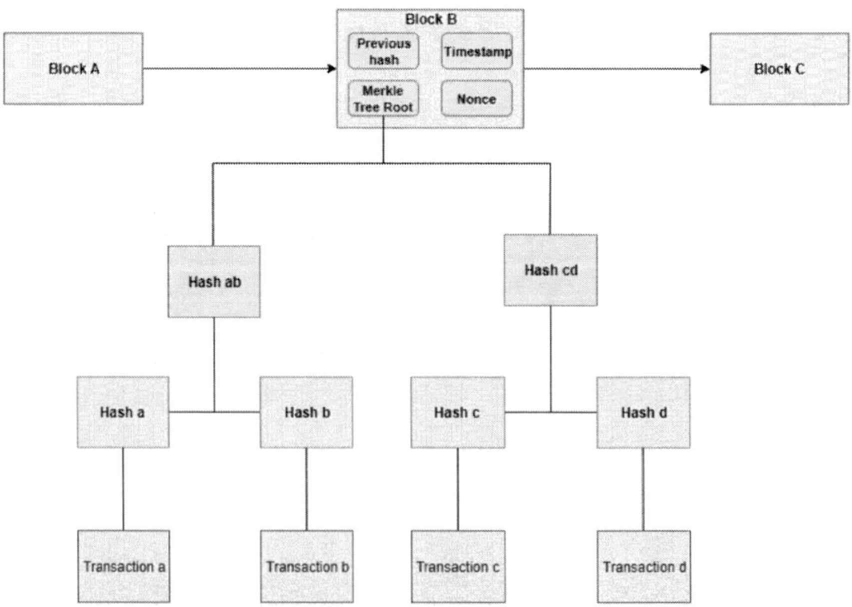

Figure 3. Block diagram of Blockchain (Chattu, V. K., 2021).

Figure 3 explains how each block, consisting of four parts, is connected with each other forming a chain.

Each block consists of:

- Previous hash
- Timestamp
- Nonce
- Merkle tree root

Big Data Technology and Uses

Data sets that are large and complicated, in which the conventional applications are incapable for data processing, are termed as big data (Dimitrov, D. V., 2019).). Big data technology is used to create, capture, search, share, store, analyze, transfer, and visualize data, as depicted in Figure 4. Big data analytics is a mechanism to find the pattern and correlation among large amounts of data. Using big data analytics, multinational companies and organizations can deduce information that can benefit them to get advantage which extends the scope of big data technology.

Figure 4. Big data technology.

In this technology, data is collected from various resources like emails, images, audio, videos, online transactions, health records, social networking sites, and applications. After this, data is stored in a database. Since the data is so vast, it can't be analyzed and visualized with traditional database software.

Use of Blockchain in Big Data

Network of decentralized data records is the key feature of Blockchain. Each record or transaction is verified and authenticated by trusted servers and can't be forged. Invalid data can't be modified into the sequence which is the best reason for using Blockchain in big data.

There are five different methods to embed Blockchain with big data technology:

1. Ensuring Data Integrity

The data recorded on each block is valid as it is gone through various process like authentication and verification, which ensures the quality of the data. Also, transparency is the other key feature as all the transactions on Blockchain can be simulated (Mallikarjuna, B., et al., 2021a).

In 2018 A, Lenovo explains how Blockchain technology can reveal the forged documents. The organization used digital signatures to legalize the important documents. The authentication of the document is done by using Blockchain record.

Data integrity can be ensured with the automatic verification of data block with details like the source and concerned transactions. Blockchain network is reinforced by number of devices called nodes, which ensures the transaction (Mallikarjuna, B., et al., 2020a).

2. Preventing Malicious Activity

In Blockchain technology, cryptographic algorithm and digital signature is applied to validate each transaction to prevent possible threat. Any node which shows invalid data is removed from the network (Mallikarjuna, B., et al., 2020b).

The authentication scheme for Blockchain technology is so powerful that it can't be surpassed by a single malicious node and require group of nodes to create feasible computational power to modify data.

3. Making Predictions (Predictive Analysis)

Blockchain technology can be used to analyze data and predict conclusion. Using Blockchain technology organized data can be formulated from different devicse.

Small organizations can also apply predictive analysis because of the decentralized nature of Blockchain. Data scientists can utilize the computational capability of the various nodes interconnected within a Blockchain network. Also, social outputs can be analyzed with the help of a cloud-based service.

4. Real Time Data Analysis

Transactions in Blockchain are real-time irrespective of the geographical boundaries with fastest speed which makes the innovators of several traditional banks to scrutinize Blockchain.

Similarly, Blockchain can be used in organizations that need real time analysis of huge amount of data. Using Blockchain technology, banks and organizations can monitor malicious activities, identify possible forgery, examine real time data modification (Mallikarjuna, B., et al., 2021b).

5. Manage Data Sharing

Using Blockchain technology, data retrieved from various studies can be stored so that others are not able to reuse the analyzed data. Data scientists can collaborate by exchanging analyzed data on a Blockchain platform (Mallikarjuna, B., et al., 2022b).

How Blockchain and Big Data Support Eachother

Blockchain and big data are two most popular technologies in this decade. The most important feature of Blockchain is decentralization. To store and transmit information, Blockchain is the best database technology which is cryptographically secured and distributed. Each block in the Blockchain consists of transaction date and previous block link.

Data Quality and Privacy

To analyze the huge amount of data and making conclusions is the most priority of the various organizations today. However, Big data technology suffers with lack of security and privacy issues.

Due to rapid increase of big data on the internet, there is exponential hike in data size. Due to the insecure environment data circulation and development of industry is facing difficulties. However, this issue can be resolved using Blockchain technology. Using smart contracts with non-tempering and traceable feature, default instructions can be automatically executed (Bazel, M. A., et al., 2021).

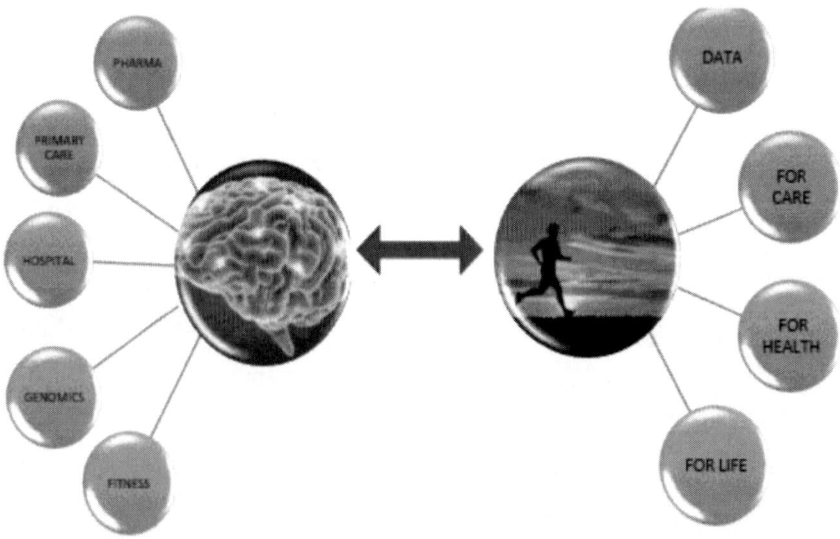

Figure 5. Hospital management system.

To enhance the security in big data, Blockchain is the suitable technology as it can support various digital data.

Figure 5 explains how Blockchain technology can be used in hospitals to make sure that the data about patient is secured and updated. Using Blockchain, all hospital workers can access the data from a single, non-modifiable, source of data.

Blockchain technology reduces the risk of incorrect diagnosis, unaltered or misplaced lab test results (Khezr, S., et al., 2019). As all the data is stored is secured, there are less chances of getting anomalies if two doctors are treating the same patient.

Data Transparency and Automation

Blockchain is a latest storage system for digital data, which is encrypted and distributed. Only those users can access the data who have authority and thus ensures the integrity of data (Mallikarjuna, B., et al., 2022c).

Using Blockchain technology, rises the issues of privacy because of its transparency feature. Data scientists are worried as it may rise the possibility of fake user profiles.

Blockchain combined with big data technology aims in preventing the possibility of data leaks. One the record is stored, permissions are required to access the data. So, it is very difficult to modify the data.

For the purpose of tracking, understanding and explaining the conclusions made by AI, Blockchain can be used. Conclusions made by AI are difficult for us to interpret as they can access huge amount of data and are able to extract the important data (Mallikarjuna, B., et al., 2020c).

For example, AI algorithms are anticipated to be used in making conclusions regarding the authenticity of a transaction. Accuracy of the conclusions made by AI, must be checked by humans, which becomes tedious task when data is large.

Big Data and Blockchain: Quantity and Quality

Blockchain technology is beneficial to cover the limitations faced by big data.

These benefits include:

- Security: One of the main features of Blockchain technology is security. All the blocks in a Blockchain are non-modifiable.
- Transparency: The transparency feature in Blockchain architecture can be used to find the source point of data.
- Decentralization: Blockchain stores data in distributed manner. Even if any node is malicious, still data is protected.
- Flexibility: Variety of data can be accumulated in Blockchain as this is secured and non-modifiable which makes Blockchain flexible in nature.

Decentralization

Earlier, centralized services were used, in which all the data is stored in a single entity. To access the required information, this single entity has to be interacted.

The best example of this system is banks. Figure 6 explains the client-server model of traditional banks. For any transaction, banks need to be contacted.

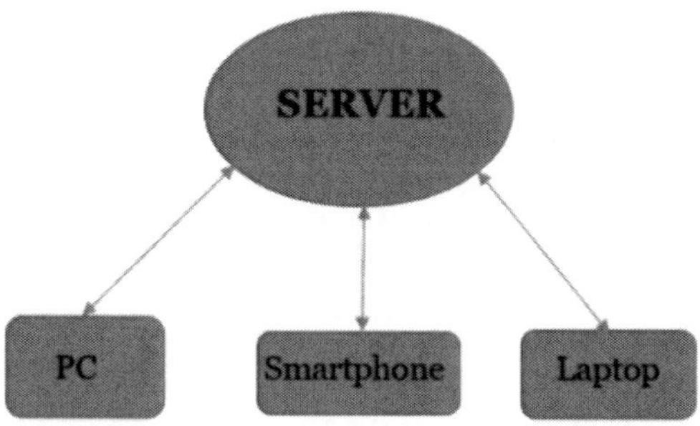

Figure 6. Client-server model.

In a client-server architecture, the user creates and sends the request to the server, which gets back the information to the requested user, such as a Google search. Centralized systems have some drawbacks which are listed below:

- Since all the data is stored in a single entity, there is potential threat of hacking and insecurity.

- Software updating process can pause the entire system in case of centralized system.
- Data will be lost if the centralized system is shut down.
- If the centralized entity gets attacked by the hacker, then all the data can be altered.

In a decentralized system, data is distributed in the nodes connected in the network.

In this network there is no third party, same methodology is adopted by bitcoin. Any transaction can be done directly without using third party. Figure 7 explains a decentralized system in a bank.

Figure 7. Example of data transaction.

Transparency

In Blockchain technology, transparency and privacy are the most important feature. Blockchain ensures privacy by hiding the details of the identity of the user with the help of cryptography. Users are only denoted by their public addresses.

All the transactions are transparent but the user's identity is private. This feature was not present in the traditional systems. This feature adds more variety which is required by bigger organizations (Mayer, A. H., et al., 2020).

However, most of the bigger organizations don't use cryptocurrency for transactions as it is transparent. Also, if all the transactions are made using cryptocurrency and integrated with supply chain, then it will the major concern for the big organizations.

Immutability

In Blockchain technology, once data is entered, it can't be altered, which is immutability feature.

In hashing, a variable length string is converted into a fixed length. Similarly, cryptocurrencies like bitcoin uses SHA-256 hashing algorithm, which takes transactions as inputs and convert it into fixed length (Mallikarjuna, B., et al., 2021a).

Big Data Challenges

Nowadays raw data is growing exponentially. Big organizations are finding the different aspects of this data, which can be used to benefit the customers, increase the likeability of a product and services offered. big data has so many advantages to offer but is still in developing and evolving phase.

Data privacy, insufficient knowledge, and inadequate analytical capabilities of companies are the major challenges faced by big data technology. Many organizations are facing problems due to lack of expertise in the field of big data (Mallikarjuna, B., et al., 2020a).

Beside this issue, organizations are facing other challenges as well which they encounter while adopting into big data environment. Some of these challenges are discussed in the following sections.

Handling Big Data

Size plays a vital role while big data is concerned. To manage the exponentially growing data is major concern for the bigger organizations. To overcome this challenge, processors are replaced with faster processor to keep up with the large amount of data. Since data is growing more rapidly than the hardware resources, increasing CPU speed is becoming stagnant. However, more cores are being incorporated in CPU due to power constraints.

There is remarkable increase in the accessibility of data. Previously, organizations were able to access a small chunk of data as compared to the current scenario. With the increase of data, organizations using statistics and analytics can access the data about consumer's likes, popularity of a product or ratings of a newly opened restaurant (Mallikarjuna, B., et al., 2020b).

Not only there is rise in unstructured data but also in the different formats of data. Hybrid databases are adopted to manage the data, in which RDBMS and NoSQL are connected like MongoDB. Also, to manage the distributed data Hadoop can be used.

Security Aspects and Constraints

Many organizations are claiming the issues with security of data. Along with other data-centric issues, security is the major challenge for them. Due to the wide range of involvement in data with various authority, data security might be compromised (Mallikarjuna, B., et al., 2020b).

To collect the data, organizations use different methods which makes data inaccurate, inconsistent and the ultimately the analysis of data is being compromised. It may cause security issues. To reduce these security issues, best security practices must be adopted (Mallikarjuna, B., et al., 2020b).

Efficiently Processing Unstructured and Semi Structured Data

Unstructured data in warehouses are not processed properly. In big data read/write operations are concurrent in nature for most of the users. With the increase of data, algorithms might become invalid. The CAP theorem states that it is impossible for a dispersed system to have all the three; we can choose only 2 out of 3. NOSQL is introduced as a new processing approach, since it is challenging to process the robust data using traditional processing methods.

An ideal big data is measured by the following 5Vs:

1. Variety
2. Volume
3. Veracity
4. Value
5. Velocity

In data analysis, firstly data must be organized. Example: Consider a patient having multiple records like lab reports, operation reports, admissions and lifetime consultation. These records are unstructured and are not organized. Without structured data, data analysis process is challenging, which is the major concern for big data.

Computations

In big data technology, useful information is extracted from the raw data by performing specific computation. However, to avoid the loss of data, altered results and insecure computations, security and privacy is must (Mallikarjuna, B., et al., 2021b).

Communication

In big data, there are number of clusters, each of them having several nodes that are distributed all over the world. Communication between nodes and clusters are managed through traditional private and public networks. However, to deduce important conclusions, customize inter-node communication can be managed. Therefore, big data need advance network protocols (Mallikarjuna, B., et al., 2022a).

Access Control

To invalidate any suspicious entity from accessing the storage server, big data needs a robust access control mechanism. Node with the permission and admin powers can only manage and access the data. Additionally, any alterations in the state of clusters must be interrogated by a process to authenticate and protect the system from mischievous nodes (Mallikarjuna, B., et al., 2022b).

Random Distribution

Using parallelism methodology, big data analytics gathers huge amount of data and processes various clusters. Clusters are scattered all over the world, which resembles a power station. The actual location of data and process is not known, which makes this methodology challenging. This creates many problems like security and regulation issues. To distribute the data and processes according to the norms and sensibility is the major challenge faced by big data (Mallikarjuna, B., et al., 2022c).

Solutions to Big Data Using Blockchain

Blockchain technology is popular for the ongoing research in various aspects. However, it is still in evolution phase and considered as modern solution for issues like trust, identity, decentralization, data ownership, and data-driven decisions. Furthermore, rapid growth in variety and quantity of data is another challenge for the modern technology. Blockchain technology is best suited technology to store large amount of data, organize it and process it. Whether it would be management of data in decentralized environment, IOT based communication or smart documents have huge impact on the evolution of big data (E. Karafiloski and A. Mishev, 2017).

Implementation of SHA 256 with Blockchain for Big Data Technology

In Blockchain technology, hashing is the most important process. To write new records in the Blockchain, hashing is used. An input of variable length string is given to a function and it gives a fixed length string as an output. This is termed as hash-function and the output is known as hash, which is executed with a hashing algorithm SHA256. The size of input is insignificant in hash function. SHA256 produces an output of 256 bits length (Mallikarjuna, B., et al., 2022c).

Following are the characteristics of a secure hash function:

- Deterministic: Which indicates the result or the hash value must be same if same input string is given multiple times.
- The hash function must generate the hash value rapidly.
- For each hash H(f), it should ne not feasible to calculate an input f from H(f).
- For every minute changes in input must affect the output significantly.
- The hash values must be unique and should not match with other hash value.

For each output value Y, to find the value of an input X must be infeasible, as:

$$H(k|X) = Y$$

Here k is any random value of high minimum entropy Khezr, S., et al., (2019).

There are a number of hash-functions available in the Blockchain technology most commonly used once are: *SHA* 256 *:Used in Bitcoin*

To store data in Blockchain, there are two data structures that are needed, pointer and link list. Figure 8 explains pointers, which stores the address of another variable. Pointers stores the hash-value for last block in Blockchain technology.

So basically, Blockchain is a linked list where each node is storing the hash value of the previous node and a data header which stores the data of that block.

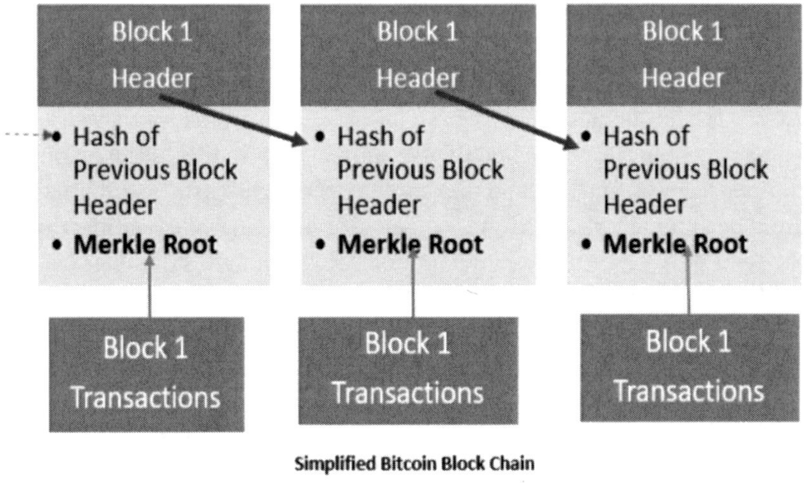

Figure 8. Simplified Blockchain structure (Khezr, S., et al., 2019).

Mining Process

The procedure of adding a fresh block in the Blockchain is known as mining. Whenever any new transaction occurs, miners verify the transaction and add it in the Blockchain if valid.

In a Blockchain network there is a time limit to create a new block, 9-10 minutes in bitcoin. The chances of the collision of hashes may occur if the rate of creating new blocks is faster. If new blocks are created rapidly, it might happen that few blocks are not added in the Blockchain. Therefore, to avoid this issue a threshold value is defined for hash. Likewise, in bitcoin, when a fresh block is created, all the transactions in the block are converted to hash code by the hash-function. A random string is generated as a concatenated hashed result, known as nonce.

Fresh block is added in the Blockchain only if the result is less than the difficulty level. Nonce is modified and the procedure gets repeated until the result is matched with the required standard value.

For each output value W, to find the value of an input X must be infeasible, as:

$$H(k\ X) = W$$

W = difficult level,
k = nonce,
X = hash of previous block.

Implementaiton of Digital Signature-Based Security in Big Data Management

The validation mechanism to authenticate and check the integrity of a message, software and digital document is digital signature. An algorithm like Diffie Hellman key exchange algorithm is used in digital signature. It is similar to signature and seal but is more secure and can solve the issue of alterations and forgery in digital communication. It also validates the authenticity of the sender. Digital signatures are accepted legally in many countries.

It is based on public key cryptography technique. Public key algorithm like RSA can create two keys: private and public (Saif, S., et al., 2020). The sender creates a digital signature with their private key and encrypts the signature. To decrypt this signature sender's public key is used.

Public Key Infrastructure (PKI) for Big Data Security

A third party is used to inspect and assure the identity of user with the help of cryptography using private and public key and issues a certificate.

This mechanism is known as PKI. It consists of the following entities:

- Client software system
- Certificate authority server
- Smart Cards
- Operational methods

Public key cryptography which is an advanced topic in IT security permits the exchange of keys in an open network. It provides security which is not present in traditional cryptography.

In this technique, there are two keys private and public key but doesn't involve the key exchange process. Since private key is private and the public key is verified and authenticated, this technique can be trusted. These key pairs are managed by public key infrastructure (PKI) (Saif, S., et al., 2020).

Authentication of Public Key Infrastructure

The first step in the authentication process is to validate the identity of the user, which is done by a certificate authority. The certificate authority is a third party and provides certificate independently. In this case, some of them may allow users just because of digital certificate, which contains only user's name and email id. However, certificate authority user could also opt personal interviews and background check. After this, private and public keys are provided to the user.

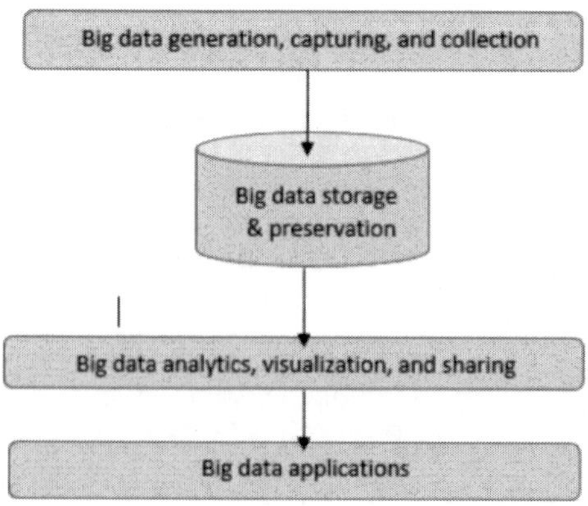

Figure 9. PKI model (Saif, S., et al., 2020).

For example, a user wants to send an email to his colleagues and signs it using digital signature with the help of a private key. This email is encrypted now and will only be decrypted by the user's public key. In this process, no secret key is shared in advance. Figure 9 explain how PKI is used in medical application systems (Saif, S., et al., 2020).

Uses of PKI

- To encrypt the email, important documents and authenticating sender's id.
- To authenticate the SMART CARD login system application users.
- To enable the secure communication using bootstrap.
- To integrate the security infrastructure to encrypt, digitally sign and certificate authority.
- To create a reliable network environment, encryption and decryption enabled digital signature PKI is introduced.
- Transparency and simplicity are two main features of PKI. It adds more security to the platform with security management skills.
- To improve security, comfort and way of digital signature are the important benefits of public key cryptography. It is fully trusted system and there is no limitation in the accessibility. Without third party intervention, users can manage certificates and data shared between client and server.

Data Manipulation of Blockchain and Big Data Technology

Blockchain is considered to be the most important technological advancement after the internet, because of huge range of applications. One of the most researched ideas is to combine Blockchain with big data. Since the data in Blockchain is already verified, there is no requirement to authenticate the data. It is impossible to manipulate data in a Blockchain as it requires high computation power. Blockchain technology integrates hashing and cryptography together. Data is more vulnerable to hacking if stored in a centralized system. The goal of Blockchain technology is to give more power to the user and provide variety of applications by integrating with big data.

Medical Record System

One of the most important applications of Blockchain is in the domain of healthcare. The medical data consist of reports, documents, images and videos. Due to unavailability of medical record systems, centralized storage systems are required. With the increase of medical data, storage is the major concern in this scenario. Also, many doctors are insecure and worried about the possibility of the legality in case things go wrong and are not comfortable sharing records with other doctors as well. To protect the privacy of both patient and doctors, security is required.

Duplicate transactions are prevented by Blockchain by accepting only the first transaction and rejecting the others. Digital signature can be used to remove duplicate records. The Blockchain process can be incorporated directly on medical database, hardware that have been used to secure the data from the risk of alteration. Furthermore, hash values and digital signatures can add more strength to protect data from modification.

To encrypt all the medical data and protect it from unauthorized access Blockchain process is applied. Also, digital signature can be used to check the integrity of the medical records. All records are arranged serial wise in a Blockchain.

Blockchain emphasize on the data integrity and is best suited technology for record management systems. However, it can't deal with the issue of exponential growing data.

Banking and Management

Due to the contribution of Blockchain technology with big data, banking sectors are interrupted. Since there is a gap between the research and implementation of Blockchain with big data, negative effect can be seen in banking sector, which is explained in the Figure 10.

Blockchain is considered as a threat to the traditional banking techniques and thus the current relationship between Blockchain and banking is complex (Al Omar, A., et al., 2019).

To prevent criminals to use the benefits of banks services in the form of money laundering and terrorism, KYC is the most critical aspect. Therefore, verification and authentication are the most frequent and important issues for a bank.

Security is the major concern for banking sector. With Blockchain technology security can be ensured. Any modification in data can be reported and monitored to track any suspicious activity.

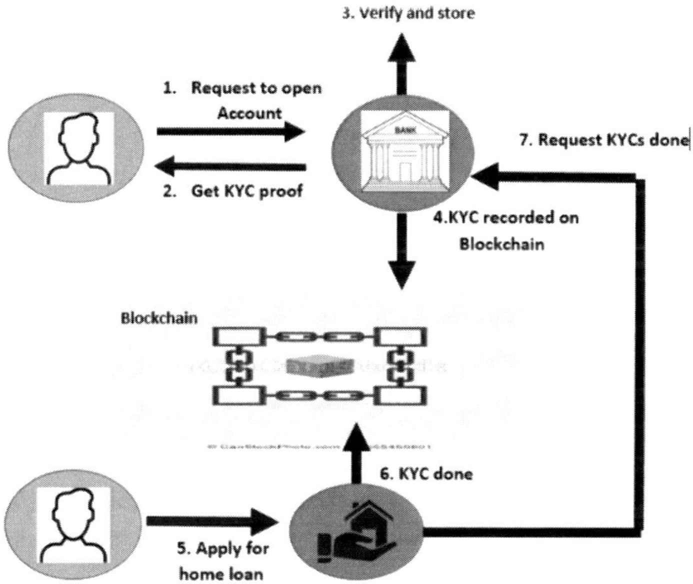

Figure 10. Blockchain use in the banking sector (Al Omar, A., et al., 2019).

The transparency feature of Blockchain enables the regulatory bodies to inspect financial activity. With Blockchain, only authenticated user can access the data and more security is added due to encryption capabilities.

The security feature in Blockchain technology is considered as both a scope and challenge in banking.

Besides all the advantages, data privacy is still major concern in Blockchain technology, as transactions are visible to nodes in network that produces meta data which leads to pattern recognition. Another major concern is anonymity, which can lead to the rise of money laundering and difficulty in calculating tax.

Social Media Data

Blockchain is considered as the improvised version of internet. To handle data more securely and promote user responsibility on internet (Chattu, V. K.,

2021), Blockchain technology is introduced. Previously, the main focus of Blockchain technology was cryptocurrency but now it is shifted to online business and social media platforms. Since data can't be altered in Blockchain technology, it can reduce the fake content and with proper authentication users' integrity can be maintained.

To increase the security of data, Blockchain has forced the reorganization of data sharing algorithms, payment methods and security policies in social media platform. For companies that depend on social media for advertisement, Blockchain is thinking about incorporating cryptocurrency transactions (Chattu, V. K., 2021).

Presently, users are having multiple accounts on social media. These platforms have the full access to the user's data which can be traded with the stakeholders. Using this data, companies' focus is on the highly targeted ads. Privacy and data security issues can be handled with Blockchain technology using decentralized social media channels having secured and encrypted communications (Chattu, V. K., 2021).

Space Data

Current space giants like NASA, ESA, CNSA and Roscosmos are still implementing national space programs having secured and reliable communications and are not willing to share national authority crypto enthusiast (Mallikarjuna, B., et al., 2021a). According to ESA, distributed ledger systems are not yet best suited for space operations and earth observer (EO) data exploitation. They claim that most of the advantages of Blockchain are theoretical and need demonstration on how Blockchain is being utilized to solve the concern pertaining in EO. Due to the advantages of different technologies like big data, AI and machine learning EO is growing. M2M communications are becoming more common and dynamic.

According to ESA, due to rise in these dynamic networks there is requirement of secured, data distribution and tracking of each step. EO and other space operations are more exposed to attack.

Scenario-Based Analysis of Blockchain Towards Big Data

Because of the better performance over the typical database systems, Blockchain technology is more tempting for data scientists. With Blockchain technology there is a possibility of unaltered and non-modifiable data. The following section discusses the three different methods in which Blockchain disrupts big data analytics (Mallikarjuna, B., et al., 2021a).

Accessibility of Decentralized Tools

High price is the main hurdle when incorporating big data analytics into existing environment. Earlier, only big organizations could use big data and get the benefits of it. However, this scenario has changed with the rise of subscription-based services. By applying decentralizing, Blockchain-inspired services goals to extend this cost-effective access to data analytics applications (Mallikarjuna, B., et al., 2021a).

The predictive analysis service, Endor, is a startup company jointly working with big organizations. A new Blockchain protocol is introduced which is considered as the Google of predictive analysis. Artificial intelligence and analytics are merged together to simplify the user interaction and get correct predictions. To promote predictive analysis, Endor is planning to combine data providers, developers and users. By using such tools, the cost of predictive and big data analytics is decreasing.

New Forms of Data Monetization

In today's world the most important thing is data. To remove the third party and monetizing data analytics, Blockchain and big data are combined together. This would be beneficial for the users to gain more powerful agreements in business and controlling the accessibility of data.

The following changes are being incorporated with the increase of data monetization due to Blockchain (Mallikarjuna, B., et al., 2021a):

- All the parties participating in a transaction will access the same quantity and quality of data that will improve data quality and analytics.
- To eliminate the necessity for multi systems to store all the transactions occurred, a single file is maintained.
- To eliminate the dependency on third parties to manage and control data.

Wibson is platform which encourages to monetize the information shared by data owners. It allows users to monetize their infrastructure. Due to transparent nature of Blockchain, data owners can track their information.

Fluent Data Exchange

In many multinational companies, data is being leveraged. Not only the best analytics tools but also the data is the most important factor. Due to the cost factor, smaller companies and research teams are not able to access the large amount of data and are constrained about data exchange.

Dock is a data exchange platform, in which the job profiles of expertise are managed under a single platform (Girardi, F., et al., 2020). Rather than going through multiple job sites, one can find valid and verified information in a single place. To create solid profiles, Dock stores all the experience and certification data on Blockchain. Forrester, a research team claims that around 73% of company's data can't be used for data analytics. However, Blockchain can surely make an impact on these numbers and make data exchange process more secured and simpler (Mallikarjuna, B., et al., 2021a).

Applications of Big Data with Blockchain

Presently there are so many applications of big data and Blockchain which are discussed in the following sections.

Stori

Since Blockchain is decentralized, all the transactions are accessed on a peer-to-peer basis. These transactions are verified by each user in the network and hence is secured and maintains integrity. Previously Blockchain was confined to cryptocurrencies but now you can store any type of data securely in Blockchain (Durneva, P., et al., 2020).

Privacy and security are the best advantage. Data is not stored at a single place which makes it less vulnerable for attack. Using distributed algorithm, so that data availability is maintained in case of power failure. 100 PB data is stored in stori. A loan service is also available to fund data storage.

File Coin

Just like Stori, the aim FileCoin is to completely transform the data storage, security and decentralization of internet. Taking example of the shutdown of the web in Egypt, the developers are hoping for a decentralized internet. Filecoins can be earned by offering data storage (Saif, S., et al., 2020).

Omnylitics

Blockchain and big data analytics are combined together in the recent technology, named as omnilytics. In this process AI and ML are used with marketing, forecasting and intelligent financing. According to them if Blockchain technology is utilized efficiently it can disrupt big data. The open nature of the network ensures trust and transparency. The performance of the data and price can be tracked by the data partners.

Datum

Data Access token is utilized by a storage network which is decentralized, known as datum. Its main emphasis on those who want to monetize the data in internet. It's much better than the currently popular data giant like Facebook. Rather than using their services and making the organization's money, users can have full authority and make money for themselves. Blockchain make sure that there are no violations. It provides more secure system to the user (Al Omar, A., et al., 2019).

Rublix

To check the genuineness and integrity of traders, a simple trading platform Rublix is introduced which aims to combine the investors of cryptocurrency all over the world. Most of the new investors are bounded by the platforms they are choosing and are suffering from the wild west approach. Rublix goals for the amalgamated platform which is secured and verifies the investment by data analytics (Yaqoob, I., et al., 2021).

Provenance

The main focus of provenance is to setup trust. To track the product journey, get accurate information about the product's ingredients and origin and the consequences on environment. With product tracking, more profit can be observed.

Producers and retailers can also get the information about products feedback and likeability which in turn can be beneficial. To build transparency in the supply chain is the main goal of provenance (Girardi, F., et al., 2020).

Conclusion

This chapter described how big data analytics and Blockchain amalgamation are done to implement Blockchain in healthcare systems. Blockchain validates the integrity of the healthcare data described. This chapter demonstrated that big data analytics in healthcare makes the system more accurate. This chapter overall monitors the healthcare data management and remote monitoring using big data analytics and Blockchain technology, Blockchain-powered EHR in pharmaceutical Industry.

References

Al Omar, A., Bhuiyan, M. Z. A., Basu, A., Kiyomoto, S., & Rahman, M. S. (2019). Privacy-friendly platform for healthcare data in cloud based on Blockchain environment. *Future Generation Computer Systems,* 95, 511-521.

Bazel, M. A., Mohammed, F., & Ahmed, M. (2021, August). Blockchain technology in healthcare big data management: Benefits, applications and challenges. In *2021 1st International Conference on Emerging Smart Technologies and Applications (eSmarTA)* (pp. 1-8). IEEE.

Chattu, V. K. (2021). A review of artificial intelligence, Big Data, and Blockchain technology applications in medicine and global health. *Big Data and Cognitive Computing,* 5(3), 41.

Dagher, G. G., Mohler, J., Milojkovic, M., & Marella, P. B. (2018). Ancile: Privacy-preserving framework for access control and interoperability of electronic health records using Blockchain technology. *Sustainable Cities and Society,* 39, 283-297.

Dimitrov, D. V. (2019). Blockchain applications for healthcare data management. *Healthcare Informatics Research,* 25(1), 51-56.

Dubovitskaya, A., Baig, F., Xu, Z., Shukla, R., Zambani, P. S., Swaminathan, A., .& Wang, F. (2020). ACTION-EHR: Patient-centric Blockchain-based electronic health record data management for cancer care. *Journal of Medical Internet Research,* 22(8), e13598.

Durneva, P., Cousins, K., & Chen, M. (2020). The current state of research, challenges, and future research directions of Blockchain technology in patient care: Systematic review. *Journal of Medical Internet Research,* 22(7), e18619.

Girardi, F., De Gennaro, G., Colizzi, L., & Convertini, N. (2020). Improving the healthcare effectiveness: The possible role of EHR, IoMT and Blockchain. *Electronics,* 9(6), 884.

Khezr, S., Moniruzzaman, M., Yassine, A., & Benlamri, R. (2019). Blockchain technology in healthcare: A comprehensive review and directions for future research. *Applied Sciences,* 9(9), 1736.

Mallikarjuna, B., Sathish, K., Krishna, P. V., & Viswanathan, R. (2020a). The effective SVM-based binary prediction of ground water table. *Evolutionary Intelligence,* 1-9.

Mallikarjuna, B., Viswanathan, R., & Naib, B. B. (2020b). Feedback-based gait identification using deep neural network classification. *Journal of Critical Reviews,* *7*(4), 661-667.

Mallikarjuna, B. (2020c). Feedback-based resource utilization for smart home automation in fog assistance IoT-based cloud. *International Journal of Fog Computing (IJFC),* 3(1), 41-63.

Mallikarjuna, B., Shrivastava, G., & Sharma, M. (2021a). Blockchain technology: A DNN token-based approach in healthcare and COVID-19 to generate extracted data. *Expert Systems,* e12778.

Mallikarjuna, B., Kiranmayee, D., Saritha, V., & Krishna, P. V. (2021b, June). Development of efficient e-health records using IoT and Blockchain technology. In *ICC 2021-IEEE International Conference on Communications* (pp. 1-7). IEEE.

Mallikarjuna, B., Addanke, S., & Anusha, D. J. (2022a). An improved deep learning algorithm for diabetes prediction. In *Handbook of Research on Advances in Data Analytics and Complex Communication Networks* (pp. 103-119). IGI Global.

Mallikarjuna, B., Anusha, D. J., & Sabharwal, M. (2022b). An effective video surveillance system by using CNN for COVID-19. In *Handbook of Research on Advances in Data Analytics and Complex Communication Networks* (pp. 88-102). IGI Global.

Mallikarjuna, B., Addanke, S., & Sabharwal, M. (2022c). An improved model for house price/land price prediction using deep learning. In *Handbook of Research on Advances in Data Analytics and Complex Communication Networks* (pp. 76-87). IGI Global.

Mayer, A. H., da Costa, C. A., & Righi, R. D. R. (2020). Electronic health records in a Blockchain: a systematic review. *Health Informatics Journal,* 26(2), 1273-1288.

Saif, S., Biswas, S., & Chattopadhyay, S. (2020). Intelligent, secure big health data management using deep learning and Blockchain technology: An overview. *Deep Learning Techniques for Biomedical and Health Informatics, 187-209.*

Siyal, A. A., Junejo, A. Z., Zawish, M., Ahmed, K., Khalil, A., & Soursou, G. (2019). Applications of Blockchain technology in medicine and healthcare: Challenges and future perspectives. *Cryptography,* 3(1), 3.

Yaqoob, I., Salah, K., Jayaraman, R., & Al-Hammadi, Y. (2021). Blockchain for healthcare data management: Opportunities, challenges, and future recommendations. *Neural Computing and Applications,* 1-16.

Chapter 5

Framework for Approaching Big Data: Blockchain, Big Data Algorithms, Gathering Data, Data Preparation, Choosing a Model and Evaluation

M. Kavitha*, R. Srinivasan and R. Kavitha
Department of Computer Science and Engineering,
Vel Tech, Tamil Nadu, India

Abstract

Scientific and engineering disciplines have become increasingly interested in big data over the last few years. There are several concerns regarding big data, such as big data security, privacy, and management, which need to be resolved before the quality of service can be improved. Big data applications and services can be enhanced by Blockchain's decentralization and security. A variety of modern innovations, such as low energy consumption, high speed, smartness, and intelligence, are available to interact with one another. The Blockchain-based big data approach allows physical devices to communicate securely with others in heterogeneous environments. Throughout IoT technology configurations, this technology establishes a new Blockchain-based computing model. This approach, which uses Blockchain as an underlying technology, can improve the reliability of IoT authentication. This will strengthen Blockchain technology and the cloud, allowing IoT pervasive environments for secure communications between physical objects. This article provides a comprehensive survey of Blockchain-based big data applications, focusing on the most recent approaches, opportunities, and

* Corresponding Author's Email: mkavi277@gmail.com.

In: Blockchain Technology Based Big Data for Healthcare
Editors: Basetty Mallikarjuna, Niranjanamurthy M, Sheng-Lung Peng et al.
ISBN: 978-1-68507-968-0

future directions. The first section of this article will discuss the overview of Blockchain and big data, followed by the integration of Blockchain with big data. Next, we survey several Blockchain-based big data services, including the collection of data, storage of data, and transmitting data securely. Following that, we also discuss the preparation of data for analysis, various learning algorithms, the Selection of models, and finally various performance metrics used to evaluate the model.

Keywords: Blockchain, big data, learning algorithms, evaluation, model, IoT

Introduction

"Big data" is a term specifically used for the enormous increase in global data traffic during the past 10 years (Chauhan, P., & Sood, M., 2021). Several vertical industries, such as healthcare, retail, transportation and logistics, manufacturing, media, and entertainment, will reduce expenditures significantly with the growth of big data, which is expected to reach 229.4 billion dollars by 2025. Hu, H et al., (2014) considered big data from three perspectives, including attribution, computation, and prediction.

The term big data refers to a new paradigm in data processing and analysis that focuses on analyzing large amounts of data and capturing their points of interest (high velocity, knowledge discovery, and analytics). The massive amounts of data that are often called big data are datasets with extreme dimensions and sizes that can't be stored, managed, analyzed, or captured by traditional database tools (Manyika, J et al., 2011). Data with extreme volumes, velocity, and representation are referred to as big data from an architectural perspective. These data require extensive horizontal scaling methods for efficient processing (Pouyanfar, S et al., 2018).

A variety of techniques and solutions have been examined to protect private information and data confidentiality. As to Su, Z., & Xu, Q. (2017)., one method of securing mobile social networks utilizes a coalitional game in tandem with matching theory. Reinforcement learning was used by Wu, J et al., (2016) to design a smart grid algorithm with security in mind. Blockchain was shown to be a powerful tool for manufacturing industrial Internet of Things applications in Liu, C. H et al., (2018). An incentive scheme based on Blockchain technology for securing mobile ad hoc data collection has been proposed by Liu, G et al., (2020). The concept was then applied to edge computing servers to improve the quality of data and enable the IoT devices to handle compute-intensive tasks in a secure manner (Xu, X et al., 2019). Creating a new Blockchain-based system In the architecture of smart cities, a big data analytics framework can be a valuable framework for improving the performance of communication security in a heterogeneous environment. Blockchain is a distributed ledger technology innovation. With more securities, the Blockchain operates in a decentralized manner (Alam, T., & Benaida, M. 2020). The transactions were recorded in the blocks. Each new transaction is recorded in a new verified block. The Blockchain connects all of these blocks. These blocks contain massive amounts of data derived from transactions. Massive blocks of data that contain a complete record of each transaction are required for evaluation. The Blockchain provides ledger credibility without requiring evaluation. As a result, big data occurs, as do corresponding analytics techniques.

Big data is a massive collection of measurements (Karafiloski, E., & Mishev, A. 2017). Because the data is so large and complex, traditional data analysis technologies could not handle it. Today, there is a high demand for predictive big data analytics. The main reason for such a large market is the ever-increasing demand for real-time big data programs. Municipal governments collect data such as traffic congestion, energy consumption, and air pollution using cameras, infrastructure, and mobile applications. This information could then be used to improve community infrastructure, including services, transportation, and public security (Alam, T., & Benaida, M., 2018). The Blockchain has the potential to improve the efficiency of online data processing. At the most advanced level, the distributed infrastructure could provide multiple remote accesses. Multiple groups store transaction data in separate databases in the event of a transaction (Alam, T., 2020).

Analytical Framework

Literature Review

The author, Banafa, A. (2017) published an article about IoT and Blockchain convergence. He discussed how these two technologies are integrated. IoT and Blockchain Convergence were discussed in a 2017 article written by Ahmad Banafa. The author discussed the incorporation of Blockchains and the Internet of Things in this article. Using Blockchains, millions of intelligent devices could be monitored, enabling the exchange of information and collaboration among them. Blockchain technology is a major benefit to IoT technology developers.

Through collaborative approaches like these, a less unstable environment can be developed for gadgets, reducing specific failures. Blockchains, in general, are more secure due to the use of cryptosystems. In the context of business transactions, Blockchains have proven useful for facilitating private, peer-to-peer communication. The primary goal of Blockchains is to enable secure communications between parties through a peer-to-peer infrastructure based on a shared database. A central authority will verify transactions and provide authentication evidence in place of any third-party verification. In addition to cryptocurrency-related apps, Blockchains can be used in areas such as banking, storage, healthcare, and robotics. With Blockchain technology, distributed applications can be built as an accessible system (Florea, B. C., 2018). In aspects of advanced social systems, the Internet of Things and Blockchains play a greater role. Efficiency and network performance are boosted across the entire organization. Jo, B. W et al., (2018) proposed a new plan that was used as part of the experiment of autonomy system management and surveillance proved to be similar to that of success. IoT devices can now be trusted via Blockchains (Di Pietro., 2018). Authentication measures are necessary for the implementation of IoT because it involves a moving object of risk. Smart devices are used in a wide variety of situations, from highly scalable ones to business-oriented ones. For enterprise-related systems such as IoT as well as highly scalable scenarios, IoT protection is necessary. Several security strategies and processes were implemented. IoT devices can be protected using Blockchain frameworks (Minoli, D., & Occhiogrosso, B., 2018).

In a Blockchain-based big data approach, communication between smart devices is made more secure by combining big data and a Blockchain. Smart cities can benefit from this approach. IoT activities are being recorded in real-time by IoT nodes that communicate on a Blockchain-based, decentralized, distributed, public network based on Blockchain technology (Dai, H. N et al., 2019). Blockchains are a series of linked blocks. Each block is linked to the nodes before it. Besides the public key, each block will have the previous block's hash and metadata (Wang, X et al., 2019). There have been several Blockchain-based big data processes developed as a way to transmit data between IoT nodes (Conoscenti, M et al. 2016). People, places, objects, and resources can be connected to increase efficiency and security with the Internet of Things (IoT). Smart cities are gaining in popularity, and measures to protect them are increasing on account of their desired future. Blockchain technology can play a major role in improving the quality of life in smart cities (Alam, T., & Benaida, M., 2020).

Blockchain and Big Data: An Overview

Blockchain

Current Blockchain technologies are leading to new finance and industrial services (Zhou, Q et al., 2020). A Blockchain network consist of blocks of records, whereas in contrast to other technologies, the Blockchain network is decentralized, meaning that participants have complete power to monitor the activities of all other participants (Viriyasitavat, W., & Hoonsopon, D., 2019). Cryptography, distributed computing, software engineering, and the creation of an infrastructure based on the security of digital assets are all component parts of Blockchain technology. Cryptoeconomics is the integration of all of these concepts, and it facilitates peer-to-peer trading of assets between computer systems via peer-to-peer networks.

Blockchain-based crypto-currency is a way of supporting the transparency and security aspects of financial transactions in the present and future. The digital market is filled with various forms of cryptocurrencies. Bitcoin was invented by Satoshi Nakamoto, and since then, 1600 cryptocurrencies have been created based on the Bitcoin concept (Shalini, S., & Santhi, H., 2019). In the case of Bitcoin, every sender initiates a transaction, which is transmitted over the public bitcoin network to the receiver. Network miners verify the identity of users and ensure the sender has enough bitcoins to send to the receiver without blocking the network's basic functioning. A transaction is added to the Blockchain as soon as the miner approves and verifies it. Each node updates the ledger of all participants if an appropriate transaction for the block is executed across all nodes.

A Blockchain platform can be classified in three ways based on its application space: public, private, and hybrid. Everyone has access to a public Blockchain since it has no owner. Decentralised Blockchains, such as Bitcoin, are public and open to all participants, granting them access to the consensus process. On the other hand, a private Blockchain is permissioned, limiting network members' access to its contents. Hybrid Blockchains are only accessible by a small group of people. Essentially, it is a partially decentralized framework in which all parties support a set of rules regarding Blockchain control and access.

The following are some of the key characteristics of Blockchain:

1. Immutability: Since Blockchain contains a permanent and unalterable network, it cannot be corrupted. Traditional banking systems are distinguished by the fact that each node maintains a copy of the digital ledger. A transaction is validated and authenticated by nodes before being added to the ledger. As a result, any transaction can only be successful if all nodes agree, making this framework transparent and secure. Furthermore, it eliminates corruption, which is of particular importance in a public Blockchain that makes transactions public, but does not allow any modification of the data recorded on it (Mallikarjuna, B., et al., 2021a).
2. Decentralization: There are several independent nodes maintaining the network rather than a single authority. Blockchain data is accessible via the web and using private keys the data is replicable (Mallikarjuna, B., et al., 2020a).
3. Security: Blockchain gives high levels of security due to its decentralized and immutable nature. A cryptographic algorithm acts as a firewall against unauthorised attacks. Hashing conceals the true nature of each piece of information while simultaneously providing a unique identifier. The ledger in the chain is immutable because each block contains its own hash and the previous block's hash. The framework is also irreversible because of hashing. Thus, it is impossible to generate a private key from a public one, and corrupting a network would essentially mean changing every record (Mallikarjuna, B., et al., 2020b).
4. Consensus: A Blockchain framework's operation depends on its associated consensus algorithms, which determine how many ethereum nodes are active on the network. The speed and efficiency of transaction validation is increased (Mallikarjuna, B., et al., 2021b).
5. Faster Financial Settlement: Blockchain is a much faster method to process financial transactions than traditional banking systems. Money transfers to foreign workers and international travelers are made much faster using this technology. A Blockchain-based smart contract can also facilitate the settlement of contractual accounts.

Big Data

Big data can be characterized by four Vs: volume, velocity, variety, and veracity.

These features are briefly summarized here:

1. Volume: The volume of a dataset can only be one factor to determine whether it is considered big data, or the amount of data it consists of. Big data processing usually faces several challenges, including an incapability to load/store the entire dataset, the curse of class imbalance, and the curse of dimensionality (many features and attributes exist).
2. Variety: The second component represents a variety of data types such as video, text, and audio, which are usually composed of structured, semi-structured, and unstructured data types. The complexity of data, the heterogeneity of data, dirty data, and the lack of ability to store data in one location are some of the significant challenges that result from variety.
3. Velocity: This is the rate at which data is generated to meet demand. Streaming platforms, high-definition videos, and video gaming are excellent examples of how data has grown unrelentingly (e.g., YouTube and IBM Cloud Video). Depending on the application, data flow rates can be different. This feature is also known as variability in some literature. The presence of a large number of vehicles on the road may cause a vehicular crowdsensing system to generate more data during peak hours.
4. Veracity: In the context of data collection, veracity refers to the quality of the sample, given that low-quality and noisy samples can be collected. This is reasonable given that there are malfunctioning or uncalibrated IoT devices, as well as untrusted devices, that can generate data that can be transmitted through fading networks as well as dynamic wireless networks.

Blockchain and Big Data Integration

A wide range of real-world problems can be solved with big data and Blockchain technologies, both of which are heavily financed by governments and private organizations. The amount of data being generated daily increases as more and more people conduct transactions online. As digital data generation increases exponentially, industries can gain more insight into consumer behavior, buying patterns, and trends. As industries gain insights into customer purchasing patterns, big data analytics is a key tool for analyzing massive datasets with data mining and statistical models. But the tremendous growth of big data presented several challenges. Data sharing, the reliability of data sources, security, privacy, and dirty data are a few of the challenges of big data. To overcome these challenges, the Blockchain's unique properties such as immutability, decentralization, transparency, and consensus mechanisms can be applied. Following are the reasons to use Blockchain with big data.

Improving Big Data Security and Privacy

Cloud computing can be used to improve data security and privacy as the number of devices connected to the Internet grows, as do the amount of data stored in cloud storage. Inquisitive parties posing threats to data integrity or data breaches are among the new challenges. Firewalls do not offer traditional solutions for big data security, because organizations do not have control over the data because it is not contained within the organization's network perimeter. Big data can be stored using Blockchain technology, which solves this problem. Due to decentralised data storage and encrypted data on the Blockchain network, it's extremely challenging.

Enhancing Data Integrity

Humans can manipulate big data records in order to manipulate predictions made by big data analytics. As a result of the Blockchain's immutability, it makes it nearly impossible to tamper with or alter its data. The Blockchain network provides a way to change data by changing at least half of nodes in the network at once, which is close to impossible in practice. In addition, Blockchain networks are trusted because of their immutability (Mallikarjuna, B., et al., 2022a).

Detection of Fraudulent Transactions

By analyzing historical data, existing big data solutions identify fraudulent transactions. As a result, big data cannot address the issue of fraudulent financial transactions. With Blockchain's ability to store large amounts of data, financial institutions can monitor activities in real time, which allows them to catch potential fraud in its earliest stages. Integrating Blockchain technology into big data can therefore help financial institutions prevent fraud and safeguard customers (Mallikarjuna, B., et al., 2022b).

Big Data Analytics in Real-Time

Since the Blockchain stores every transaction, big data analytics are possible in real-time. Due to the integration of Blockchain and big data analytics, banks and financial institutions can utilize cryptocurrency to settle cross-border transactions in near real-time. Furthermore, banks are also able to monitor and react to changes in data in real-time, allowing them to halt transactions immediately after they have been blocked (Mallikarjuna, B., et al., 2022c).

Enhancement of Data Sharing

By combining big data and Blockchain technology, service providers can share data with other stakeholders while minimizing data leakage risks. By storing big data generated from multiple sources in Blockchain, each experiment carried out can be recorded, which avoids the repetition of data analysis.

Enhancing Big Data Quality

Data scientists spend much of their time integrating large data sets from multiple sources with various formats. Data quality can be improved because of Blockchain's structure and completeness. Data scientists are able to use high-quality data to make real-time predictions (Mallikarjuna, B., 2020c).

Simplifying Data Access

By streamlining data access online, Blockchain technology will simplify the management of big data analytics. As a result, the integration of multiple departments within an organization into a single Blockchain allows authorised users to access data that is secure, trusted, and not subject to multiple checks.

Blockchain Services for Big Data

The number of large organizations and corporations using advanced analytics tools to store, visualize, and analyze data has grown tremendously over the past several years. As a result of massive data use and transmission, big data security poses a significant challenge. Although cloud computing has some security concerns, big data services made extensive use of cloud computing.

Third-party applications and intruders may easily steal sensitive data and crash servers if proper security mechanisms are not implemented. The collection of big data, the sharing of data, the storage of data, and the analysis of big data pose numerous challenges. The purpose of this paper is to investigate Blockchain-based big data approaches and services. Figure 1 illustrates how Blockchain services can be applied to the big data environment, including big data collection, transmission, and storage, along with big data analytics and the preservation of privacy.

Blockchain-Based Big Data Approach

Big data based on Blockchain will allow IoT nodes to analyze secure transaction information. In a Blockchain-based big data environment, both public and private data can be shared. A complex network of IoT nodes is made possible by the devices' connectivity. A user could track and move activities between IoT networks wherever communication was possible. According to Wikipedia, a Blockchain is a chain of cryptographic or authenticated blocks which is controlled by a computer which is connected to the entire network. Blockchains are used to store and transmit data blocks.

Several advantages can be derived from this integration model:

(i) Stakeholder trust: Because of its extensive additional functionality, the Blockchain-based big data approach will establish relationships between numerous wireless technologies. Because a miner would first verify each block of the transaction before connecting to the Blockchain, only verified devices can communicate with the framework.
(ii) A Blockchain-based big data technique may reduce costs because it operates efficiently without the involvement of a third-party vendor. It destroys all third-party clusters that exist between the sender and the receiver.
(iii) Blockchain-based big data saves a lot of time. This method reduces transaction time from hours to seconds.
(iv) A Blockchain-based big data approach ensures device and information privacy and security.
(v) A Blockchain-based big data approach creates connected networks for both social and community services. Connected devices can communicate and share data with one another.

(vi) Using this method, money can be exchanged securely without the use of a third party. It offers quick, secure, and financial information services. It shortened the transfer time and cost.

(vii) This strategy is critical in the investigation or elimination of the asset or activity's potential for loss.

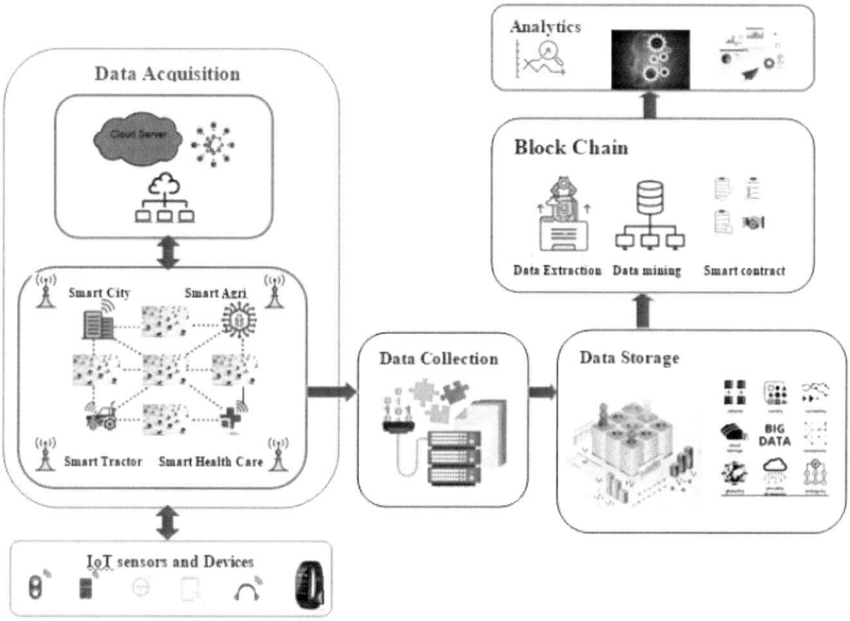

Figure 1. Services of Blockchain in big data framework.

A Blockchain-based big data approach may face a number of challenges, including scalability, storage, skill levels, and detection, among others.

Because of the high transaction volume, it could be hung. Because IoT is being integrated with Blockchain, expect the load to be heavier than it is now.

1. The IoT node will keep track of a digital transaction in a Blockchain-based big data system. During the majority of the time, it will increase its processing power, making it a difficult task or putting a significant strain on the connected devices or routers.
2. With the Internet of Things, Blockchain has evolved into a radical revolutionary innovation. This technology is known to some people all over the world.

3. Identifying the nodes is a challenge in this strategy for all smart devices. IoT can discover their connected nodes, but when it integrates with Blockchain, this task becomes more difficult.
4. The ledger will be distributed freely among all connected nodes. Each node has access to the Blockchain's activities. As a result, privacy has been a significant challenge in the integrated solution.
5. Blockchain can be of the personal or public variety. Interoperability between public and private Blockchains would thus be an impediment to the integrated approach.
6. Because Blockchain-based big data will be used globally, it will be subject to a number of regulations in order to carry out the policy.

The Use of Blockchain in Big Data Acquisition

The data collected by big data applications is unstructured, and it can be in a variety of formats. It is impossible to process these data in their native form. In order to make various predictions on the application domain, the data must be converted to a structured format. Using a chain of blocks, you can make predictions based on structured data. Data integrity is assured by Blockchain algorithms, reducing the possibility of data attacks. In this paper, we examine two subdomains of Blockchain services: Blockchain for secure data storage, and Blockchain for data analytics.

Secure Big Data Collection Using Blockchain

The utilization of Blockchain within big data applications will provide significant security benefits. Big data applications are becoming increasingly popular, but they have also faced significant security concerns. A key phase of the data processing life cycle is data collection. The data collection process becomes vulnerable to various malicious attacks and threats when sources and links are suspicious. Data collection methodology must be secure, as such, for a variety of applications. To provide secure data collection, several studies have been carried out. Using Blockchain platform, a safe big data collection method based on mobile crowdsensing (MCS) is proposed. As a result of the rapid growth of portable smart mobile terminals (MT) and sensors, an increasing number of MCS applications have been successfully used for the industrial Internet of things (IIoT). Cloud servers and MTs are used to create a MCS framework. MTs in a specific area are selected to complete tasks published by the MCS servers. There are several challenges in collecting data, such as MTs having a limited energy supply, a variety of sensing devices, and ensuring that data is securely shared between MTs.

In Liu, C. H et al., (2018) a framework was proposed for overcoming these challenges using deep reinforcement learning (DRL) and Blockchain technology. In a distributed system, it offers both energy-efficient data collection and data sharing security. In MTs, a distributed DRL approach, based on Blockchain technology, effectively collects extensive data and provides maximum sensing device flexibility. Data reliability and security are provided by the Ethereum Blockchain platform, which MTs use to share information. Ethereum maintains its ledger without the involvement of a third party, and shares information with cooperating MTs.

IoT for Energy-Efficient Data Collection

A manufacturing plant can be considered as a 2D target area with a series of Points-of-Interest (PoIs) as obstructions and sensing points for Mobile Terminals (MTs). Data is available at each PoI for MTs to collect. In addition, it is taken into account that there are many obstacles, such as buildings and engineering works. Any mobile terminal, such as a smartphone, autonomous ground vehicle, or even low-flying drone, with mobility, communication, and computing capabilities is deployed in the factory. In order to reduce the risk of damage to the batteries, MTs are designed to collect data for fixed time slots and then return to the origin to be charged. MT receives and stores any data taken from a POI within its sensing range if that POI lies within I's sensing range. To facilitate better data mining and analysis, collected data should be evenly distributed from most points of interest, but collecting them consumes energy. Consequently, we are trying to minimize energy consumption and maximize data collection while ensuring geographical fairness.

Transmitting and Sharing Data Securely Using Blockchains

Blockchain can provide secure transmissions of big data because it is decentralized and immutable. Moreover, it facilitates the sharing of data between sources and data analytics, thereby offering an alternative to traditional data transmission protocols that have encountered security and privacy problems. Blockchain can facilitate big data transmission and prevent data theft while ensuring big data training. Various sources of information can be utilized, including reports, libraries, social media, and assistive technology. As a result, the data sharing flow is traceable and measurable, resulting in high transparency and reliable data sharing. After being added to the Blockchain with signatures and hash values, the data is shared with data analysis services. The illustration of Figure 3 illustrates a big data transmission model utilizing Blockchain.

Blockchain technology can be used for big data transmission and sharing, according to research published in the literature. With the advent of edge computing, end users are now able to optimize latency and processing time by storing more data on edge nodes. In contrast, it is difficult to share sensitive information without proper authorization. At the edge node, the model introduces a trust-based data-sharing approach using Blockchain technology. During this process, the authors use proof of collaboration to reduce the computational workload at the edge nodes. Furthermore, the authors propose a Blockchain-based futile transaction filtering algorithm that can access data from the cache layer rather than the storage layer to reduce response time and storage overhead. To boost network efficiency in the proposed model, the authors proposed express transactions and hollow blocks. Smart contracts with express transactions were created to support transactions that do not happen simultaneously.

A Blockchain-Based Storage System for Big Data

Enhanced access to images, reports on diagnostics, infectious diseases, etc. are becoming increasingly common as a result of rapid advancements in information technology, and significant quantities of medical data are generated daily.

In addition to allowing for better treatment outcomes, the proper utilization of medical data allows for the early prediction of infectious diseases. As a result, it makes sense to investigate how to effectively utilize medical data. E-medical records can provide physicians with accurate information about a patient's treatment and experiences. Medical information sharing can be used illegally to compromise patient privacy. It is, therefore, crucial to control access to medical information. Access control can be implemented most effectively using attribute-based encryption (ABE) in the current environment. Cloud-based servers allow medical institutions (e.g., hospitals) to manage encrypted medical data, thereby reducing their costs and saving storage space at the same time. Additionally, Blockchain technology has been applied to medical scenarios in the past, but such data cannot be efficiently retrieved. The literature and apply the Blockchain and cloud server together to provide both security and the ability to retrieve data; however, the cloud server being centralized means that if one server fails, it affects the entire cloud server. Our storage platform for this purpose will be the InterPlanetary File System (IPFS).

The IPFS protocol was designed to deal with redundant files. Users can locate specific files by referring to their hash addresses, which are assigned to each stored file. As IPFS is decentralized, it does not have single points of failure. The encryption of medical data and the profile of our users (including physicians, nurses, patients, researchers, etc.) are determined based on attributes before storing them. User attributes are associated with the private key, but policy attributes are associated with the ciphertext. By using the user's private key, the ciphertext can only be decrypted if and only if the ciphertext's access policy is met. In addition, Blockchain can be used to record data storage and retrieval processes, making it possible for us to track both the source and the process of retrieval of medical data. Furthermore, the Blockchain can store hashed values of medical data, which serves as an accurate verification tool for the users. For a secure storage environment and to deal with the semi-honest and curious nature of cloud servers, attribute-based encryption may be an option.

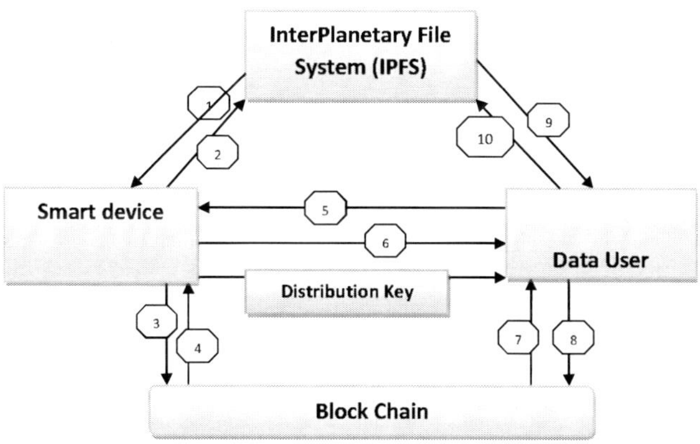

Figure 2. Process of data storage.

Record Storage Model

The scheme consists of four main entities: Blockchain, InterPlanetary File System (IPFS), smart device and data user (DU). The IPFS will ensure the system's data is private, searchable, and verifiable. Figure 2 illustrates the main processes.

A system consisting of user and smart device is responsible for encrypting and saving records. The Encrypt and Index algorithms are implemented first, followed by integration with Blockchain to encrypt records and generate indexes. Next, the IPFS hash address is recorded on the Blockchain, followed by the hashes of the recorded records. Smart devices are primarily used to register all personnel, identify their attributes, and assign a secret password associated with their account. A data user (DU) can be a person associated with the system. The system can assign a key pair to each DU that is associated with its attributes. In order to find a requested record, DU must create a request to the system. It will return a token for users to use to search for the records they need if the smart device confirms that they have the proper access to the system.

Flow of the Model

For convenience, provably secure storage is implemented and a scheme is also introduced for the access of electronic medical records. The doctor establishes a medical record after diagnosing the patient's condition and registering them with a hospital system. In case of data loss, the records must be preserved so the patient can regain access to his information and the researcher can find out more information at any time.

Since medical records are personal information that needs to be encrypted, they must be protected. Step 1.: Before uploading the records to IPFS for storage and indexing, the user encrypts and signs them. Step 2: The user receives the hash address for the stored file from IPFS. Step 3: To broadcast the hash value along with the encrypted hash address, IPFS requires that the user encrypt the hash address with a random number and hash it with the SHA256 hash function. Step 4: The Blockchain will return an ID for the transaction. The data storage phase is complete once the Blockchain provides the transaction ID. Whenever the user returns the record, they must first review the previous records. Steps 5 and 6 illustrate how the DU will submit a keyword-enhanced access request to the model, further DU's access rights is verified, and give a token to the DU following his confirmation. By comparing the hash address contained in the token and the Blockchain hash address indicated in steps 7 and 8, the DU is able to determine whether the hash address contained in the token was counterfeit. In steps 9 and 10, DU downloads the ciphertext from IPFS using the verified hash address.

In addition, the original records are obtained from DU using its secure private key to decode the ciphertext. Finally, DU checks whether its hash value matches that of the Blockchain.

Big Data Preparation

When data is first collected, it is often unclean, noisy, incomplete, or even redundant. Even the most powerful machine learning algorithms will produce less accurate results when fed such data into a machine learning model. As a result, Data Preprocessing is required. Preprocessed data, combined with the right machine learning algorithms, results in models with high throughput and efficiency rates. The ultimate goal of data preprocessing is to clean it, extract features from it, and normalise it.

1. Clean Data

This is the process of removing noisy, missing, or incomplete data from acquired data.

Filtering Noisy Data

The use of filtering techniques such as the Ensembler Filter demonstrated that filtering noise out of data maintained a high level of performance accuracy. The Iterative Partitioning Filter (IPF) and the use of Denoising Autoencoders are two other prominent algorithms for filtering noise out of data.

Missing/Incomplete Data

Missing or incomplete data causes inconsistencies and degrades a system's overall performance. Missing values in data are common as a result of unforeseen events such as incomplete downloads or data collection equipment failure. Dealing with missing data may entail removing such data from the whole, determining statistical relationships such as the mean, median, mode, and so on for quantitative data, and applying other methods such as Bayesian or Decision trees to generate new data to fill the void.

2. Extracting Features from Data

This enables the selection of special features from a large set of data, i.e., the selection of a subset of great interest from a large set of data. The curse of dimensionality as a result of big data is lifted through feature selection. Feature extraction reduces the dimensionality of data, which can help increase response time and reduce system complexities. Principal Component Analysis, Autoencoders, Image Data Thresholding, Hough Transforms, and other algorithms are used to extract the features.

3. Normalizing Data

Data normalisation is the process of organising data in order to achieve cohesion in data entities. This aids in the removal of data redundancies as well as the reduction of data size. After preprocessing, data can be fed into the model to perform specific automated tasks via continuous learning.

Big Data Algorithms for Analysis

Learning Algorithms for Big Data

Science and engineering are rapidly expanding their use of big data. Despite the considerable potential inherent in these massive data sets, fully addressing the various challenges will require novel thinking and learning approaches. Our paper outlines a literature review on recent developments in machine learning research related to the big data processing addition to highlighting new insights into machine learning techniques, a wide variety of advanced learning methods are discussed, such as representation learning, deep learning, parallel and distributed learning, transfer learning, and active learning. Learning systems and algorithms are formally defined areas of study in the field of machine learning. It combines ideas from a variety of scientific, engineering, and mathematical disciplines, including artificial intelligence, optimization theory, information theory, statistics, cognitive science, optimal control, and many more. A wide range of machine learning applications has deep implications on society and science since machine learning is applied to almost every scientific field. This approach can be applied to a variety of applications, including recommendation engines, recognition systems, information processing, and autonomous control. There are three major categories of machine learning: supervised learning, unsupervised learning, and reinforcement learning. Supervised learning is a process of training using data that contains desired outputs and has been labeled accordingly. Unsupervised learning, on the other hand, requires no labeled training data, and inputs are provided without any targets. In reinforcement learning, feedback is received through external interactions. These three learning paradigms have led to the development of numerous theory mechanisms and application services for data task handling. Several Google products, including Google Translate, Google Street View, Android Voice Recognition, and Image Search, use machine learning algorithms to analyze large quantities of messy Internet data. Figure 3 shows how various learning algorithms are applied to big data.

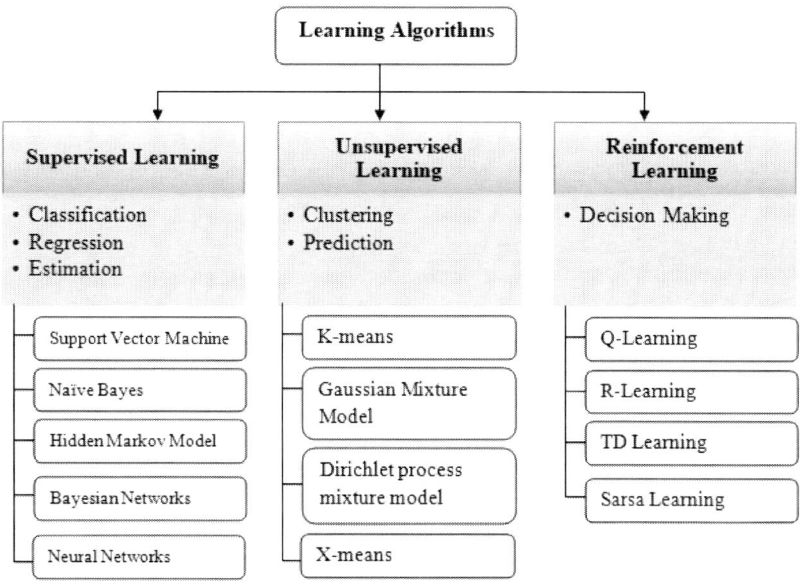

Figure 3. Learning algorithms.

Advanced Learning Methods

Our focus in this section will be on some recent, promising learning methods that might help solve big data problems. The distinguishing feature of these approaches is that they emphasize the learning process rather than a single algorithm.

Representation Learning

Discriminatory Learning: A growing number of datasets contain high-dimensional features, which challenge existing learning algorithms. Recent advances in representation learning have made it easier to extract useful information during the development of classifiers or other predictors due to their meaningful representations of data representation learning aims to capture as many possible input configurations in a studied representation as possible.

This can increase computational efficiency as well as statistical power. A representation learning problem can be divided into three subtopics: feature selection, feature extraction, and distance metric learning. Recent studies suggest a number of techniques to improve ML's capabilities, including ARMA, biased representation learning, and cross-domain representation learning. Scientific activity on representation learning has exploded in recent years, spawned by and sustained by a series of impressive empirical successes.

Deep Learning

Right now, deep learning is one of the most exciting research trends in machine learning. By contrast, deep learning automates the discovery of hierarchical representations by utilizing both supervised and unsupervised strategies in deep architectures. Traditional learning methods are not often able to capture complex, hierarchically launched statistical patterns of input, and deep architectures can often outperform hand-made features in capturing these patterns. Two well-established deep learning research approaches and directions are deep belief networks (DBNs) and convolutional neural networks (CNNs). Both have demonstrated significant potential for future research in the deep learning field. Recent years have seen an increased interest in deep learning from academics due to its top-notch performances in fields like speech recognition, computer vision, language processing, and information retrieval. Increasing processing power along with advances in graphics processors will enable deep learning to play an increasingly important role in providing solutions for predictive analytics for large data sets. Microsoft's Bing voice search and IBM's brain-like computer have both benefited from big data analytics via deep learning techniques. Figure 4 shows the use of Deep Learning when the amount of data increases.

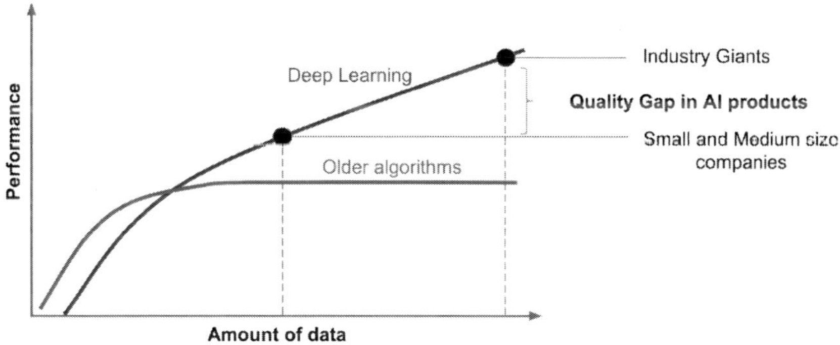

Figure 4. Use of deep learning.

Distributed and Parallel Learning

In today's world of unimaginable amounts of data, fascinating information can often be found. Scientists and engineers will be able to develop more intelligent systems as a result of learning from these massive amounts of data. In contrast, most learning algorithms are not able to use all of the data efficiently in order to learn. As a result, distributed learning would appear to be a promising research area since it is a natural way to expand the learning algorithms across multiple workstations. A distributed learning framework, in contrast to traditional learning frameworks, facilitates learning by disseminating data. A number of recent distributed machine learning algorithms were developed, such as distributed boosting, stacked generalization, and meta-learning. Distributed learning eliminates the need to gather data into a single workstation, which saves time and energy since distributed computing is able to handle huge amounts of data. Similar to distributed learning, parallel machine learning is also used to scale up traditional learning processes.

Transfer Learning

The high heterogeneity of the collected data, however, destroys the hypothesis with the explosion of data from a variety of sources. This problem is addressed by transfer learning, which enables knowledge to be applied from one or more source tasks to a target task by combining knowledge from different domains, tasks, and distributions. As a result of transfer learning, it is possible to solve problems more quickly by applying previously learned knowledge. A transfer learning approach can be divided into three types based on domains and tasks: inductive, transductive, and unsupervised. Inductive transfer learning involves distinct source and target tasks regardless of whether those tasks are in the same domain. Comparatively, transductive transfer learning uses a separate target domain for the task and source tasks. Unsupervised transfer learning involves transferring knowledge unrelated to the source task but separate from it.

Active Learning

In many real-world applications, we encounter situations like this: huge amounts of data are available, but labels are hard to find. Data having enormous volumes of unlabeled properties is frequently tedious and time-consuming to analyze. It seeks to address this issue by labeling only those instances which are most critical. Therefore, the active learner is motivated to use as few labeled examples in its data collection as possible in order to maximize accuracy while minimizing labeling costs. Active learning involves three main scenarios: the synthesis of membership queries, stream-based sampling, and pool-based sampling.

Kernel-Based Learning

Kernel-based learning is a powerful technique for increasing computational power based on the design of efficient nonlinear learning algorithms. The kernel method is distinguished by the large number of samples that can be implicitly mapped into an infinitely dimensional space of features, in which inner products can be directly calculated. For example, kernel-based learning uses a nonlinear mapping to project data 'y' in the input space 'Y' onto the much higher dimensional feature space 'f':

$$\phi : Y \rightarrow f \, ; \, y \mapsto \phi(Y) \tag{1}$$

As a result, we can work with mapped data ϕ (y) $\in$ f, rather than y $\in$Y for a given learning problem (Equation (1)). Various mappings can be used to project data from the input space onto different features spaces. Despite the diversity of feature spaces, in practice it can be difficult to select a mapping that is appropriate for a problem.

Kernel tricks can be used to create nonlinear variants of the most widely used linear statistics without having to know the mapping in advance. With the use of a kernel function, in place of an inner product operator, one may determine the similarity between feature pairs. An appropriately designed kernel k can transform a nonlinear problem into a linear formulation in a higher-dimensional space f.

$$k(y,y') = (\phi(y), \phi(y'))_f \; \forall \; y,y' \in Y \quad (2)$$

In kernel operation, Gaussian kernels or polynomial kernels are two of the most frequently used functions. Data is implicitly mapped onto high-dimensional, if not infinite-dimensional spaces with such kernels. Kernel functions allow insight into big data in a nonlinear way, and their use can lead to significant performance improvements compared with linear functions at the expense of increased computational complexity.

Selection of Models

Selecting the best model can be achieved by comparing each against the required criteria.

Methods for Resampling

Resampling methods are used to arrange the data samples to see whether the model is performing well on the given data samples which is not been trained.

Random Split

Random Split is used to divide the data samples into training data, testing data and validation datasets. It prevents biasing and test data can be used for evaluating the model at the time of selecting the features and tuning the model. This helps in producing the accurate results on test dataset. Finally validation dataset can be used for final evaluation.

Time-Based Split

Time series data is used to describe the frequently used data and the data can be split into training and test data. For example training data will include last three years and also the data from the last 10 months from current year. The test or validation data will be the last 2 months. Using smaller test data will be help to establish the model and it also prevents overfitting. The events or data points in time-series data are not independent of one another, which is considered as disadvantage.

Cross Validation by K-Fold Method

K-Fold The training dataset is divided into k folds during cross-validation. The first k-1 folds are used for training, while the remaining fold is kept for testing, and the process is repeated for K-folds. The mean accuracy for all of these folds is returned after fitting and evaluating a total of K folds. This methods fails for imbalance classes, so as a solution, split can be done in stratified manner, which is known as stratified K fold cross validation.

Bootstrap

Bootstrapping is a resampling technique which is used to stimulate samples from a data set. It infers data about a population, calculates standard errors, and ensures that data is thoroughly tested.

The following steps is adopted in Bootstrap resampling technique:

1. Sample size is chosen randomly.
2. An observation is randomly picked from the training dataset.
3. The chosen observation is combined with earlier chosen samples.

Akaike Information Criterion (AIC)

AIC is a method of calculating information loss. As a result, the model with the lowest level of uncertainty is recommended as the best model.

$$AIC=2K-2\log(L)/N \tag{3}$$

- K is the independent variable
- L is the maximum likelihood estimation
- N is the data points in the training set

AIC's is not good at generalising models, generally it desires for complex models where loss of information is less.

Bayesian Information Criterion (BIC)

Bayesian probability, is used and this model is used for estimating maximum likelihood (next page):

$$BIC = K*\log(N)-2\log(L) \quad (4)$$

- K is the independent variable
- L is the maximum likelihood estimation
- N is the data points in the training set

BIC is suitable for large dataset.

Structural Risk Minimization (SRM)

Overfitting occurs when the model becomes biased to the training data. SRM attempts to balance the model's complexity by fitting on the data successfully.

Evaluation of Models

Models can be evaluated using a variety of metrics. Evaluation metrics are vital and often depend on where the problem is located and what is being solved. Having a deep understanding of two or more metrics can assist the evaluator in finding a good fit between the problem statement and the metric.

Classification Metrics

Table 1 presents a confusion matrix, which is used to determine the number of test cases that are classified correctly or incorrectly. The target classes are 1 (Positive) and 0 (Negative). The TN classifies those cases that are correctly classified as negatives. TP signifies cases that are correctly classified as positives. FN denotes positives that are incorrectly classified as negatives. Negative cases that are incorrectly classified as positive cases are FN.

Table 1. Confusion matrix

	Actual 0	**Actual 1**
Predicted 0	True Negatives (TN)	False Negatives (FN)
Predicted 1	False Positive (FP)	True Positives (TP)

Accuracy

Accuracy is calculated by dividing the number of correctly classified test cases by the total number of test cases.

$$\text{Accuracy} = \frac{(\text{TP} + \text{TN})}{(\text{TP} + \text{TN} + \text{FP} + \text{FN})} \tag{5}$$

Precision

Precision is a metric used to determine classification accuracy.

$$\text{Precision} = \frac{(\text{TP})}{(\text{TP} + \text{FP})} \tag{6}$$

Using equation (6), we can determine the percentage of correct positive classifications relative to total positive classifications. In general, larger the fraction, greater the precision, and therefore the model's accuracy in identifying positive groups.

Recall

The number of correctly identified positive cases out of the total number of positive cases is indicated by recall.

$$\text{Recall} = \text{TP}/(\text{TP} + \text{FN}) \tag{7}$$

F1 Score

The F1 score is the harmonic mean of both Recall and Precision, thereby equalizing their strengths.

$$\text{F1 Score} = 2 * \frac{(\text{precision} * \text{recall})}{(\text{precision} + \text{recall})} \tag{8}$$

AUC-ROC

Figure 5 shows the ROC curve, which plots the true positivity (recall) versus the false positivity (TN/(TN+FP)). AUC-ROC represents the region under the receiver operating characteristics. As the area grows, the performance of the model increases. As long as the curve stays close to the diagonal line of 50%, the model predicts the output variable randomly.

Log Loss

In a log loss method, the likelihood function, which indicates the probability of observed conditions, is equivalent to -1*log (likelihood function). A better model will have a lower loss score if the likelihood function is converted to log and then a negative value is added.

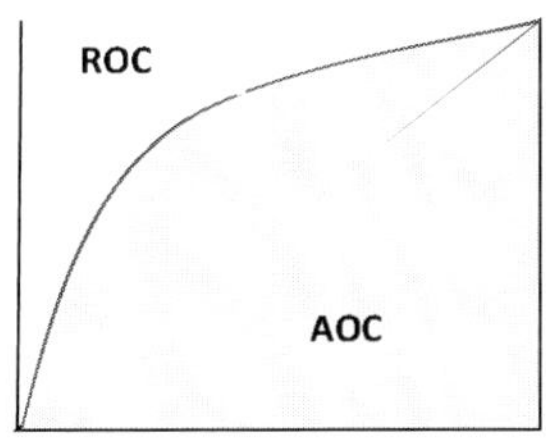

Figure 5. AUC-ROC.

Gain and Lift Charts

Gain and lift charts are similar to confusion matrices in terms of evaluating model performance, but with significant differences. Models are evaluated on their accuracy on the entire population or test set using confusion matrices, while gains and lift charts evaluate the model on subsets of the entire population. Thus, a score can be calculated for each percentage of the population (x-axis). Models that perform better than random predictions are measured by lift charts. 'Lifts' refer to the improvement in accuracy.

K-S Chart

The K-S charts, also known as Kolmogorov Smirnov, shows how positive and negative class distributions are separated from each other. When the difference between the positive and negative cases is large, the model is more accurate at distinguishing them.

Metrics of Regression

In contrast to classification models, which have discrete output variables, regression models have continuous output variables. As a result, the metrics for evaluating the regression models are designed accordingly.

Mean Squared Error or MSE

Using MSE, a comparison between actual and predicted values is computed, squared, and then the mean of all errors is calculated. Even if a model is well-fitted and there are a few outliers, MSE will produce high error values.

$$MAE = \frac{1}{n}\sum_{i=1}^{n}(y_i - \widetilde{y}_i)^2 \quad (9)$$

Root Mean Squared Error (RMSE)

RMSE is the root of MSE, and it helps make the errors more understandable by bringing the scale of errors closer to the actual values

Mean Absolute Error or MAE

The MAE is the average of the absolute error values. By removing the square terms, MAE effectively reduces the penalty associated with outlier values or ignores outlier values to some degree.

$$MAE = \frac{1}{n}\sum_{i=1}|x_i - x| \quad (10)$$

Root Mean Squared Log Error or RMSLE

A logarithm is added to the actual value and prediction to calculate the RMSE. Value x represents the actual value, and value y represents the prediction. As a result, the higher error rates with the log function are downplayed, reducing the impact of outliers. Logs also enable RMSLE to capture a relative error (by comparing all error values).

$$RMSLE = \sqrt{\frac{1}{n}\Sigma_{i=1}^{n}(log(x_i + 1)) - (log(y_i + 1))^2} \quad (11)$$

R-Squared

By using independent variables or predictors, the R-Square measures how much of the target variable's variance can be captured.

$$\text{R-Squared} = 1 - \frac{\text{UnexplainedVariation}}{\text{TotalVariation}} = 1 - \frac{\text{Variance(model)}}{\text{Variance(Average)}} \quad (12)$$

Adjusted R-Squared

R-inability Square's to reduce in value with added features is addressed by Adjusted R-Square. As more features are added, the score suffers.

$$adjR_2 = 1 - (1 - R^2)\frac{n-1}{n-m-1} \quad (13)$$

A magic element is the common denominator in this case, which increases as the number of features increases. Thus, increasing R2 is needed to increase the overall value.

Clustering Metrics

Using distance-based metrics is advantageous since clustering algorithms predict the grouping of data points.

Dunn Index

Dunn indexes clusters that have low variance across all members and are compact. It is also crucial that the mean value of each cluster is as far apart as possible.

$\delta(Xi, Yj)$ represents the distance between intercluster points, or between Xi and Xj.

$\Delta(Xk)$ represents the distance within the cluster Xk, i.e., its intercluster distance.

Dunn index disadvantages include increased computation costs as the number of clusters and dimensions grow

Silhouette Coefficient

Basically, the silhouette coefficient evaluates the proximity of points within one cluster to those within another cluster in the range from -1 to +1.

A higher Silhouette value indicates that the distance between different clusters is substantial.

If 0 is present, then the points are close to the decision boundary.

If a cluster is incorrectly assigned to the points, the value of -1 is indicated.

Elbow Method

According to the elbow method, the number of clusters in a dataset is calculated by plotting the number of clusters against the percentage of variance explained. In the x-axis, the point at which the curve abruptly bends (the elbow) represents the optimal number of clusters.

Bias vs. Variance

A model can be biased when assumptions are made, such as linear regression models, which assume a straight line relationship between the output variable and the independent variables. Underfitting occurs when there is not a linear relationship between the data and the independent variables. Models that focus too much on the training set or learn the variations too closely lose their generalisation ability. This leads to overfitting. As bias and variance are indirectly proportional, the optimal model must be sacrificed for variance in order to achieve low bias. To meet this requirement, the bias and variance should be intersected in the model. In order to accomplish this, hyper-parameters of the model is fine-tuned iteratively. A suitable metric should be selected after each iteration of the model.

Learning Curves

Training or building up a model is best tracked through learning curves. In the process of selecting and evaluating models, these curves can help establish the optimal combinations of hyperparameters. Learning curves are usually used to track the development of models with a y-axis showing performance improvement and a x-axis showing time or experience.

Learning curves typically follow the following two patterns:

Learning Curve for Training

A plot of an evaluation metric's score over time during training, for tracking a model's learning or progress.

Curve of Validation Learning

This curve shows the evolution of the evaluation metric score by time on the validation set.

Conclusion

With its high level of security and efficient network management capabilities, Blockchain technology has drawn considerable interest as a disruptive ledger technology for supporting big data system management.

An innovative analysis of big data using Blockchain was conducted in this article. The first part of the meeting consisted of a discussion of recent developments in Blockchain and big data, as well as the motivation for combining both technologies. Several big data services, including data acquisition, performance metrics, and model evaluation, have been examined extensively using Blockchain. Learning from these vast amounts of data has the potential to provide significant gains to a variety of industries. Traditional machine learning approaches cannot predict and cover a wide variety of observations regardless of their type, volume, speed, uncertainty, incompleteness, and value density. As a result, machine learning techniques shall be adapted to deal with large amounts of data.

This chapter provides a brief overview of traditional machine learning algorithms, followed by an analysis of several contemporary advanced learning techniques. In the discussion, it was evident that scalable Blockchain platforms for big data involve a lot of technical challenges during implementation and integration. By combining big data and Blockchain, the challenges of Blockchain can be addressed. With the help of the Blockchain, big data can be safely managed and secured. As data accumulation grows, a decentralized, immutable ledger, combined with advanced technology, can ensure data integrity, while big data analytics will provide more valuable insights for making valuable predictions.

References

Alam, T. (2020). A reliable framework for communication in internet of smart devices using IEEE 802.15. 4. *Authorea Preprints*.

Alam, T., & Benaida, M. (2018). CICS: cloud–internet communication security framework for the internet of smart devices, *International Journal of Interactive Mobile Technologies (iJIM)*, 12(6).

Alam, T., & Benaida, M. (2020). Blockchain and internet of things in higher education. *Universal Journal of Educational Research*, 8, 2164-2174.

Alam, T., & Benaida, M. (2020). Blockchain, fog and IoT integrated framework: Review, architecture and evaluation, *Technology Reports of Kansai University*, 62(2).

Banafa, A. (2017). IoT and Blockchain convergence: benefits and challenges. *IEEE Internet of Things*.

Chauhan, P., & Sood, M. (2021). Big Data: Present and Future. *Computer*, 54(04), 59-65.

Conoscenti, M., Vetro, A., & De Martin, J. C. (2016, November). Blockchain for the Internet of Things: A systematic literature review. *In 2016 IEEE/ACS 13th International Conference of Computer Systems and Applications (AICCSA)* (pp. 1-6). IEEE.

Dai, H. N., Zheng, Z., & Zhang, Y. (2019). Blockchain for Internet of Things: A survey. *IEEE Internet of Things Journal*, 6(5), 8076-8094.

Di Pietro, R., Salleras, X., Signorini, M., & Waisbard, E. (2018, June). A Blockchain-based trust system for the Internet of Things. *In Proceedings of the 23nd ACM on Symposium on Access Control Models and Technologies* (pp. 77-83).

Florea, B. C. (2018, June). Blockchain and Internet of Things data provider for smart applications. In *2018 7th Mediterranean Conference on Embedded Computing (MECO)* (pp. 1-4). IEEE.

Hu, H., Wen, Y., Chua, T. S., & Li, X. (2014). Toward scalable systems for big data analytics: A technology tutorial. *IEEE Access*, 2, 652-687.

Jo, B. W., Khan, R. M. A., & Lee, Y. S. (2018). Hybrid Blockchain and internet-of-things network for underground structure health monitoring. *Sensors*, 18(12), 4268.

Karafiloski, E., & Mishev, A. (2017, July). Blockchain solutions for big data challenges: A literature review. In *IEEE EUROCON 2017-17th International Conference on Smart Technologies*, (pp. 763-768). IEEE.

Liu, C. H., Lin, Q., & Wen, S. (2018). Blockchain-enabled data collection and sharing for industrial IoT with deep reinforcement learning. *IEEE Transactions on Industrial Informatics*, 15(6), 3516-3526.

Liu, G., Dong, H., Yan, Z., Zhou, X., & Shimizu, S. (2020). B4SDC: A Blockchain system for security data collection in MANETs. *IEEE Transactions on Big Data*.

Mallikarjuna, B., Sathish, K., Krishna, P. V., & Viswanathan, R. (2020a). The effective SVM-based binary prediction of ground water table. *Evolutionary Intelligence*, 1-9.

Mallikarjuna, B., Viswanathan, R., & Naib, B. B. (2020b). Feedback-based gait identification using deep neural network classification. *Journal of Critical Reviews*, 7(4), 661-667.

Mallikarjuna, B. (2020c). Feedback-based resource utilization for smart home automation in fog assistance IoT-based cloud. *International Journal of Fog Computing (IJFC)*, 3(1), 41-63.

Mallikarjuna, B., Shrivastava, G., & Sharma, M. (2021a). Blockchain technology: A DNN token-based approach in healthcare and COVID-19 to generate extracted data. *Expert Systems*, e12778.

Mallikarjuna, B., Kiranmayee, D., Saritha, V., & Krishna, P. V. (2021b, June). Development of efficient e-health records using IoT and Blockchain technology. In *ICC 2021-IEEE International Conference on Communications*, (pp. 1-7). IEEE.

Mallikarjuna, B., Addanke, S., & Anusha, D. J. (2022a). An improved deep learning algorithm for diabetes prediction. In *Handbook of Research on Advances in Data Analytics and Complex Communication Networks*, (pp. 103-119). IGI Global.

Mallikarjuna, B., Anusha, D. J., & Sabharwal, M. (2022b). An effective video surveillance system by using CNN for COVID-19. In *Handbook of Research on Advances in Data Analytics and Complex Communication Networks*, (pp. 88-102). IGI Global.

Mallikarjuna, B., Addanke, S., & Sabharwal, M. (2022c). An improved model for house price/land price prediction using deep learning. In *Handbook of Research on Advances in Data Analytics and Complex Communication Networks*, (pp. 76-87). IGI Global.

Manyika, J., Chui, M., Brown, B., Bughin, J., Dobbs, R., Roxburgh, C., & Hung Byers, A. (2011). *Big Data: The Next Frontier for Innovation, Competition, and Productivity*. McKinsey Global Institute.

Minoli, D., & Occhiogrosso, B. (2018). Blockchain mechanisms for IoT security. *Internet of Things*, 1–2: 1–13.

Pouyanfar, S., Yang, Y., Chen, S. C., Shyu, M. L., & Iyengar, S. S. (2018). Multimedia big data analytics: A survey. *ACM computing surveys (CSUR)*, 51(1), 1-34.

Shalini, S., & Santhi, H. (2019). A survey on various attacks in bitcoin and cryptocurrency. In *2019 International Conference on Communication and Signal Processing (ICCSP)*, (pp. 0220-0224). IEEE.

Su, Z., & Xu, Q. (2017). Security-aware resource allocation for mobile social big data: A matching-coalitional game solution. *IEEE Transactions on Big Data*.

Viriyasitavat, W., & Hoonsopon, D. (2019). Blockchain characteristics and consensus in modern business processes. *Journal of Industrial Information Integration*, 13, 32-39.

Wang, X., Zha, X., Ni, W., Liu, R. P., Guo, Y. J., Niu, X., & Zheng, K. (2019). Survey on Blockchain for Internet of Things. *Computer Communications*, 136, 10-29.

Wu, J., Ota, K., Dong, M., Li, J., & Wang, H. (2016). Big data analysis-based security situational awareness for smart grid. *IEEE Transactions on Big Data*, 4(3), 408-417.

Xu, X., Zhang, X., Gao, H., Xue, Y., Qi, L., & Dou, W. (2019). BeCome: Blockchain-enabled computation offloading for IoT in mobile edge computing. *IEEE Transactions on Industrial Informatics*, 16(6), 4187-4195.

Zhou, Q., Huang, H., Zheng, Z., & Bian, J. (2020). Solutions to scalability of Blockchain: A survey. *IEEE Access*, 8, 16440-16455.

Chapter 6

Big Data with Blockchain Support, Inpatient Management and Medical History Management Data: Advancement of Deep Learning and Blockchain Technology in Healthcare

S. P. Ramesh
School of Computing Science & Engineering,
Galgotias University, Uttar Pradesh, India

Abstract

Cryptocurrency and Blockchain technology have been among the most important innovations and technological achievements in recent times, and they are becoming increasingly important in the business world. A positive aspect in Blockchain technology is that it is undergoing continual upheaval and establishment, which seems to be a good thing. When individuals are separated by large distances, it is a sequence of blocks that secures information and helps them keep confidence in one another. Because of the fast expansion of crypto currency technology in recent years, academics and industry professionals have been pushed to investigate creative methods to integrating distributed ledger technology across a broad range of fields. For developers, the fast expansion of Blockchain technology has opened the door to a plethora of new application options, many of which are in the healthcare business. This research provides an in-depth assessment of the development of Blockchain-based healthcare technology and its applications, as well as the consequences of these developments. This inquiry calls attention to the unsolved research challenges in this rapidly developing field, and we

In: Blockchain Technology Based Big Data for Healthcare
Editors: Basetty Mallikarjuna, Niranjanamurthy M, Sheng-Lung Peng et al.
ISBN: 978-1-68507-968-0

go into further detail about them in this report. The potential of digital currency in the transformation of the healthcare sector is also demonstrated.

Keywords: Blockchain, healthcare technologies

Introduction

A consequence of the growing use of digital technology in health-care services, massive amounts on electronic patient data have been created. In light of this development, it is predicted that the security of healthcare information throughout its collection, use and sharing will continue to be unsurpassed in the industry. With the development of Blockchain technology as a transparent and accountable data storage and processing method, it has opened the door to new potential to tackle key data confidentiality, security and integrity concerns, such as those in the health sector, amongst other things. Recently, both the business sector and the academic community have expressed a large level of investment in Blockchain technology, which is not surprising. On a daily basis, Blockchain development applications and scientific articles are being developed and published. Blockchain technology is defined as a decentralized peer-to-peer (P2P) computer data network technology that may be transmitted to all users, either publicly or privately, and that can be stored to any type of information in a reliable and verifiable manner, according to the definition.

Analytical Framework

Literature Review

Increasing usage of communications technology in healthcare has resulted in massive amounts of electronic patient data. This development places tremendous demands on public health data security in terms of collection, use, and sharing. In the medical services sector, for instance, the coming of Blockchain innovation as a capable and straightforward method of storing and moving information opens up a universe of opportunities for settling significant information protection, security, and honesty issues. Blockchain innovation has been broadly used because of the new flood in business and scholastic interest. A new Blockchain application or examination article is being made pretty much consistently (Michael, J.; Cohn, A.; Butcher, J.R, 2018). Cryptocurrency is characterized as an appropriated record for electronic data cash exchanges between peers in a peer-to-peer (P2P) network this may be public or private and scattered to each client, empowering any sort of data to be kept in a reliable and certain manner (Yli-Huumo, J.; Ko, D.; Choi, S.; Park, S.; Smolander, K, 2016).

Blockchain innovation is a public Blockchain for computerized data moves on a peer-to-peer (P2P) network that might be scattered openly or secretly to each client. Blockchain innovation is turning out to be more famous. Besides, a crucial idea of the Blockchain is the shrewd agreement, which is a legally enforceable approach comprising of an effectively customizable arrangement of rules for which diverse assented to connect with one another in the way of dispersed automation (Andoni, M.; Robu, V.; Flynn, D.; Abram, S.; Geach, D.; Jenkins, D.; McCallum, P.; Peacock, 2019). A brilliant agreement is a legitimately enforceable arrangement comprising of an effectively flexible arrangement of rules under which various gatherings consent to partake in appropriated automation with each other.

Keen agreement applications have been created in an assortment of fields, including energy assets (et al., Fanning, K.; Centers, D.P, 2016), monetary administrations, casting a ballot, and medical care. The accessibility is enhanced by Blockchain technology, which removes this need third-party controllers or mediators by eliminating the need for them. When conducting a transaction in a distributed Blockchain and unpredictable environment (et al. Nakamoto, S, 2008), consensus techniques and cryptography are employed to ensure that the transaction is legitimate. As part of a decentralized Peer to peer network of transactions that is built on Blockchain technology, the receiving node checks messages and, if they are legitimate, includes them in the next block of transactions. This requires the use of a consensus mechanism to confirm the data contained within within every block, which is referred to as "Proof of work" (PoW). After the consensus process is finished, that block would be added to the chain, and every node in the network will accept it, enabling the chain to expand forever (Engelhardt, M.A, 2017). The block will be added to the Blockchain once the conventional wisdom process is completed, and every node may approve the transaction, allowing the chain to grow indefinitely.

Among the most promising uses of Blockchain technology is in the field of medicine, which is becoming more popular. When it comes to the healthcare industry, Blockchain offers the most potential because of its ability to address issues such as data confidentiality and protection, along with information sharing and storage (Al Ridhawi, I.; Aloqaily, M.; Kotb, Y.; Al Ridhawi, Y.; Jararweh, Y. A, 2018). Interoperability must be a must in the healthcare industry, and it must be one of the criteria for success. For the purposes of this definition, that is the capability of multiple parties, whether people or machines, to exchange information in a manner that is accurate, efficient, and consistent. The objective of interoperability in medical care is to empower information to be imparted all through the climate and conveyed by various clinic frameworks, fully intent on working with the trading of wellbeing related data, including electronic wellbeing records (EHRs), between medical services suppliers and patients (Gordon, W.J.; Catalini, C, 2018). The ability to safely trade patient clinical records (expecting that the patient has allowed consent to do as such) is empowered by similarity, that nitty gritty incorporated to do as such paying little heed to the supplier's geographic area or the reliable series of interconnected that current between them (Zhang, P.; Schmidt, D.C.; White, J.; Lenz, G, 2018).

In regard to the fact that patient information is obtained from a number of sources, this is extremely important. It is possible to solve this aspect of interoperability through the adoption of Blockchain technology, which now has demonstrated the potential to secure store, maintain, and transfer electronic health records (EHRs) between healthcare organizations (et al. Lin, I.C.; Liao, T.C, 2017). A significant pressure has been placed on the economies of numerous countries by the growing costs of healthcare infrastructure and software in the industry. In the healthcare industry, distributed ledger technology is being used to improve organizational performance, improve patient satisfaction, improve patient data management, increase compliance with regulations, reduce prices, as well as permit more effective utilisation of healthcare-related data (et al. Mackey, T.K.; Kuo, T.T.; Gummadi, B.; Clauson, K.A.; Church, G, 2019). Distributed ledger technology is being used to improve organizational performance, improve patient satisfaction, improve patient data management, increase compliance with regulations (Peter, H.; Moser, A., 2017), and enable more effective use of healthcare-related data (Zheng, Z.; Xie, S.; Dai, H.N.; Wang, H, 2016). As per the first conversation, there is likewise the likelihood that Blockchain innovation will affect the progression of medications and clinical gear in a long and complex medical care production network. Fake medications are a huge risk to people from one side of the planet to the other, particularly in agricultural nations. This peril can possibly be wiped out by incorporating Blockchain innovation into the medical services inventory network. In the current examination stage, there is a review into the conceivable utilization of Blockchain innovation in a wide assortment of medical care applications, including information the board and storage, gadget association, and security in the web of clinical things, among others (IoMT).

As indicated by the discoveries of the review, most of partners and end clients, including patients, parental figures, analysts, drug organizations, and insurance agencies, announced a positive effect on the nature of their experience (QoE) because of the advantages gave by Blockchain innovation in the previously mentioned application regions. Correspondence of medical care information without the risk of giving and taking clients' protection and information security is a basic advance in making the medical care framework more astute, working on the nature of medical care benefits, and further developing the general client experience, which are all significant objectives to accomplish. Giving an exceptional outline of the employments of Blockchain innovation in medical services, just as their impact on medical services financial matters, patient nature of involvement, and the rise of new plug prospects in the sector, is the point of this review. Many audit articles on the utilization of Blockchain innovation in various regions have been distributed, including finance, the web of things (IoT) (et al. Ølnes, S.; Ubacht, J.; Janssen, M, 2017), the energy sector, administration, protection and security (Mettler, M, 2016), and the web of things (IoT). In any case, in spite of the fact that there have been a couple of audit articles distributed on the utilization of Blockchain innovation in medical services, there has not been a careful basic evaluation of the most ebb and flow research on Blockchain-based medical services applications.

A brief assessment of Blockchain-enabled healthcare applications is provided by Mettler. M (2016), who claims that his article offers a short overview of the technology. In all, three fields are investigated in the study: public health management, user-oriented medical care, and pharmaceutical fraud and forgery. The research, however, is not primarily focused with the functional characteristics and advantages of Blockchain technology, despite the fact that it was the first to offer such an overview of possible Blockchain-based healthcare applications. Later in that year, a second review study on the possible applications of Blockchain technology in healthcare and biological sciences was published by Kuo et al. (2018). Conventional Blockchain technology (such as the features of bitcoin) and its design, according to Kuo et al. (2018), are the major subjects of debate. As a further step, the authors describe how Blockchain technology may be utilized for a variety of applications, including medical record administration, insurance claim processing and scientific research, as well as a health data ledger, among others. The writers did not go into depth on the technological aspects of how knowledge will be transmitted from a central place, which was a major oversight. The findings of a similar study, conducted by Stagnaro and colleagues by Siyal, A.; Junejo, A.; Zawish, M.; Ahmed, K.; Khalil, A.; Soursou, G (2019), propose a variety of applications for Blockchain technology in the area of healthcare, including in particular, the integration of claims adjunction and patient care records. And also found that supply chain management and supply chain management were the major focal points as has been the case in the previous study (SCM). The study's main flaw is that it only covers a few use scenarios and does not look into future Blockchain-based healthcare applications. Hölbl and colleagues by McGhin, T.; Choo, K.K.R.; Liu, C.Z.; He, D (2019) examined the applicability of Blockchain in healthcare applications. The authors conducted a comprehensive evaluation of the literature between 2008 and 2019. However, it does not evaluate the experiments performed in the application areas in question [52]. The authors of another linked study investigated the applicability of Blockchain technology in medicine, namely in the fields of health insurance, electronic health records (EHR), pharmaceutical distribution, biomedical research (BMR), procurement processes (PP), and medical education, among other things.

As has been the case with prior research, a number of key Blockchain-based healthcare applications, such as smart contracts, data sharing, interoperability, and cloud storage, were left out of the analysis. Siyal et al. (2017) addressed a wide range of Blockchain-based healthcare applications, including fraud detection, neurological research, clinical research, and electronic health records (EHR). In Siyal et al. (2017) study, the most significant issue is that several newly released articles are left out of the mix, which is a serious oversight. McGhin and colleagues (2019) performed research on the needs for the healthcare sector to protect patients' medical information using Blockchain technology. The findings were published in the journal Health Information Technology. This study [54] found that only a small number of healthcare applications were addressed, including OmniPHR (Roehrs, A.; da Costa, C.A.; da Rosa Righi, R, 2017), Pervasive social network (PSN), and Healthcare Data Gateway. OmniPHR (McGhin and colleagues, 2019) is a patient health record system that was developed by the University of Pennsylvania.

A detailed taxonomy of Blockchain technology in healthcare applications has not yet been published, based on our results from the literature study that we performed. This shortcoming will be addressed by providing the reader with a technical foundation in a range of Blockchain-based healthcare applications, with a special emphasis on the most recent advances and accomplishments inside this sector. It is the purpose of this article to include a detailed technical study of existing Blockchain technologies that have been implemented in the healthcare industry, as well as an evaluation of their advantages and disadvantages. The future of Blockchain technology is also addressed in the course of the presentation. Also included are the most up-to-date research problems, prominent topics, and research views in each of the healthcare application areas, as well as research directions prospects in the field of healthcare technology. The following are the most significant contributions made by this article, summarized as follows:

Compiling a list of the many existing applications of Blockchain technology in the healthcare business and evaluating them.

Identifying and exploring the most important concerns relating to healthcare applications in the context of Blockchain technology.

Explaining and underlining the recommendations for additional study, as well as the lingering challenges connected to Blockchain-based healthcare applications.

The distribution of information about the advantages and disadvantages of currently available Blockchain-based applications.

Methods

Applications in Healthcare Using Blockchain Technology

When it comes to data modelling and governance, Blockchain technology is revolutionizing the way many healthcare applications are designed and implemented today. Since its introduction, it has gained widespread acceptance for its versatility and capability for segmenting and protecting medical data while also exchanging services in a previously unthinkable manner. At this time, Blockchain technology is being utilized in the United States to support a range of healthcare-related operations. Blockchain-based medical care arrangements are hypothetically isolated into four levels, every one of which is made out of four sorts of information sources, a Blockchain innovation, a medical care application, and partners, in addition to other things. An illustration of a Blockchain-based work process with regards to medical services applications is displayed in Figure 1. The information gathered from clinical gadgets, labs, online media, and different sources is collected and turned as unique data prior to being moved up to turn out to be large information as the measure of information increments. Huge information is the aftereffect of this increasing. Basically, that data is the main part of the entire Blockchain-based medical care framework, and it is additionally the main part that prompts the advancement of the primary level of the progression, which is simply the Blockchain.

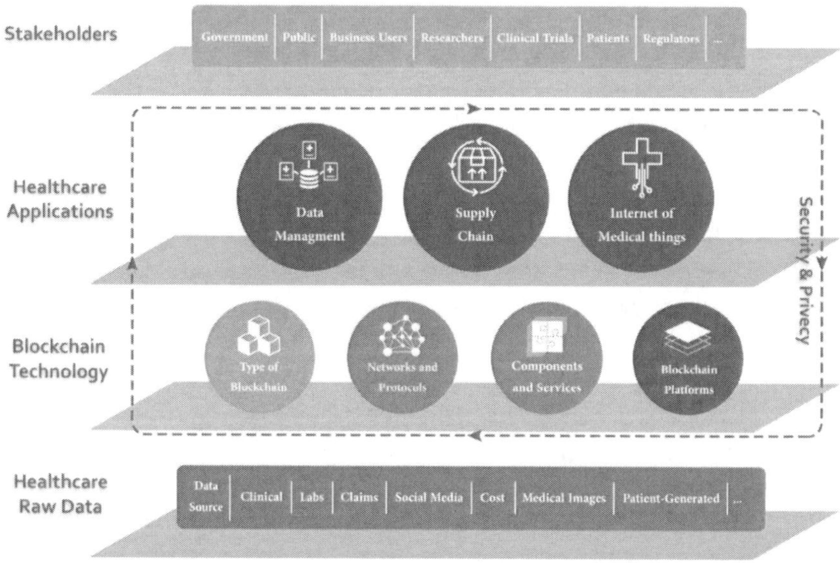

Figure 1. The process for Blockchain-based healthcare applications.

Blockchain innovation is respected the major structure block in the mission of a protected medical services design, with the crude information layer being perceived as the key establishment. Blockchain innovation is based on top of the crude information layer, which is parted into four parts (Frost, J.H.; Massagli, M.P et al., 2008). There are critical varieties across Blockchain frameworks, remembering contrasts for agreement strategies and conventions. Utilizing Blockchain advances, clients might make and oversee exchanges all the more effectively since the frameworks make it simpler for them to do as such. Various stages, including Ethereum, Ripple, and Hyperledger Fabric (Liang, X.; Zhao, J.; Shetty, S.; Liu, J.; Li, D, 2017), are using Blockchain innovation, which was made and is right now being used.

Brilliant agreements, computerized marks, a Blockchain wallet, occasions, participation, and advanced resources are only a couple of the many components that make up the Blockchain. When imparting across various organizations, a wide assortment of conventions could be utilized to achieve this objective.

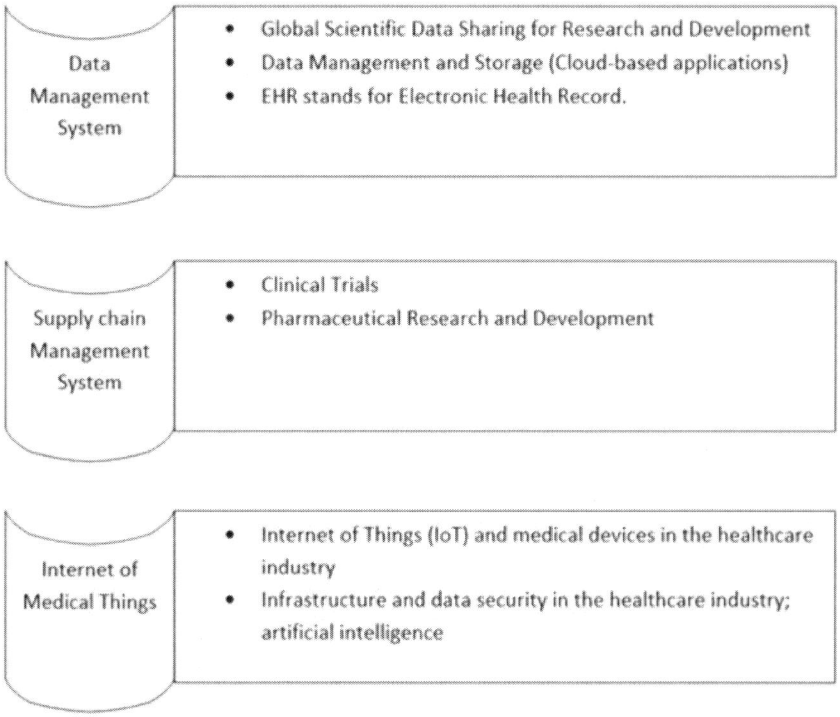

Figure 2. Healthcare applications based on Blockchain technology.

It is possible to pick from a variety of P2P, centralized, decentralized, and distributed network configurations. Depending on the range of criteria that must be satisfied, policymakers may select for public, private, or even federated choices to achieve their objectives. Following the development of the platform via the use of Blockchain technology, the next stage is to guarantee that the applications are properly linked into the overall system. There are three main categories of applications for Blockchain technology in healthcare, each of which is discussed below. It is critical to first and foremost focus on data management, which encompasses international scientific data interchange for research and development (R&D), data administration, data storage (for example, cloud-based applications), and electronic health records (EHRs). Clinical trials and pharmaceuticals are examples of items in the second class of SCM applications, which also covers other sorts of products. The Internet of Medical Things (IoMT) is covered in the third class, which encompasses the convergence of healthcare IoT and medical devices, healthcare IoT infrastructure and data security, as well as artificial intelligence (AI). Healthcare applications that may be implemented on the Blockchain in the future are shown in Figure 2 as a depiction. In addition, the stakeholder layer is situated at the very top of the hierarchy and is composed of parties who stand to profit from Blockchain-based healthcare applications, such as business users, researchers, and patients, among other individuals and organizations. Users' main concerns at this layer are the ability to communicate, process, and manage information in a timely manner without compromising the security and privacy of the information that is being shared or processed.

Applications for Healthcare Management Using Blockchain Technology

Patients' ability to access and share their own health data is becoming easier as a result of advancements in electronic health-related data storage and retrieval, cloud-based healthcare information flash memory, and patient data privacy protection legislation [64]. It is extremely valuable for any information-driven organization to manage the smooth integration of data storage, transaction management, and integration management. As a matter of fact, this is especially true in the healthcare sector, because Blockchain technology has the potential to relieve these important problems in an efficient and effective way. A healthcare data management process on Blockchain is depicted in Figure 3, and each of the seven stages is discussed in greater detail later in this document. There are a number of Blockchain-based applications in this area that are discussed in greater detail below, including data sharing and management, data storage (for example, cloud-based applications), and electronic health records (EHR).

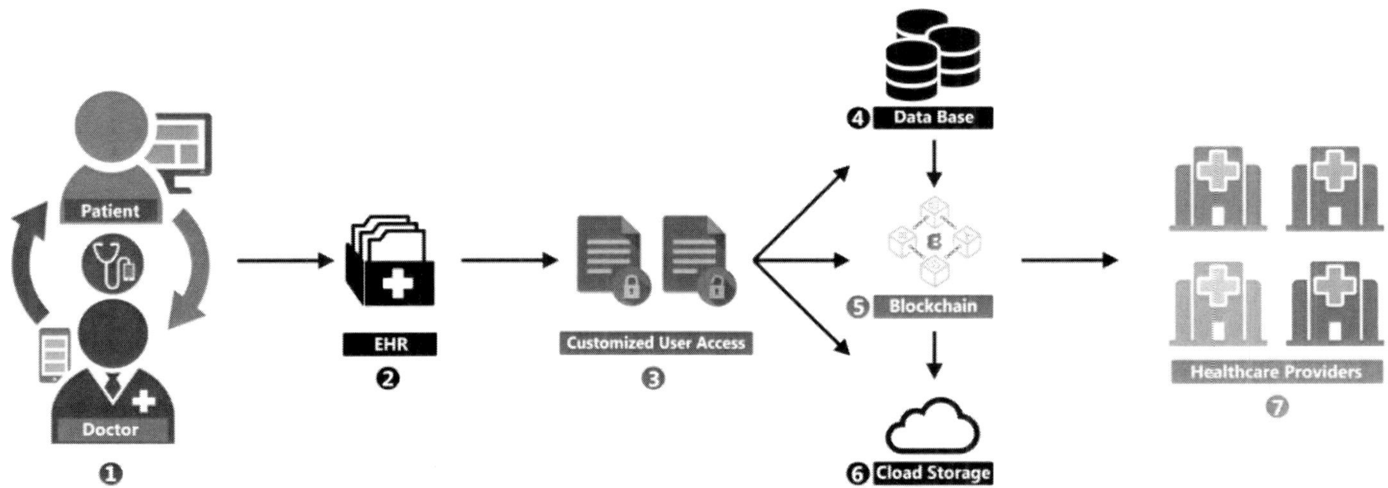

Figure 3. Blockchain technology used to handle healthcare data.

Step 1: Raw data is collected through a patient's relationships with their doctors and other experts, such as specialists and other health care providers. You'll discover information on your medical history, a present issue, and other physiological data in this area.

Step 2: Based on the main data collected in the previous step, an electronic health record (EHR) is generated for each individual patient in the system. Nurses' notes, medical imaging studies, and prescription histories are all examples of the kinds of medical information that may be found in an electronic health record (EHR).

Step 3: The individual patient who owns critical EHR information is recognized, and personalized control is given exclusively towards the holder of that specific property.

Step 4: In order to get authorization for the use of such sensitive information, interested parties must first make a request for authorization. This request is then passed on to the EHR owner, whom he or she will decide who will be given access to the data.

Step 5: This process, which comprises the database, the Blockchain, and cloud storage services, is centered on these three phases, which are also referred to as the "heart of the process." Record storage is accomplished in a distributed manner through the use of database and cloud storage systems, and a Blockchain provides total secrecy and authenticity by requiring only customized legitimate user access to the system.

Step 6: Final users (such as ad-hoc clinics, community health centers, and hospitals) that are interested in obtaining access to a safe and sound care delivery system that has been authorized by the owner are identified.

Step 7: Regardless of where you are treated, your health history will also be viewable and searchable on your phone. It will also be validated via the use of a distributed ledger such as Blockchain, to which healthcare providers will contribute over time et al. Fan, K.; Wang, S.; Ren, Y.; Li, H.; Yang, Y (2018).

International Scientific Data Exchange

A significant and fundamental initial phase in working on the nature of healthcare suppliers while likewise making the healthcare system wiser (et al. Yue, X.; Wang, H.; Jin, D.; Li, M.; Jiang, W, 2009) is to energize the trading of healthcare and medical information among them. Shared health records are an individual choice that people make with each other. Allow us to consider the circumstance of a patient who wants to unveil his medical history with a specialist at their underlying visit (Ji, Y.; Zhang, J.; Ma, J.; Yang, C.; Yao, X, 2018). A patient who decides to impart his medical history to an insurance agency or an exploration association, for instance, would be considered to be in a sharing situation. For sure, the actual data might be moved across public lines (Shen, B.; Guo, J.; Yang, Y, 2019). Nonetheless, as recently expressed, the working component of the present health-care systems has a few impediments. In particular, one of the main hindrances is that patients have restricted admittance to their medical records. Thus, people are totally unconscious that their own health data hosts been revealed to unidentified third gatherings (Vo, H.T.; Kundu, A.; Mohania, M.K., 2018). In the healthcare area, Blockchain innovation can possibly make a huge commitment by empowering and getting a basic strategy for the trading of electronic health information. Blockchain innovation can possibly make a critical commitment by further developing commitment and participation with the healthcare area. As recently expressed, (et al. Zhu, L.; Wu, Y.; Gai, K.; Choo, K.K.R, 2019), this is generally viewed as perhaps the main contribution made by Blockchain-based healthcare. A few of the commitments that have been made in this space will be examined more meticulously in the accompanying areas. For instance, Castaldo and Cinque (2018) introduced an information recording system that would improve and build the trading of electronic health information across various European nations in the most solid way conceivable, utilizing private Blockchain innovation as its establishment. Medical information sharing application named Healthcare Data Gateway (HGD) made by Yue and partners (2017) is presently accessible for download. The application, named Healthcare Data Gateway (HGD), is based on the Blockchain design and is accessible for download. Customers may effortlessly oversee and impart their information to others utilizing the gave arrangement without agonizing over their security being compromised. It is a brilliant strategy for expanding the insight of healthcare systems while at the same time ensuring the protection of patient information. Utilizing Blockchain innovation as a conveyed information store to build up a record of radiological examinations and direct picture sharing using custom-made client consents, Vishal Patel (2018) has proposed a system for cross-area picture sharing. It was created by Fan et al. (2017) with regards to a comparative exploration venture to address information the executives and data sharing issues in an electronic medical records (EMRs) system and to further develop medical data trade. Patient admittance to electronic medical records (EMRs) from various organizations is made conceivable through MedBlock, which takes out the requirement for recently gathered health data to be isolated into independent data sets.

Moreover, emergency clinics might profit from information trade and participation empowered by Blockchain innovation to acquire a superior comprehension of their patients' medical narratives preceding gathering with them for an interview with them.

A few scientists, including Ji and associates (Wang, H.; Song, Y, 2018), have proposed a staggered area sharing system dependent on Blockchain innovation. The objective was to utilize Blockchain innovation to permit telecare medical data systems to share area data while keeping up with namelessness, which was accomplished. They can set up the essential models for area sharing decentralization, mystery, changeability, staggered security assurance, hopelessness, and unforgeability, in addition to other things, using Merkle trees and request safeguarding encryption. In view of the test discoveries, apparently the plan is reasonable and feasible for the two patients just as medical staff, and that it very well may be utilized to get area information in telehealth data systems. The MedChain system, created by Shen et al. (2019), is a meeting-based healthcare information trade system that is effective and depends on Blockchain innovation. The MedChain convention utilizes a condensation tie geography to guarantee the trustworthiness of a common medical IoT information stream, which is basic for medical IoT information security. In addition to other things, this is being done to address the failure of current systems, for example, Medrec and MedBlock. Introduce the discoveries of the (Al Omar, A.; Bhuiyan, M.Z.A.; Basu, A, 2019) assessment show that MedChain can possibly build efficiency while likewise meeting the security prerequisites for healthcare information trade.

Information and Data Management

Data security and privacy are continually violated, either unintentionally or maliciously, by third parties, despite the fact that many businesses, particularly healthcare institutions, are data-driven and that the volume of data generated at this or other times in the future, such as the Internet of Things, is increasing significantly (et al. Kaur, H and team, 2018). Several businesses have experienced substantial reputational and financial damage as a result of this procedure. Various users of health data have a variety of responsibilities, and access to data should be controlled by the rights that have been assigned to each of these responsibilities, as described above. This type of access may be made possible through the usage of Blockchain technology in a seamless and efficient manner. Several Blockchain technologies have been developed specifically for this purpose, and we will discuss them in greater detail in the following section. When compared to traditional electronic medical record management systems, Medicine is a decentralized electronic medical record management system in which data authorization and operation are stored in the Blockchain and execution is performed by smart contracts, rather than traditional EMR management systems. MedRec collaborates with suppliers to gather all of their medical information in order to guarantee that authentication, confidentiality, auditing, and sharing requirements are met. This provides patients with comprehensive, unalterable medical information and services. The researchers (Zhu et al., 2019) developed a technique for establishing regulated Blockchain data management in the cloud environment in order to address the concerns of users who were concerned that they did not have control over the data that was put on the Blockchain. They came to the conclusion that the approach was feasible. The trust authority node was created in their model to allow users the ability to terminate and halt any potentially harmful activities regardless of whether or not they are being attacked by a majority of users. An additional piece of work (Macrinici, D et al., 2018) presented a novel concept for redefining consent management in the healthcare system, which primarily allows users to control the entirety of their health record data through the use of Blockchain technologies. Despite the fact that they have been implemented, they do not have an authorisation design or access control in place.

Organizing and Managing Information

Information security and protection are constantly abused, either inadvertently or vindictively, by outsiders, in spite of the way that numerous organizations, especially healthcare foundations, are information driven and that the volume of information produced at this or different occasions later on, like the Internet of Things, is developing fundamentally (Genestier et al., 2017). Numerous associations have experienced huge reputational and monetary harm because of this interaction. An assortment of clients of health information has an assortment of obligations, and admittance to information ought to be constrained by the rights that have been allocated to every one of these obligations thus. This kind of access might be guaranteed in a consistent way using Blockchain innovation. A few Blockchain advancements have been grown explicitly for this reason, and we will talk about them more meticulously in the following segment. As opposed to conventional EMR the executives' systems, Medicine is a decentralized electronic medical record the board system wherein information approval and activity are put away in the Blockchain and execution is performed by brilliant agreements. MedRec teams up with providers to accumulate all of their medical data to guarantee information confirmation, privacy, inspecting, and sharing prerequisites are met. This furnishes patients with thorough, unchangeable medical information and administrations. The specialists (Zhu et al., 2019) fostered a technique for building up controlled Blockchain information the executives in the cloud climate to address the worries of clients who were worried that they didn't have authority over the information that was being presented on records. They arrived at the resolution that the procedure was attainable. At the point when they fostered their model, they incorporated a remarkable trust authority hub that permitted clients to end and stop any conceivably unsafe exercises even in case of a larger part assault. An extra piece of work (Genestier et al., 2017) introduced a clever idea for reclassifying assent the executives in the healthcare system, which principally permits clients to control the whole of their health record information using Blockchain innovation. In any case, regardless of the way that they have been carried out, they don't have an approval plan or access control components.

Electronic Health Record (EHR)

Medical records in the traditional sense are paper-based, and keeping track of the progression of a patient's health condition over time takes a significant amount of time. A further problem is that they have a tendency to provide incorrect information, which can result in patients receiving substandard care. With the presentation of electronic health records (EHRs), data innovation gave the chance to ease a portion of this weight. Because of the accessibility of electronic admittance to health records, doctor rehearses have had the option to essentially work on the nature of their consideration. Besides, electronic health records (EHR) take into account better sickness the board and more elevated levels of safeguard therapy in light of the utilization of innovation. A significant advantage of using a digital record is that it provides improved decision-support capabilities as well as greater cooperation among caregivers, both of which are important. As a result, its significance is becoming increasingly recognized among those who work in the healthcare industry. The development of Blockchain technology for the purpose of securing, sharing, and storing electronic health record data both within and between institutions has been the subject of numerous studies. Chen and partners (2019) fostered a solid distributed storage system for patients' touchy medical records determined to create a protected Blockchain structure for medical information trade utilizing Blockchain innovation. In this system, medical information the executives is refined using a computerized file that is ensured by access control rights to the data having a place with its proprietors and that stores medical records. Introducing cloud encryption at the lower part of the order chain is the means by which this data is put away. In a connected report, Guo et al. (2018) fostered a property-based mark technique that utilizes Blockchain innovation and an assortment of specialists to guarantee and confirm electronic wellbeing records, and they distributed their discoveries on the web. It makes bunch message broadcasting simpler, and it could be more impervious to intrigue assaults because of this element. Wang and Song (2018) proposed a protected cloud-based electronic wellbeing record system dependent on Blockchain and trait-based cryptography, which they accept will be safer than current systems. The analysts utilized a mix of personality-based encryption and character-based marks simultaneously for medical information encryption, which they alluded to as "computerized signs."

Table 1. Electronic health record study population data sources from cohort

Data Source	Sample Size	References
Single psychiatric inpatient unit	728-2010	82, 97
Specialized center/clinic	544-10017	15, 40
Prison Network	370, 511	8
Multiple Hospital	467-55492	23, 47
Multiple primary care practices	1074-25241	53, 105
Health Care System	7925-345,143	44, 74
Consortium	2537- 919, 873	25, 48
Centralized anonymized repository	8709 -233, 844	28, 83

Notwithstanding Blockchain, different strategies are utilized related to Blockchain to guarantee the respectability and recognizability of the medical foundation. While the three investigations referenced above have essentially centered around the cryptographic parts of getting EHR blocks, Roehrs et al. (2017) have addressed an assortment of difficulties identified with the unification of dispersed wellbeing records and the entrance the board of partners from the healthcare supplier local area in their exploration. A disseminated model for incorporating individual wellbeing records (PHR) was proposed to resolve these issues. It utilizes a parallel information base to store PHR in squares and joins primary semantic interoperability with a current vision of various PHR designs. OmniPHR was made to address these two concerns. Subsequently, Hussein et al. (2018) embraced something else altogether and fostered a structure for securing medical records dependent on Blockchain innovation and discrete wavelet changes, which depended on hereditary calculations. The proposed approach utilizes an altered cryptographic hash generator to produce the necessary client security key to ensure the client's information. Furthermore, MD5 strings (a message-digest method that utilizes a hash capacity to get a 128-bit hash esteem) were utilized to assemble another critical configuration by including a discrete wavelet change into the MD5 strings. Further developed generally system security, just as protection from different assaults, are accomplished through the use of this method. Table 1 gives an outline of the healthcare information the board techniques that are right now accessible with regards to Blockchain development execution.

Applications of Blockchain Technology in Healthcare Data Management

Health Education

In spite of the way that the Blockchain is principally utilized for recording exchanges including the Bitcoin computerized money, it can possibly be applied in the field of training [92, 93]. Sharing data and abilities from an assortment of sources frames the premise of instructive undertakings. It is predicated on the reason that each of the people included are dependable. As internet learning turns out to be more famous, it is turning out to be harder for administrative specialists to direct the alteration of data in medical instruction (Alonso, S.G, 2019). As per Funk et al. (2018), the utilization of Blockchain innovation by wellbeing professions teachers can possibly work on the nature of training just as the instructive effect on numerous ages of understudies in the wellbeing professions. Also, it could be helpful in deciding the general significance of different instructive drives. Aside from that, any foundation that takes on Blockchain innovation will actually want to give affirmation all alone, without the requirement for an outsider to mediate. With the formation of timestamped, confirmed duplicates of diary articles, Blockchain can possibly essentially affect medical library organization in an assortment of ways. This includes the collection, preservation, and dissemination of authoritative material, as well as the creation of timestamped, verified copies of journal articles. Utilizing Blockchain innovation in healthcare, we can guarantee that patient data is secure and that it isn't modified in any capacity throughout treatment. For instance, putting away instructive data in records utilizing Blockchain innovation would simplify it for wellbeing instructors to follow the effect of their endeavors as their understudies progress through the instructive pipeline and in the long run give their insight to the following class, which would help everybody. Keeping track of which learning modules are the most frequently used and effective will also be made much easier as a result of this. Furthermore, certification may be granted to the appropriate individuals without the involvement of a third-party organization. These examples demonstrate some of the potential benefits that Blockchain technology could have in the fields of health and medical education.

Management of Enrollment Information

When people enroll in health care plans, they generate administrative data about their enrolment. This information incorporates data about healthcare conveyance, qualification rules, and credentialing records. Notwithstanding the way that the essential makers of this data are government organizations, for example, the central government and state governments (Dehgani, R, 2019), we might utilize information created by little, medium, and surprisingly enormous healthcare suppliers. The manual technique for managing an enormous and changed element of information has been in need for quite a while, and it requires a tedious course of confirming references, capabilities, and qualification before it very well may be executed. As a result, the entire procedure is delayed to a certain extent. A large amount of administrative assistance to deal with slows down the entire enrolment process and becomes a hindrance to the smooth operation of a productive healthcare system, as shown in the following chart. It is possible, on the other hand, to store this information on a Blockchain in order to verify reliable references and relevant data in the shortest amount of time possible. This may be advantageous to an administrative assistant who is attempting to improve the efficiency of the enrolment process because it simplifies the enrolment process, allows for eligibility queries, allows for network management, and allows for coordination, among other things.

Due to its significance in overcoming the security issues associated with electronic health records in healthcare (et al. Manag, 2019), the Blockchain technology has experienced tremendous growth in the healthcare industry (Clauson, K.A, 2018). It is possible that electronic health records (EHRs) will improve the delivery of health-care services in the future [99]. A patient's admission to a clinic, a clinician's finding of a patient, or the section of an analytic outcome, for example, a MRI check, into an electronic wellbeing record system all outcome in the age of this code. Thusly, the security of such computerized data is given the most elevated need, and Blockchain innovation is currently being utilized to guarantee the wellbeing and security of healthcare information, among different applications. Blockchain innovation is basic for information the executives in healthcare since it assists with protecting the worth of information while additionally bringing down capacity costs. Due to a remarkable element of Blockchain innovation, it is the main answer for securing advanced data, and in light of its broad use, it will keep on assuming a basic part in the eventual fate of corporate information the executives.

Logistics and Supply Chain Management

Considering best practices from business, an essential inventory network the board (SCM) system is created with the full intent on smoothing out the whole conveyance measure, from requesting to supply (Jayaraman, R, 2019). Because of the scattered requesting settings for medical supplies, drugs, and basic assets, production network the board (SCM) is a troublesome suggestion in the healthcare business. There is an intrinsic danger of giving and taking the production network measure, which could straightforwardly affect patient security. As per research led by the World Health Organization (WHO), in excess of 100,000 individuals bite the dust in Africa consistently because of erroneous measurements of fake medications acquired from obscure or deceitful merchants (Benchoufi, M, 2017).

To sweeten the deal even further, notwithstanding item and drug forging, the shortfall of an item library and bundling blunders in a healthcare organization might make critical disturbance the generally SCM. A significant observing device, Blockchain, is particularly significant in acquiring knowledge into the entire course of drug and medical item transportation. The way that all exchanges are recorded on the record and that each hub in the Blockchain keeps a record of every exchange makes it simple to affirm progressively where a prescription came from, who offered it to whom, and who circulated it. Besides that, the dispersed record of the Blockchain permits healthcare specialists and doctors to confirm and approve the accreditations of providers (Shae, Z, 2017).

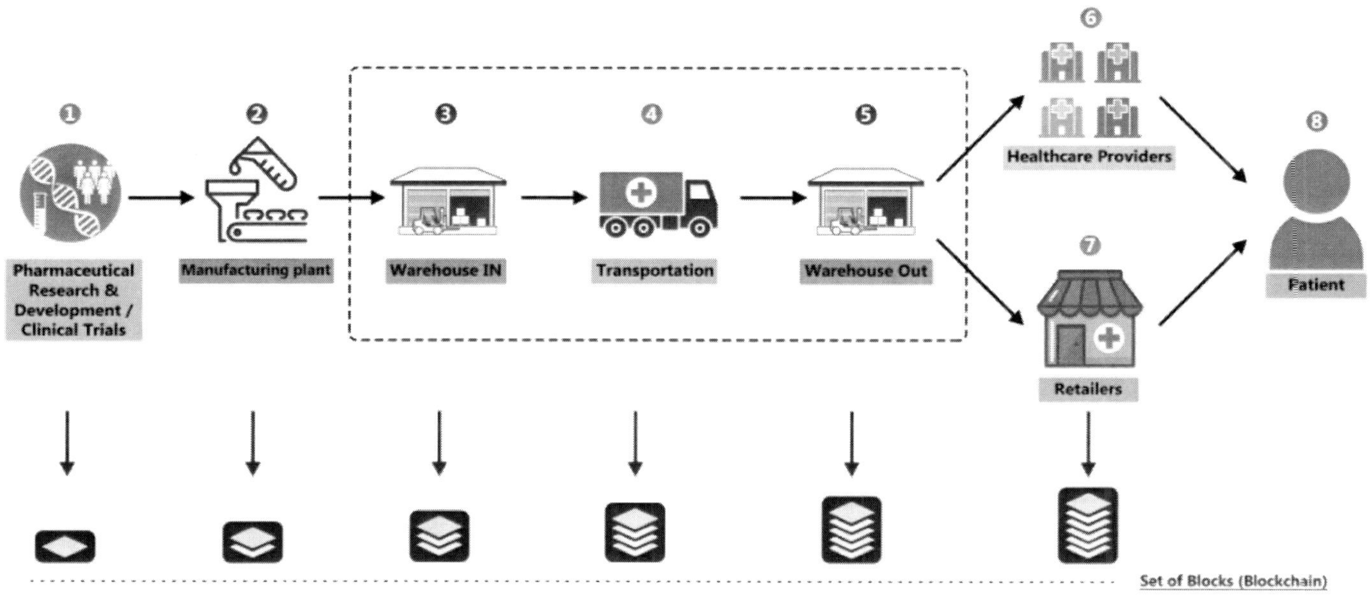

Figure 4. Supply chain management in the era of Blockchain technology.

Drug stores and healthcare suppliers will actually want to ensure that the progression of certified meds keeps on arriving at the patients who need it the most in the event that they have more noteworthy perceivability into the inventory network because of a decent and opportune validation methodology. In this regard, Blockchain innovation offers huge potential for the foundation of a confided in organization of sellers that will empower healthcare directors to shield patients from dishonest merchants. Besides, Blockchain innovation can possibly make huge upgrades sought after estimating, information provenance, extortion counteraction, conditional security and proficiency, among different spaces of utilization. Blockchain innovation is delineated in Figure 4 as a feature of a drug production network the executives technique that utilizes the innovation.

Step-1: A road obstruction is set up after the improvement of a creative medicine or medical therapy, which incorporates patent security and an extended course of clinical investigations. It is recorded in the computerized record as an exchange and is open to any client who wishes to see it.

Step-2: If the clinical exploration is a triumph, the patent is moved to the assembling plant, where it will be utilized in the formation of a test model and, at last, in the production of enormous amounts. Every item on the Blockchain has an interesting character that is associated with one more exchange or square, just as to whatever other significant information that might be contained in the exchange or square.

Step-3: Following the fulfilment of large-scale manufacturing and bundling, the prescription is gathered and put away in a stockroom in anticipation of future circulation. In the Blockchain, data like the date, the time, the part number, the standardized tag, and the termination date are totally put away together.

Step-4: Information about transportation is additionally put away in the Blockchain. This data can incorporate things like the time it takes to get from one stockroom (IN) to another, the technique for transportation utilized, who was approved to move the merchandise and different subtleties.

Step-5: An outsider dissemination network is oftentimes liable for appropriating prescriptions and medical supplies to healthcare specialists and shippers around the United States. To do this, every outsider has an active stockroom (OUT), which is associated with all dispersion endpoints using a solitary outbound distribution center (OUT). The Blockchain contains a second exchange that is disconnected to the first and is hence excluded from the past exchange.

Step-6: To check and forestall the offer of fake items, medical services suppliers, for example, clinics and centers are obliged to report data, for example, bunch number and part number, just as item proprietor and lapse date, to the Food and Drug Administration. What's more, this is a component of the Blockchain innovation.

Step-7: The means done by a shop are very like the means made by a trader in Stride 6 of this strategy.

Stage-8: Authenticity ought to be checked by patients all through the whole interaction, as the Blockchain inventory network gives straightforward data to planned buyers to confirm the authenticity of an item.

Clinical Trials

A few hardships go up against clinical preliminaries in medical care, including individual information insurance, information trade, and patient enlistment. Blockchain innovation can assist us with defeating these troubles. Models for trading clinical preliminary information that advance receptiveness and repeatability while keeping up with security have been created. Nugent et al. (2016). recommended keen agreements on a private Ethereum organization to settle trust corruption and to build information straightforwardness in clinical preliminaries to address trust debasement and increment information straightforwardness. There was a need to improve the logical believability of clinical preliminary outcomes, which might be hurt by issues like missing information and particular distributing. The objective of this examination was to achieve that objective. Shae and Tsai (2017) have made four extra framework parts on top of the customary Blockchain to work on the limit of clinical preliminaries and accuracy medication. These parts are depicted exhaustively beneath. Among the parts are: a Blockchain-based dispersed and equal figuring model for enormous information examination; an information the executives part for information incorporation; a character the board part for security assurance of Web of Things gadgets; and an information sharing administration part for a collective exploration biological system (Marucheck, A, 2011). In another examination, Choudhury et al. (2019) introduced another information the executives system dependent on consent Blockchain innovation and brilliant agreements, which they called "Authorization Blockchain Information: The Board Structure." Explicitly, the objective of this review was to limit the authoritative weight just as the time and exertion needed to guarantee information honesty and security in multi-site clinical investigations. Benchoufi et al. (2017) fabricated an assent work process on top of clinical preliminary procedure to work on the effectiveness of the cycle. Their Blockchain evidence of-idea framework, which depends on time stepping assent gathering, joins brilliant agreement enlistment as a component of the confirmation of-idea measure. The recorded recognizability of such extremely touchy information offers an opportunity to ensure the evidence and straightforwardness of such information, in any event, when the entire archive is kept in a public stockpiling, like a devoted openly open site.

The Pharmaceutical Industry

Drug firms are continually endeavoring to upgrade the nature of medicine just as foster novel medicines for a wide scope of diseases and issues. Such drugs should go through an extensive endorsement methodology to guarantee patent assurance, wellbeing, adequacy, measurable legitimacy, and endorsement from administrative organizations prior to being made accessible to people in general.

Typically, this interaction requires quite a while, starting with disclosure and finishing with commercialization, with clinical preliminaries representing a huge piece of the time (Sylim, P, 2018). Subsequently, inferable from an absence of safety and security, a particularly extensive technique is defenseless to prescription review and forging. The utilization of Blockchain innovation across the entire drug fabricating interaction might eliminate this staggering point. It is feasible to keep up with namelessness and assurance security by means of the utilization of Blockchains conveyed record, which makes it conceivable to guarantee that each preliminary occasion is recorded in the Blockchain hubs, which is sealed. To ensure that all drug organizations go along to the support of patent security, a private Blockchain might be used. This might be cultivated by means of the utilization of a shrewd agreement, which guarantees trustworthiness, recognizability, and straightforwardness as of late as 2015, an exploration found that around a little over half of drug firms are either chipping away at or trying different things with Blockchain, showing the capability of Blockchain in the drug area.

Real drugs are hard to find all through the world, presenting huge risks to the overall population and clients. The Blockchain drug store observation framework made by Sylim et al. (2018) was tried in the mimicked organization to check whether it was plausible to utilize the innovation and its standards in a drug observation framework. To upgrade the discernibility of fake drugs, the venture was dispatched. Misrepresentation of customary drug supply chains, which is a significant issue in certain Asian countries, is forestalled by the technique. Note that Gcoin, otherwise called Worldwide Administration Coin, offers a powerful job to every one of the hubs in a progressive association, which is used in medicine inventory network the board. This is valid in numerous ways. Tseng et al. (2018) recommended that a Gcoin Blockchain be utilized as the establishment for the information stream of medications to create straightforward information on drug exchanges. Makers, wholesalers, retailers, drug stores, medical clinics, and customers all advantage from this procedure for sharing data.

The recording of medication exchanges can possibly change the medication store network from one of guideline (government reviews) to one of checking (by all members cooperating). Moreover, the medicine production network's administrative model might be altered from one of assessment and review to one of a reconnaissance net, which would supplant the assessment and examination model.

Table 2. Pharmaceuticals companies' PE

Company	Pe Ratio	References
Sun Pharma	169.55	12
Dr. Reddy's Labs	43.87	7
Divis Labs	51.51	9
Cipla	37.95	5
Biocon	78.18	11
Aurobindo Pharma	15.77	1
Lupin	0	14
Torrent Pharma	40.33	6

Throughout 10 years, radio recurrence recognizable proof (RFID) innovation has been viewed as a dependable possession preserver. Notwithstanding, outside of the RFID confided in area, for example, the post-production network organization, this distinguishing proof can be fashioned by cloning the RFID label's extraordinary ID number. Utilizing the Ethereum stage and its wallet, it is feasible to eliminate such weaknesses across the entire store network line, starting with the maker and finishing with the end customer. Table 2 gives an undeniable level outline of the SCM strategies utilized in Blockchain innovation.

Supply Chain Management Applications of Blockchain Technology

The executives of Cases and Charging Data: notwithstanding the expenses of giving medical care benefits, the entire area is presently worth a trillion dollars, and the figure is developing quick. The course of clinical charging is a fundamental part of the medical care industry. This is because of the way that, without proper invoicing, it is difficult to ensure powerful assistance conveyance. From the second a patient is conceded to the medical clinic until the time the individual is looked at, this methodology is followed. Many cycles are involved, fusing checking in with the protection office, finding money related commitment, coding and charging consistence, sending the case, and getting portion from protection offices. The whole charging system may be puzzled, especially since a part of the costs are totally covered by the patient's solitary medical inclusion plan, while others ought to be paid by the patient out of their own pocket.

Quite possibly the most significant issue in clinical charging is superfluous charging, which happens due to a shortfall of openness and trust between specialists, patients, and assurance providers. Claims and charging in the medical consideration industry are being exploited reliably, yet this may be tended to or decreased by executing a direct system that is accessible to all accomplices. It is feasible to ensure that a particularly straightforward framework is kept up with by keeping everybody required all through the entire cycle and taking out doubt among them. A drug is considered fake on the off chance that it incorporates improper parts and is sold fully intent on disguising or mimicking its starting point, authenticity, or even viability (Chiuchisan, I, 2014).

Quality administration: Moreover, item and drug falsifying altogether affect SCM. With regards to their exhibition in the drug business, they are serious qualities that essentially affect the proficiency, genuineness, and solid productivity of a specific medical services industry. When shopping in a worldwide economy, clients are frequently uninformed about the exact beginnings of the merchandise they purchase and eat. On the grounds that this sort of drug is unsafe to the patient, it is a possibly hazardous issue all around the globe. Besides, the picture of the first drug organizations is imperiled, provoking prescription producers and merchants to go through a lot of cash in countermeasures.

As indicated by the discoveries of the exploration, strategies, for example, spectroscopy and chromatography are valuable for distinguishing fake items since they can identify dynamic substances just as the structure of the picture test. Because of the way that it is subject to electromechanical gear, it has its cutoff points and in this way builds the overhead expenses. One way to deal with resolving these issues is to store drug makers' data on the Blockchain, including item chronic numbers and bundle numbers, so drug organizations, drug makers, and clients would all be able to confirm the realness of the information by associating with the Blockchain and cooperating with it. Quality control, item enrolment, prescription following, and medication duplicating are totally made conceivable through the utilization of this strategy (et al. Yuce, M.R, 2010), which is minimal expense and proficient.

Internet of Medical Things

A significant job in the advancement of wellbeing and medical data systems is performed by Internet of Things (IoT) innovations (Rani, A.A.V, 2019). Medical care gadgets, for example, heart screens, body scanners, and wearable devices may now assemble, investigate, and trade information continuously through the Internet attributable to Internet of Things innovation. Utilizing the Internet of Medical Things (IoMT) worldview, healthcare specialists might snap a picture, recognize threatening parts or even questionable cells, and afterward discuss this information with people who have the legitimate consents to get to the data.

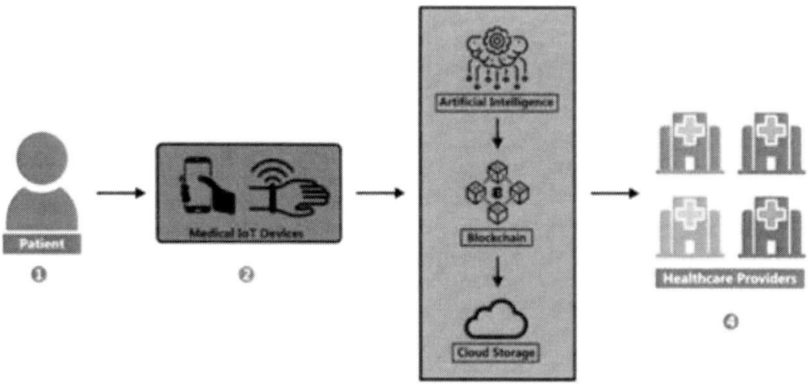

Figure 5. Internet of medical things (IoMT) in a Blockchain environment.

The advancement in healthcare IoT and brilliant medical gadgets in the AI field is the accentuation of the accompanying segments, which are parted into three regions. Figure 5 shows an illustration of IoMT with regards to Blockchain innovation.

Stage 1: In the domain of IoMT, each snippet of data begins from the patient.

Stage 2: Medical Internet of Things gadgets are habitually either connected personally to the patient's body or checked distantly, bringing about an enormous amount of information being made.

Stage 3: Data made in sync 2 is saved money on blocks or in distributed storage (see beneath) (see underneath). Simulated intelligence will help Blockchain in the development of savvy virtual specialists, who thus will actually want to fabricate new records all alone. In case of crucial medical information, where security is the first concern, a decentralized man-made reasoning system might help Blockchains in acquiring the greatest degree of assurance.

Stage 4: Healthcare suppliers are the end clients who look for admittance to the system to give free from any danger treatment to their patients, which has been endorsed by the proprietor.

Internet of Things in Healthcare and Medical Devices

Consider the Internet of Things an assortment of PC gadgets with novel identifiers that are equipped for moving information over an organization utilizing the Internet convention without the requirement for any human-machine cooperation. This is exactly what the Internet of Things is. It has been suggested that the Internet of Things (IoT) plays a crucial role in the healthcare system (Zanjal, S.V, 2016) because of its strong seamless connectivity. The Internet of Things (IoT) is now concentrated on wearable technology and medical devices. In the healthcare business, remote body-region organization (WBAN) systems, which are a basic part of Internet of Things (IoT) systems, are quite possibly the most fundamental component. With respect to remote checking of physiological pointers, remote body region organizations (WBAN) are quickly acquiring fame and are turning into a significant empowering influence innovation for a wide assortment of utilizations, outstandingly in the medical and healthcare fields. As well as helping individuals to remember arrangements and changes in their circulatory strain, Internet of Things gadgets may likewise be utilized to follow calories consumed and various different things (et al. Catawba, 2019). The conversation that will follow will give an outline of the current situation with the workmanship in the reconciliation of Blockchain innovation with Internet of Things (IoT) gadgets. Griggs et al. (2018) developed a solid continuous patient observing and medical mediation system that was fit for performing medical therapies progressively. The system was based on the Blockchain and utilized keen agreements. In view of tweaked edge esteems, the exploration suggests that Blockchain innovation be coordinated to execute brilliant agreements that assess data got by a patient's Internet of Things healthcare hardware. This is done to resolve the issue of reporting information move exchanges in a healthcare system that depends on the Internet of Things. Rahman and Associates (2020) made a keen dyslexia examination system in which a decentralized enormous information storehouse is utilized to store and afterward share information across healthcare gatherings, organizations, and people. The system depends on Blockchain innovation. With regards to getting to data and pleasure, versatile media is an expression that alludes to the utilization of compact electronic gadgets. The wellbeing information accumulated all through the dyslexia testing measure is kept in a decentralized huge information vault, where it will later be made accessible to different analysts for future clinical investigations and factual examination purposes. At the point when Otoum, S et al. (2019) fostered the principal primary wellbeing observing system, they utilized the Internet of Things (IoT) and Blockchain innovation. In their idea, they proposed another method where both locally and around the world decentralized appropriation are enacted by isolating the organization into edge and center organizations, along these lines empowering both locally and worldwide decentralized dispersion.

As a consequence of the adoption of the Blockchain system, the efficiency and scalability of the system are improved. A proposal for employing a PSN-based healthcare system that is safe and secure was created. Data security is one of the most challenging issues associated with this method, particularly when information is sent between PSN nodes. In order to resolve this issue, the authors devised a number of methods that were implemented. An improved version of IEEE802.15.6 was first created. This protocol establishes secure connections for mobile devices and sensor nodes with limited computing resources by balancing the computational demands of the devices and sensors. The second protocol, on the other hand, makes use of Blockchain technology in order to exchange health data across PSN nodes throughout a large geographical area. A mobile health system based on Blockchain technology was developed by Mitsuo Ichikawa and Colleagues (2019) in order to ensure the integrity of data. The framework was designed to prevent tampering with data. The researchers set out to develop a mobile health system for cognitive behavioral therapy of insomnia, with the objective of ultimately putting it into practice. They used a smartphone application to do this.

Internet of Things Infrastructure and Data Security in Healthcare

A variety of networks and Internet of Things (IoT) devices, such as terminals, sensors, diagnostic instruments, wireless access points, and other similar devices, are used in the field of healthcare information and communication technology (ICT). Numerous healthcare innovations, for example, wearable gadgets and remote observing administrations, are empowered by this foundation to impart and trade information about a patient's fundamental conditions with guardians, permitting them to give better treatment to the patient. It is unavoidable that information might travel by means of obscure correspondence organizations (for instance, wide region organizations) eventually during the transmission interaction, and that this information will be defenseless against security and protection breaks. Indeed, there are various occasions (for instance, three Phishing assaults caused a patient individual information break that cost Catwaba Valley Medical Center in North Carolina 20,000 dollars [148]) in which vindictive aggressors are perseveringly looking for any intense shortcoming through which they can enter the healthcare organization and compromise the specialist co-op's important data.

For the Internet of Things in healthcare, researchers are experimenting with a number of approaches to secure users' data from unwanted access in order to meet the security problems stated above, which include An SDN, according to Nikoloudakis and Colleagues (2019), is a system that virtualizes existing network infrastructure into various abstraction layers in order to provide a resistance mechanism against malicious assault. As an extra proposition, the creators fostered a haze registering design that, utilizing the OpenVAS structure, assesses the weaknesses of current and recently added gadgets in the healthcare Internet of Things (IoT). In particular, the recommended model has a basic imperfection in that the normal assessment span for a solitary gadget is approximately 7 minutes and 21 seconds, which is excessively long and brings up mar issues about the system's versatility. This issue may be taken care of using Blockchain innovation in light of the fact that the Ethereum Blockchain-based stage has a square mining season of 10–15 seconds, which is quicker than different stages. In [150], Nausheen and

Begum (2018) introduced an elective methodology, depending on application solidifying techniques, for example, code confusion and application program interface (API) insurance to get basic rationale and portable applications, individually. Following the finishes of the review, approaches, for example, return-situated programming and check adding ought to be utilized to offer an additional a layer of protection from figuring out. As opposed to mainstream thinking, in spite of the way that this review gives phenomenal help with the security insurance of embedded medical gadgets devices, heterogeneous advances should be coordinated to accomplish aggregate productivity, which expands the general system's degree of intricacy to the detriment of expanded effectiveness.

With the goal of improving the performance of Intrusion Detection Systems (IDSs) in Internet of Things (IoT) networks, researchers at the University of California, Berkeley (2018) developed an Adaptively Supervised and Clustered Hybrid (ASCH-IDS) technique that categorizes potential intruders based on aggregated sensor data. Anomaly detection (ADS) and Misuse detection (MDS) outperform each other in terms of performance as a result of the difference in the amount of aggregated sensory traffic supplied into each subsystem, respectively. The system performs commendably in any event, when the rate change is raised, and it acquires the most significant levels of affectability and explicitness when the tactile information extent on misuse location is 25 percent, as displayed in the table underneath. This method proposes that the deliberate rate has expanded because of the strategy. In an ensuing report, similar creators utilize Restricted Boltzmann Machine-based Clustered IDS (RBC-IDS), a profound learning-based system, to screen basic foundation for potential interlopers utilizing three secret layers, bringing about an expanded exactness of 99.91 percent contrasted with 99.80 percent in the earlier review. Contrasted with the recently suggested worldview's overhead costs, the overhead expenses of this new trial are twice pretty much as high as those of the earlier test. As oneself driving independent vehicle (SDAV) keeps on modifying the current transportation system, its utilization in healthcare is turning out to be progressively fundamental, outstandingly in the healthcare store network the board (SCM).

Utilizing an interruption discovery system, Aloqaily et al. (2018) had the option to battle against attacks like Denial of Service, Probe, Remote to client, and other comparative kinds of assaults. Profound conviction networks were proposed by the creators for information measurement decrease, and choice trees dependent on the ID3 technique were proposed by the creators for interruption arrangement utilizing the ID3 calculation. Disregarding the systems' incredibly high location precision (99.92 percent), which is very high, the bogus negative rate (1.53 percent) is fairly huge. As indicated by the discoveries, around three interruption endeavours might enter the system for each 200 client meetings because of this weakness. As per the creators, a brilliant clinic system that is contained a crossover detecting network that uses an obliged application convention, an Internet of Things shrewd entryway, and a UI that permits outsiders to enable patients with a wellbeing observing system has been proposed with an end goal to lessen the security weakness of RFID in the healthcare Internet of Things foundation. The data received from the Internet of Things gadgets, then again, is put away in a focal data set that is defenceless against extortion and control. It is feasible to defeat this issue by utilizing a decentralized record, for example, the Blockchain, in light of the fact that information blocks are replicated across dissipated organization hubs, bringing about more straightforwardness and responsibility. Work by Robereto Saia on the internet of substances is an enhancement to the earlier work around here. On the internet of substances, he introduced an exceptional technique that separated the internet of things into two essential parts: elements like client gadgets and a tracker that permits the exchange of data to an appropriated record (Blockchain). According to the correct implementation of such a broad and complicated network may expose possible limits, such as difficulties in minimizing the processing overhead of Blockchain. Healthcare services may be provided by using this hybrid network architecture, which is a mix of wireless and Blockchain technology.

With the use of the Blockchain, Esposito et al. studied the security and privacy of healthcare data by including several types of data structures into the system and watching their outcomes. Because maintaining a large amount of health data on a Blockchain is both time-consuming and difficult, the researchers chose to utilize the hash of the data as a transaction in their study. It is important to note that this alone will not be adequate to ensure data security. In healthcare small area networks, it is difficult to decrease the overhead associated with Blockchain implementation since adding blocks to the chain in line with typical cryptographic mining methods such as Proof of Work (PoW) demands the usage of huge quantities of computer resources. To resolve this issue, Dorri and Associates proposed another lightweight plan for networks that incorporate countless Internet of Things gadgets. To decrease the measure of time needed for access confirmation utilizing the arrangement header, a nearby PC is utilized as a Miner, and various Internet of Things gadgets are bunched together with the goal that one of them is picked as the group head. This diminishes the measure of time needed for access check utilizing the strategy header. This strategy empowers the arrangement header to contain a forward-thinking adaptation of the approach. The organization head is responsible for keeping up with the entrance control list. Moreover, as recently revealed, this examination utilized a common overlay organization, where numerous information proprietors were allowed to enter information into blocks that were directed by a solitary head, as a component of its discoveries. Along these lines, clients might start to doubt the system, which may prompt more issues. A few security and protection weaknesses in the current Internet of Things ecosystem have been found because of the arrival of an audit paper by Khan and Salah [160]. These vulnerabilities will be investigated further. One of the most serious weaknesses was protection during software updates for billions of Internet of Things devices (for example, in the healthcare business), a situation in which Blockchain technology may be utilized to increase security.

By safeguarding essential Internet of Things infrastructure and sensitive data, it is feasible to prevent security and privacy concerns in healthcare. Examples incorporate the break of 3.62 million patients' information, including individual data, government managed retirement numbers, and charge card subtleties, at Banner Health in Arizona (2018), which happened in 2016. Considering the previous conversation, we might deduce that, while customary security systems give upgraded assurance, completely sealed systems are hard to achieve nowadays. Blockchain technology, among other cutting-edge technologies, is considered by many to be a promising candidate for application in small and medium-sized healthcare Internet of Things systems.

Artificial Intelligence

In tandem with the fast integration of Blockchain technology with artificial intelligence in a range of real-world healthcare applications, the power and resilience of Blockchain technologies are increasing. Among the most important driving forces behind the artificial intelligence (AI) industry are machine learning and deep learning, both of which are making significant contributions to the advancement of robotics. We may expect a machine to have increasing ability to accurately categorize and predict patterns as the amount of data we feed it increases. ModelChain is a system made by Kuo and Ohno-Machado (2014) that depends on Blockchain innovation and is planned for use in appropriated figuring conditions. It is feasible to contribute wellbeing information to prepare an AI demonstrate and further develop treatment utilizing this engineering, which utilizes a private Blockchain and doesn't expect members to unveil their wellbeing data. This engineering utilizes a private Blockchain and doesn't expect members to reveal their wellbeing data. Utilizing this kind of innovation, you might build the security and versatility of dispersed protection saving medical care prescient demonstrating across a few organizations, while likewise bringing down costs simultaneously. Utilizing fake systems, computational experimentation, and parallel execution, Wang et al. (2018) proposed a Blockchain-based parallel healthcare system (PHS) that depends on Blockchain innovation. Patients' diagnosis, condition, and treatment method were the primary focus of the American College of Physicians (ACP) in their animation. The PHS is being linked with a consortium Blockchain in order to connect hospitals, patients, the health regulatory authority, and associated communities, among other things.

Applications of Blockchain Technology on the Internet of Medical Things

There is a deficiency in the level of standardization: It has been seen in recent years that the usage of cutting-edge IoMT technology in the healthcare industry has increased significantly. Notwithstanding on-premise medical gear utilized by medical care professionals, the Internet of Medical Things (IoMT) makes the way for medical administrations that can be gotten to from any area, whenever, and from any gadget, permitting specialists to direct patients consistently. Since remote gadgets are connected to the assortment of biosignals, this is additionally the establishment for telehealth reconnaissance applications, which are turning out to be progressively famous. Therefore, the meaning of carefully designed medical information transport can't be underscored. There is an enormous level of heterogeneity in correspondence conventions, medical gadgets, and stage plans, which might be characterized as an absence of normalization among IoMT providers, because of which this issue creates. Accordingly, keeping up with the trustworthiness of an alterable yet normalized transmission medium is troublesome in the current climate. Since the presentation of Blockchain isn't influenced by the correspondence principles utilized by a framework, state of the art innovation, for example, Blockchain, can be utilized to forestall unapproved admittance to information while it is being sent over an obscure organization. Blockchain can be used to prevent unauthorized access to data when it is transmitted over an unknown network. It takes enormous processing power and unanimous agreement (51 percent) among its mining nodes to change just one Blockchain data block, which must then be broadcast to the whole network and incorporated into a chain of blocks before being included into the chain of blocks.

Conclusion

People and organizations of all kinds and types are showing a great deal of interest in Blockchain technology, which is becoming increasingly popular. It can possibly upset the customary business on the grounds that to its components, which incorporate decentralization, obscurity, persistency, and auditability. These qualities are among those that make it extraordinary. Because of the utilization of Blockchain innovation, it is normal that the medical services environment would be changed. Aside from the way that the strategy will be open and secure, the general nature of medical services will be upgraded, while costs will be kept up with to a flat out least.

All through this chapter, we analyzed the numerous Blockchain applications in the medical care area, featuring both the significant examination exercises now in progress just as planned future exploration ways in the field. We talked explicitly about flow research on wellbeing information the board, and how Blockchain innovation may enable people while likewise improving on the most common way of offering wellbeing information to other people. Because of the revelation, specialists are by and large in arrangement that, with the utilization of Blockchain innovation, patient information would be truly held and constrained by the person who created the information in the lead position.

A benefit of the Blockchain is that health data may be timestamped, making it difficult for anybody to make changes to them after they have been put to the distribution ledger. Eventually, patients will be able to pick who will have access to their data and for what purpose they want that data to be used on their behalf. The fact is that there are a lot of issues that have not been resolved and that must be addressed in more depth. Models incorporate the cross-line trade of wellbeing information in circumstances where different and once in a while clashing specialists exist, which might decrease or dispense with the advantages of information sharing empowered by Blockchain in circumstances where the advantages of information sharing empowered by

Blockchain are diminished. It is true that expectations regarding personal privacy change from one country to the next, based on the laws that govern each individual country in the world. It is also critical to do more research on legislative and standards challenges, as well as cross-border health data retrieval techniques that take into account data preservation and usage intents. Another potential issue that has gotten little attention so far is the Blockchain's ability to store and process massive quantities of data access transactions in a timely manner. This is a concern that has garnered little attention thus far. A result of the huge amount of transactions, the time it takes to finish mining blocks on private or public Blockchains would increase exponentially over time. To keep mining delays to a bare minimum, it is necessary to develop innovative approaches and algorithms.

Also discussed was current Blockchain research in the context of healthcare supply chain management, which we found to be quite interesting. The capability of Blockchain innovation to address trust disintegration and increment information straightforwardness in clinical preliminaries is explicitly investigated in this article. It has been proposed by certain scholastics that the reception of Blockchain innovation can work on the logical legitimacy of clinical preliminary discoveries, which has been called into question in the past inferable from concerns like missing information and particular distribution. The subject of medication observing came up during our conversation, and obviously Blockchain innovation will turn into a basic instrument for drug specialists and other medical services experts to precisely and immediately confirm the progression of legitimate medications and their dispersion to patients soon. In any case, more exploration on trustworthy global positioning frameworks that screen the enrolment of items is fundamental. The utilization of RFID and standardized identifications in global positioning frameworks has expanded as of late, but these frameworks are not impermeable to altering since these codes are sent as fixed qualities all through the store network measure, which might be changed or duplicated by forgers. According to this chapter, a new set of concerns for further investigation has been identified, including invoicing and payment administration, among others. A transparent technology, such as Blockchain, may be able to help address or minimize the problem of claims and billing in the healthcare business, despite the fact that this occurs on a regular basis.

Finally, we spoke about how Blockchain technology may be used in the Internet of Things (IoT). Various technologies will be used to connect patients with their providers in the twenty-first century, and these technologies will be integrated into the healthcare delivery system (e.g., remote healthcare services, wearable gadgets, and so on). Regardless of the way that these frameworks create information consistently, they might be powerless against malevolent assaults while in transmission at different levels of the hidden correspondence organization. These examination papers, which were all given in this review, are talked about in this chapter as alternative safe arrangements that utilize Blockchain innovation to guarantee the respectability of wellbeing information are offered by different scientists. In our viewpoint, the main inquiry that scholastics should settle is the way the Blockchain will work in mind boggling and differed correspondence organizations, which are presently being examination. The Internet of Things (IoT) conveyance framework will utilize correspondence networks that will be overseen by countless specialist organizations, each with its own information access control strategy, to offer administrations. Appropriately, all together for Blockchain innovation to work viably in such a climate, we should do explore on Blockchain systems that empower a solitary worldwide access strategy for the entire organization, as recently referenced. Moreover, in light of the fact that the organization is comprised of hubs and PCs that are situated in various topographical areas, synchronization instruments are fundamental to build up the request in which squares are added to the organization when they are finished. Extra investigation into state-of-the-art arrangements that help Blockchain as an assistance is additionally suggested. Blockchain as an assistance permits different gatherings (organizations, gadgets, clients, etc.) inside the IoMT worldview to get to essential cognizant Blockchain foundations on a membership premise.

References

Al Omar, A.; Bhuiyan, M.Z.A.; Basu, A.; Kiyomoto, S.; Rahman, M.S. Privacy-friendly platform for healthcare data in cloud based on Blockchain environment. *Future Gen. Comput. Syst.*, 2019, 95, 511–521.

Al Ridhawi, I.; Aloqaily, M.; Kantarci, B.; Jararweh, Y.; Mouftah, H.T. A continuous diversified vehicular cloud service availability framework for smart cities. *Comput. Netw.*, 2018, 145, 207–218.

Al Ridhawi, I.; Aloqaily, M.; Kotb, Y.; Al Ridhawi, Y.; Jararweh, Y. A collaborative mobile edge computing and user solution for service composition in 5G systems. *Trans. Emerg. Telecommun. Technol.*, 2018, 29, e3446.

Alonso, S.G.; Arambarri, J.; López-Coronado, M.; de la Torre Díez, I. Proposing new Blockchain challengesin eHealth. *J. Med. Syst.*, 2019, 43, 64.

Andoni, M.; Robu, V.; Flynn, D.; Abram, S.; Geach, D.; Jenkins, D.; McCallum, P.; Peacock, A. Blockchain technology in the energy sector: A systematic review of challenges and opportunities. *Renew. Sustain. Energy Rev.*, 2019, 100,

Benchoufi, M.; Porcher, R.; Ravaud, P. Blockchain protocols in clinical trials: Transparency and traceability of consent. *F1000Research*, 2017, 6, 66.

Benchoufi, M.; Ravaud, P. Blockchain technology for improving clinical research quality. *Trials*, 2017, 18, 335.

Cardoso, L.; Marins, F.; Portela, F.; Santos, M.; Abelha, A.; Machado, J. The next generation of interoperability agents in healthcare. *Int. J. Environ. Res. Public Health*, 2014, 11, 5349–5371.

Castaldo, L.; Cinque, V. Blockchain-based logging for the cross-border exchange of ehealth data in europe. In *International ISCIS Security Workshop*; Springer: Cham, Switzerland, 2018; pp. 46–56.

Chiuchisan, I.; Costin, H.N.; Geman, O. Adopting the internet of things technologies in health care systems. In *Proceedings of the 2014 International Conference and Exposition on Electrical and Power Engineering (EPE)*, Iasi, Romania, 16–18 October 2014; pp. 532–535.

Choudhury, O.; Fairoza, N.; Sylla, I.; Das, A. A Blockchain framework for managing and monitoring data in multi-site clinical trials. *arXiv*, 2019.

Clauson, K.A.; Breeden, E.A.; Davidson, C.; Mackey, T.K. Leveraging Blockchain technology to enhance supply chain management in healthcare. *Blockchain Healthc. Today*, 2018.

Davis, Jessica. 3 phishing hacks breach 20,000 Catawba Valley patient records. *HIMSS*, 2018. Available online: https://www.healthcareitnews.com/news/3-phishing-hacks-breach-20000-catawba-valley-patient-records (accessed on 20 April 2019).

Dehgani, R.; Jafari Navimipour, N. The impact of information technology and communication systems on the agility of supply chain management systems. *Kybernetes*, 2019.

Engelhardt, M.A. Hitching healthcare to the chain: An introduction to Blockchain technology in the healthcare sector. *Technol. Innov. Manag. Rev.*, 2017, 7, 22–34.

Envelopment analysis. *Health Care Manag. Sci.*, 2019, 1–15. [CrossRef].

Esposito, C.; De Santis, A.; Tortora, G.; Chang, H.; Choo, K.K.R. Blockchain: A panacea for healthcare cloud-based data security and privacy? *IJARIIE*, 2021, 7(4)

Fan, K.; Wang, S.; Ren, Y.; Li, H.; Yang, Y. Medblock: Efficient and secure medical data sharing via Blockchain. *J. Med. Syst.*, 2018, 42, 136.

Fanning, K.; Centers, D.P. Blockchain and its coming impact on financial services. J. *Corporate Account. Financ.*, 2016, 27, 53–57.

Frost, J.H.; Massagli, M.P. Social uses of personal health information within Patients Like Me, an online patient community: What can happen when patients have access to one another's data. *J. Med. Internet Res.*, 2008, 10, e15.

Funk, E.; Riddell, J.; Ankel, F.; Cabrera, D. Blockchain technology: A data framework to improve validity, trust, and accountability of information exchange in health professions education. *Acad. Med.*, 2018, 93, 1791–1794.

Genestier, P.; Zouarhi, S.; Limeux, P.; Excoffier, D.; Prola, A.; Sandon, S.; Temerson, J.M. Blockchain for consent management in the eHealth environment: A nugget for privacy and security challenges. *J. Int. Soc. Telemed.* eHealth, 2017.

Gordon, W.J.; Catalini, C. Blockchain technology for healthcare: Facilitating the transition to patient-driven interoperability. *Comput. Struct. Biotechnol. J.*, 2018.

Griggs, K.N.; Ossipova, O.; Kohlios, C.P.; Baccarini, A.N.; Howson, E.A.; Hayajneh, T. Healthcare Blockchain system using smart contracts for secure automated remote patient monitoring. *J. Med. Syst.*, 2018, 42, 130.

Guo, R.; Shi, H.; Zhao, Q.; Zheng, D. Secure attribute-based signature scheme with multiple authorities for Blockchain in electronic health records systems. *IEEE Access*, 2018, 776, 1–12.

Hussein, A.F.; ArunKumar, N.; Ramirez-Gonzalez, G.; Abdulhay, E.; Tavares, J.M.R.; de Albuquerque, V.H.C.A medical records managing and securing Blockchain based system supported by a genetic algorithm and discrete wavelet transform. *Cognit. Syst. Res.*, 2018, 52, 1–11.

Jayaraman, R.; AlHammadi, F.; Simsekler, M.C.E. Managing Product recalls in healthcare supply chain. In *Proceedings of the 2018 IEEE International Conference on Industrial Engineering and Engineering Management (IEEM)*, Bangkok, Thailand, 16–19 December 2018; pp. 293–297.

Ji, Y.; Zhang, J.; Ma, J.; Yang, C.; Yao, X. BMPLS: Blockchain-based multi-level privacy-preserving location sharing scheme for telecare medical information systems. *J. Med. Syst.*, 2018, 42, 147.

Joshi, A.P.; Han, M.; Wang, Y. A survey on security and privacy issues of Blockchain technology. *Math. Found. Comput.*, 2018, 1, 121–147.

Kaur, H.; Alam, M.A.; Jameel, R.; Mourya, A.K.; Chang, V. A proposed solution and future direction for Blockchain-based heterogeneous medicare data in cloud environment. *J. Med. Syst.*, 2018, 42, 156.

Liang, X.; Zhao, J.; Shetty, S.; Liu, J.; Li, D. Integrating Blockchain for data sharing and collaboration inmobile healthcare applications. In *Proceedings of the 2017 IEEE 28th Annual International Symposium on Personal, Indoor, and Mobile Radio Communications (PIMRC)*, Montreal, QC, Canada, 8–13 October17

Lin, I.C.; Liao, T.C. A survey of Blockchain security issues and challenges. *IJ Netw. Secur.*, 2017, 19, 653–659.

Mackey, T.K.; Kuo, T.T.; Gummadi, B.; Clauson, K.A.; Church, G.; Grishin, D.; Obbad, K.; Barkovich, R.; Palombini, M. 'Fit-for-purpose?'—Challenges and opportunities for applications of Blockchain technology in the future of healthcare. *BMC Med.*, 2019, 17, 68.

Macrinici, D.; Cartofeanu, C.; Gao, S. Smart contract applications within Blockchain technology: A systematic mapping study. *Telemat. Inform.*, 2018, 35.

Marucheck, A.; Greis, N.; Mena, C.; Cai, L. Product safety and security in the global supply chain: Issues, challenges and research opportunities. *J. Oper. Manag.*, 2011, 29, 707–720

McGhin, T.; Choo, K.K.R.; Liu, C.Z.; He, D. Blockchain in healthcare applications: Research challenges and opportunities. *J. Netw. Comput. Appl.*, 2019,

Mettler, M. Blockchain technology in healthcare: The revolution starts here. In *Proceedings of the 2016 IEEE18th International Conference on e-Health Networking, Applications and Services (Healthcom)*, Munich, Germany, 14–16 September 2016; pp. 1–3.

Michael, J.; Cohn, A.; Butcher, J.R. Blockchain technology. 2018. Available online: https://www.steptoe.com/images/content/1/7/v3/171269/LIT-FebMar18-Feature-Blockchain.pdf (accessed on 20 March 2019).

Moosavi, S.R.; Gia, T.N.; Rahmani, A.M.; Nigussie, E.; Virtanen, S.; Isoaho, J.; Tenhunen, H. SEA: A secure and efficient authentication and authorization architecture for IoT-based healthcare using smart gateways. *Procedia Computer Science* 52 (2015) 452 – *459.*

Nakamoto, S. *Bitcoin: A Peer-to-Peer Electronic Cash System*; BN Publishing: La Vergne, TN, USA, 2008.

Nausheen, F.; Begum, S.H. Healthcare IoT: Benefits, vulnerabilities and solutions. In *Proceedings of the 2018 IEEE 2nd International Conference on Inventive Systems and Control (ICISC)*, Coimbatore, India, 19–20 January 2018.

Nikoloudakis, Y.; Pallis, E.; Mastorakis, G.; Mavromoustakis, C.X.; Skianis, C.; Markakis, E.K. Vulnerability assessment as a service for fog-centric ICT ecosystems: A healthcare use case. *Peer-to-Peer Netw. Appl.*, 2019, 1–9.

Nugent, T.; Upton, D.; Cimpoesu, M. Improving data transparency in clinical trials using Blockchain smart contracts. *F1000Research*, 2016, 5, 2541.

Ølnes, S.; Ubacht, J.; Janssen, M. Blockchain in government: Benefits and implications of distributed ledger technology for information sharing. *Gov. Inf. Q.*, 2017, 34, 355–364.

Otoum, S.; Kantarci, B.; Mouftah, H.T. On the feasibility of deep learning in sensor network intrusion detection. *IEEE Netw. Lett.*, 2019.

Patel, V. A framework for secure and decentralized sharing of medical imaging data via Blockchain consensus. *Health Inform. J.*, 2018.

Peter, H.; Moser, A. Blockchain-applications in banking & payment transactions: Results of a survey. In *Proceedings of the 14th International Scientific Conference Pt, European Financial Systems*, Brno, Czech Republic, 26–27 June 2017.

Radanovic, I.; Likic, R. Opportunities for use of Blockchain technology in medicine. *Appl. Health Econ. Health Policy*, 2018, 16, 583–590.

Rani, A.A.V.; Baburaj, E. Secure and intelligent architecture for cloud-based healthcare applications in wireless body sensor networks. *Int. J. Biomed. Eng. Technol.*, 2019, 29, 186–199.

Roehrs, A.; da Costa, C.A.; da Rosa Righi, R. OmniPHR: A distributed architecture model to integrate personal health records. *J. Biomed. Inform.*, 2017.

Shae, Z.; Tsai, J.J. On the design of a Blockchain platform for clinical trial and precision medicine. In *Proceedings of the 2017 IEEE 37th International Conference on Distributed Computing Systems (ICDCS)*, Atlanta, GA, USA, 5–8 June 2017; pp. 1972–1980.

Shen, B.; Guo, J.; Yang, Y. MedChain: Efficient healthcare data sharing via Blockchain. *Appl. Sci.*, 2019, 9, 1207.

Siyal, A.; Junejo, A.; Zawish, M.; Ahmed, K.; Khalil, A.; Soursou, G. Applications of Blockchain technology in medicine and healthcare: Challenges and future perspectives. *Cryptography*, 2019, 3, 3.

Sylim, P.; Liu, F.; Marcelo, A.; Fontelo, P. Blockchain technology for detecting falsified and substandard drugs in distribution: Pharmaceutical supply chain intervention. *JMIR Res. Protoc.*, 2018, 7, e10163.

Tseng, J.H.; Liao, Y.C.; Chong, B.; Liao, S.W. Governance on the drug supply chain via Gco in Blockchain. *Int. J. Environ. Res. Public Health*, 2018, 15,

Vo, H.T.; Kundu, A.; Mohania, M.K. *Research Directions in Blockchain Data Management and Analytics*; EDBT: Lisbon, Portugal, 2018; pp. 445–448.

Wang, H.; Song, Y. Secure cloud-based EHR system using attribute-based cryptosystem and Blockchain. *J. Med. Syst.*, 2018, 42, 152.

Xu, X.; Lu, Q.; Liu, Y.; Zhu, L.; Yao, H.; Vasilakos, A.V. Designing Blockchain-based applications a case study for imported product traceability. *Future Gen. Comput. Syst.*, 2019, 92, 399–406.

Yaeger, K.; Martini, M.; Rasouli, J.; Costa, A. Emerging Blockchain technology solutions for modern healthcare infrastructure. *J. Sci. Innov. Med.*, 2019, 2.

Yli-Huumo, J.; Ko, D.; Choi, S.; Park, S.; Smolander, K. Where is current research on Blockchain technology?—A systematic review. *PLoS ONE*, 2016, 11, e0163477.

Yuce, M.R. Implementation of wireless body area networks for healthcare systems. *Sens. Actuators Phys.*, 2010, 162, 116–129.

Yue, X.; Wang, H.; Jin, D.; Li, M.; Jiang, W. Healthcare data gateways: Found healthcare intelligence on Blockchain with novel privacy risk control. *J. Med. Syst.*

Zanjal, S.V.; Talmale, G.R. Medicine reminder and monitoring system for secure health using IOT. *Procedia Comput. Sci.*, 2016, 78, 471–476.

Zhang, P.; Schmidt, D.C.; White, J.; Lenz, G. Blockchain technology use cases in healthcare. In *Advances in Computers*; Elsevier: Amsterdam, The Netherlands, 2018; Volume 111, pp. 1–41.

Zheng, Z.; Xie, S.; Dai, H.N.; Wang, H. *Blockchain Challenges and Opportunities: A Survey*; Work Paper; Inderscience Publishers: Geneva, Switzerland, 2016.

Zhu, L.; Wu, Y.; Gai, K.; Choo, K.K.R. Controllable and trustworthy Blockchain-based cloud datamanagement. *Future Gen. Comput. Syst.*, 2019, 91, 527–535.

Chapter 7

Blockchain with Big Data and Machine Learning in Healthcare

Ravindra Kumar* **and Basetty Mallikarjuna**
School of Computing Science and Engineering,
Galgotias University, Uttar Pradesh, India

Abstract

Big data finds its application in design of cost optimization methods and models for prevention and control of numerous illnesses. One such application is the use of health monitoring systems which are based on monitoring data received from sensors used for obtaining a patient's health status. The models so designed can also be utilized for cross-checking improvements in the patient's health after a medicine is given or validating the effectiveness of a medicine. With the emergence of internet and mobile technologies, these methods can be fully utilized in the forms of apps by the patient. This can reduce the cost of performing expensive tests or diagnostic analysis. Internet of Things (IoT) is another domain that is vastly used for such applications. The purpose of this article is to review the application of big data technologies in healthcare sector.

The important data received from sensors used for monitoring the health of a patient, is collected, cleaned, transformed, visualized and analyzed for the purpose of diagnosis. Machine learning models can be prepared for analyzing this data and making suitable decisions for prescribing medicines and then monitoring the progress of the patient's health. The visualization techniques so designed could provide an enhanced tool both for the patient and the doctor. The roles of these

* Corresponding Author's Email: ravi6387b@gmail.com.

In: Blockchain Technology Based Big Data for Healthcare
Editors: Basetty Mallikarjuna, Niranjanamurthy M, Sheng-Lung Peng et al.
ISBN: 978-1-68507-968-0

techniques are well suited for wearables and smart phone apps which are used to monitor the health of a patient, providing health awareness programs, designing a health monitoring system, and using collaborative care methods. All these applications are based on using data analysis and data interpretation techniques. This can be of tremendous help to the end user who needs to put together the outputs. Further, there could be improvements in time-consuming processes. Visualization techniques and insights obtained from big data analytics approach can prove very useful in healthcare application. This can greatly help in decision making process for the health status of the patient.

This could lead to the development of a new category of healthcare solutions. These models will process the incoming health-information, and will have the capability for interpreting and analyzing such crucial information. These models can help to a greater extent in diagnostic approaches as well as in preventing a large set of illnesses. This could lead to an entirely different life style for the patient. With an increasing demand for such models, their significance is felt to a greater extent.

Keywords: healthcare, big data, machine learning, IoT (Internet of Things), PCM (Principal component Analysis)

Introduction

Big data is characterized by a set of attributes. Some of these attributes are enumerated below:

1) Volume: Information is generated at an alarming speed and the size. For example, zettabyte is a unit for one such block of information.
2) Variety: Different types of information are generated from various sources. This can be structured, semi-structured or unstructured information.
3) Velocity: Information is generated at an alarming rate, which is at very high pace.
4) Value: This refers to bringing the correct meaning from the information.
5) Veracity: This feature refers to uncertainty and inconsistencies in the information.

The issues faced by big data are listed below:

1) To store huge and exponentially growing information.
2) How to process information which has different types viz. Structural, semi-structured and unstructured?
3) Putting this large volume of information to a computation unit.

The two main components of the big data are Hadoop and map-reduce programming paradigm. Hadoop is a framework that allows for storing and processing huge information in parallel and distributed fashion. Hadoop is comprised of HDFS (Hadoop distributed file system) and map-reduce. HDFS allows to store any type of data across clusters. The map-reduce allows for processing of the data which is stored in HDFS. Hadoop is a distributed file system, which is capable of storing exponentially growing huge information. This can store unstructured data as well. It does not require pre-dumping schema validation. This allows for processing information faster. HDFS is the storage unit of Hadoop, which is a distributed file system. It divides files into smaller chunks and stores it across clusters. The data is stored using name-node and data-node. The name-node is the master node while data nodes are slave nodes. HDFS stores the data in the form of blocks. The block size can be configured based on your requirements. The default block size is 128 MB (megabyte).

The name-node is the master node which maintains and manages the data nodes. It records metadata, e.g., location of blocks stored, the size of the files, permissions, hierarchy, etc. It receives a signal known as heartbeat from the data nodes. The data node is a slave node, which stores the actual information. It serves the read and write requests from the master node. There is a secondary name node, which is used for check-pointing. YARN (yet another resource negotiator) consists of resource manager and node manager. The resource manager has two components viz. Schedulers and applications manager. The node manager has two components viz. Application master and container.

The map-reduce is a software framework which helps in writing applications that processes large data sets using distributed and parallel algorithms inside Hadoop environment. The stages in map-reduce can be listed as input, splitting, mapping, shuffling, reducing and result phase.

The Hadoop ecosystem has Flume for unstructured data and Sqoop for structured data. The storage is HDFS. The resource managing is achieved with YARN. It is also comprised of map-reduce, Hive, Mahoot, Pig, HBase, SPARK, Kafka, SOLR, OOZIE and Zookeeper blocks.

The identity card used by the patient will link the patient, through internet to the electronic reports, which contains important information regarding the health of the patient. Doctors can use this information. Communication plays a vital role in a system like this which is based on IoT. This system can provide information for visualization and analysis. Using simulations, making a prescription, predicting and monitoring health can be achieved with such a system.

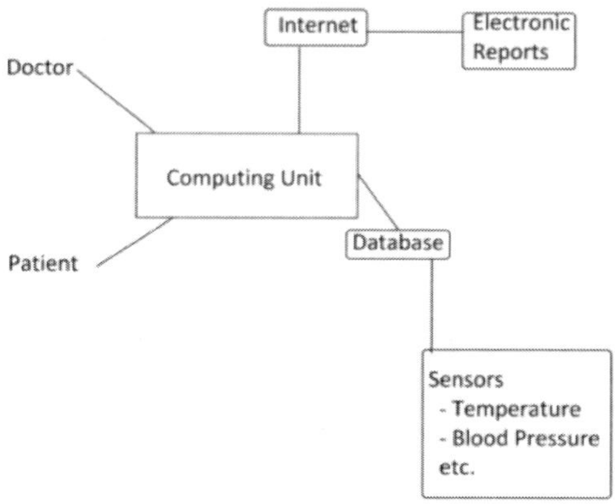

Figure 1. Working and information flow in a healthcare system based on IoT.

Figure 1 depicts the working and information flow for a healthcare system based on IoT.

New technologies and processes can be adopted for the design and developments of such models. The information used in these models can be digitized and related healthcare monitoring system can be developed using smart connected devices and IT services.

The next section contains an overview of big data technology and then describes a scheme based on machine learning techniques for optimizing cost.

Overview of Big Data

Big data can be referred to as an agglomeration of related sets of information, that is, volumetric and complicated enough such that it cannot be processed using conventional data processing tools or utilities.

The issues faced in big data are gathering information, cleaning the information, storing data, exploring data, performing analysis, and exchanging data. This change is mainly due to handling an additional data, that is, generated from the analysis of a voluminous piece of data. Nowadays, the information is generated in chunks of petabytes and terabytes. Big data normally deals with data, which is in the chunks of exabytes. This huge volume of data is being generated from numerous sources that include public, computing units, electronic devices like smart phones and gadgets, network. One such example is to gather and analyze the information received by web pages related to a specified topic.

The issue faced by big data is that the conventional database methods are not adequate. The response of time such conventional tools is not desirable. Hence, big data helps in storing such a voluminous data and analyzing the information. The three Vs of big data can be viewed in the directions of volume, speed and complexity. Volume of information is increasing at an alarming rate. Information is originated rapidly and it needs to be processed at a very high speed. Moreover, delayed response can result in lost eventuality. Some of these utilities are digital marketing and information system related to medical diagnosis, internet, smart phones and sensors' information processing systems. Another dimension in big data is variety of data, which could be structured data like tables in databases, unstructured data like audio, video and text data or semi-structured data like logging information.

Another dimension in big data could be value that represents uncertainty in the information or it can be viewed as inconsistent information.

Apart from these four dimensions, there could be other dimensions which are veracity, viscosity, variability, etc.

Big data deals with huge voluminous data. Most of this data is unstructured data. The issue faced in big data is how to store this huge data and perform computations on this data?

The main big data enabling technologies are discussed next. These are used for storing and processing this huge volume of data. Apache Hadoop comprises of two main components which are distributed file system called HDFS (Hadoop Distributed File System) and map reduce programming paradigm. HDFS is the storing unit and it decomposes big data into clusters in a distributed fashion. The properties of HDFS are that it can scale out hardware resourcing unit and it is fault-tolerant. Map reduce is a programming paradigm which is based on parallel processing. Map can be viewed as apply operation while reduce can be viewed as summarize operation. One such utility which is based on map reduce is for indexing web pages. YARN is yet another resource negotiator which is used as a scheduler and resource manager. Pig is a scripting language which is based on dataflow model. Hive is also used that is consisting of SQL like queries. Giraph is used for graph processing tasks. Spark offers high speed processing and Cassendra, MongoDB are examples of NoSQL databases. Zookeeper is a central management system, which is used for synchronizing and configuration purposes. It also maintains high availability of modules.

Map reduce is a programming paradigm which is based on parallel processing of big data. A map function is specified by the user, which processes key-value pairs and outputs intermediate key-value pairs. The reduce function summarizes all intermediate key value pairs that are related to a specific intermediate key value pair.

HDFS architecture is composed of name node and data node. Name node stores the metadata. YARN is the job scheduler and resource manager in Hadoop framework. This is used for allocation of resources to utilities that are running in the Hadoop cluster. It is also used for scheduling jobs in which needs to be executed on different cluster nodes. It is composed of a resource manager, that contains a scheduler. Different node managers work and report to resource manager. A node manager is composed of many containers.

Hive is a data management utility for Hadoop system and it is distributed in nature. It is composed of SQL like queries which are called HiveSQL or HSQL. It is used for data mining purpose. It executes on top of Hadoop.

Apache Spark is used for data analytics. It is widely used in education and industry sectors. It is a kind of fast cluster computing technology. The coordination kernel is called Zookeeper. The roles played by the Zookeeper are distributed locking system, configuration managing tasks, electing leaders, and managing work queues. This is a replica-based utility and it maintains metadata of utilities that are distributed across Hadoop system. It is a centralized system that maintains key-value pairs which can be used for coordination purposes. It runs on multiple computing units.

Conventional SQL can be used for queries related to huge volume of structured data while NoSQL is required for handling data that is unstructured. These require no specific schema. Every row in NoSQL may be having its own set of column values. NoSQL gives higher throughput in applications related to big data that has huge volume of information.

SQL databases are relational and analytical, while NoSQL are key-value, column-family, graph and document. Apache Cassandra is a distributed NoSQL. This can be used for working with huge volume of data. This can be scaled up and it is high-performing NoSQL. It is capable to handle huge volume of data because of its distributed nature. Information is put on many computing units and the replication factor is greater than one. Hence, data availability is high and there is no single point failure.

HBase is a distributed database. It is written in java language. It is capable of storing huge amount of information in chunks of petabytes and terabytes. Spark streaming is used for processing of streaming data that is available from live streaming. It can be scaled up easily. The throughput is high and it is fault-tolerant. It can process stream information which may be available from HDFS, Kafka, network sockets, flume, etc.

The machine learning module of Spark is called Spark ML and graph processing module of Spark is called GraphX, which can handle stream information. The input data received from different stream sources is fed to Spark stream block which produces batch data. This data is fed to Spark engine that outputs batch processed data. The input from stream could be any one from Kafka, HDFS, S3, flume, kinesis or twitter. The output of Spark stream block could be HDFS, databases or dashboards.

Apache Kafka is a streaming data processing software. It is written using Scala and Java programming languages. This is a streaming processing and distributed event handling software. It can process about a trillion of events in a single day and it is based on commit logging distributed system abstraction.

Spark MLib is the machine learning software which is distributed and built on top of Spark core software. This machine learning software can be scaled up and it consists of machine learning tools, algorithms and utilities. The tasks which can be performed are classification, regression, clustering, filtering and dimension reduction.

GraphX is used in Spark software for processing graphs and it extends the RDDs (Resilient distributed dataset) of Spark. The simplification of graph analysis tasks and capability to handle directed multigraphs is provided in it. This is a layer on the top of Spark core layer.

Design of a Machine Learning Technique for Cost Optimization

Machine learning (ML) techniques are currently used in a wide range of applications including health-care, customer segmentation, weather forecast, classification, etc. An application designed using ML techniques is capable of learning without explicitly writing programs. In ML design process, firstly the problem is studied, then training of ML algorithm is performed, followed by evaluation of the model. The training of the ML algorithm is based on data that is being used in the application for training purpose. Analysis of errors is also performed.

The advantage of using such a scheme is the adaptability. Machine learning algorithms have a capability to learn from data.

Data mining is another promising field for machine learning methods. Machine learning methods are useful in the situations of complex problems that are based on large set of rules, continuously changing scenarios and dealing with large volume of data sets. Classification, summarizing, forecasting index for next year, handling voice inputs, customer segmentation and recommendation systems are popular applications of machine learning algorithms.

Literature Review

Binkhonain, Manal, and Liping Zhao (2019), describe an overview of applications of machine learning algorithms in classification and identification, related to non-functional requirements. Using Support Vector Machine (SVM) for text classifications, is discussed by Tong, Simon, and Daphne Koller (2001). The machine learning algorithms comprising of Random-Forest, Artificial Neural Network (ANN) and SVM are evaluated for a specific application in supervised classification by Nitze, I., U. Schulthess, and H. Asche (2012). Somvanshi, et al. (2016), and Rebentrost, et al., (2014), describe an overview of decision-tree and SVM for big data classification. Crisci (2012), et al., Kotsiantis (2007) and Belavagi (2016), discuss supervised machine learning algorithms. A smart grid application based on machine learning algorithms is given by Ozay, Mete, Inaki Esnaola, Fatos Tunay Yarman Vural, Sanjeev R. Kulkarni, and H. Vincent Poor (2015). Machine learning application in the field of wireless sensor networks and quantification are given by C. Jiang, et al. (2017), and G. Goovaerts, et al. (2019). Machine learning applications in networks and gait analysis is discussed by L. Liu, et al. (2021), H. Zhang, et al. (2020) and, T. Bao, et al. (2019). Applications of machine learning methods for IoT based systems, reinforcement learning and Fuzzy sets are presented by C. Di, et al. (2019), A. Asadulaev, et al. (2020), and X. Lü, et al. (2020). Finally, the application of clustering, eigenvalues and ensemble SVM are discussed by J. Zhang, Z. Yin and R. Wang (2017).

Proposed Scheme

This section describes the application of Principle Component Analysis (PCA) method of machine learning is used to identify two principal components in a sample data set used in an optimization application. The data set consists of output values of three generators, overall cost incurred in the optimization application. PCA is used to reduce dimensionality such that two principal components in the given sample data set can be found. The results are shown below.

Using PCA for Finding Principal Components in a Sample Data

The steps involved in proposed PCA application is given below:

Step 1: The libraries used in this application are numpy, pandas, matplotlib and seaborn, that are available in Python.

Step 2: A sample data set, which is obtained by executing optimization program written in Python and using Lagrange multiplier method, is used in the application. Firstly, the data set has been created using a dictionary variable named "data_set_cost."

The dictionary variable has the following keys:

Data: This contains 42 records, where each record consists of values of generator output p1, output p2, output p3 and optimal cost.

Pi is representing a generator in the optimization program.

Target: This value indicates a category, which is either 0 or 1 representing either category A or category B for the output. The other keys used in the dictionary variable are description, field names.

Step 3: Create a data frame named dataframe1 and using panda's library. The records in the Data key are used in the data frame.

The first five records in the dataframe1 are shown in Figure 2.0.

Step 4: Using standard scaler utility, which is available in preprocessing library, the values used in the data frame are normalized.

Step 5: PCA module is imported from Sklearn library (Python).

Step 6: An instance of PCA module is created with a value of two for 'number of components' argument.

Step 7: The scaled data which is obtained in Step 4 is used to fit in the instance of PCA.

	Value of P1	Value of P2	Value of P3	Optimal cost
0	214.23	80.51	15.00	3577.13
1	212.74	81.04	16.01	3582.40
2	208.87	80.93	20.28	3582.65
3	206.55	80.91	22.80	3582.94
4	205.05	80.91	24.41	3583.18

Figure 2. A sample dataset (dataframe 1).

Step 8: The output obtained after fitting scaled data is PCA components. The two components created with PCA are used for clustering the data points in the data set. The categories can be assigned now with these components. Supervised learning algorithms which are based on KNeighbors classifier, Random Forest classifier or Decision Tree classifier can now be used. The classifier can be evaluated using accuracy, precision or F1-Score. Confusion matrix offers a view of the outputs of the classifier.

Illustration and Results

The outputs obtained from PCA technique are presented here. The output showing clustering of data set points is shown in Figure 3.0.

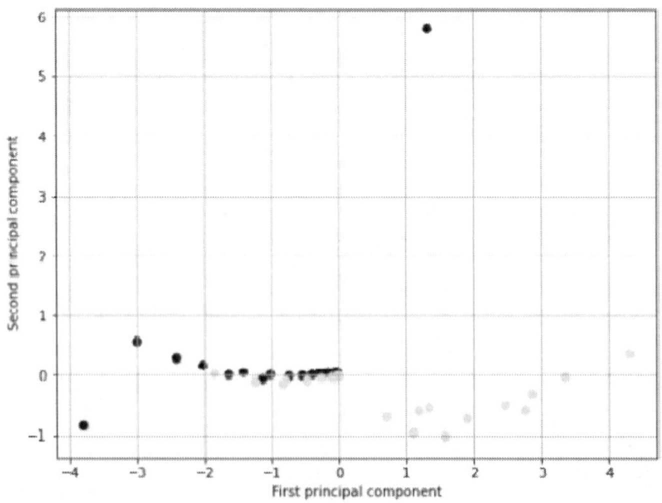

Figure 3. PCA clustering on a sample dataset.

The two PCA components are shown in Figure 4.0.

	Value of P1	Value of P2	Value of P3	Optimal cost
0	-0.592596	0.231474	0.592146	0.494583
1	0.048211	0.944151	-0.052065	-0.321781

Figure 4. Output for two components in PCA.

The heatmap from seaborn library is shown in Figure 5.0.

Figure 5. Heatmap of PCA components in the model.

Conclusion

The machine learning algorithms are quite beneficial for designing a model for optimization. This paper has shown one such application of PCA technique for clustering data points in a sample data set. The PCA components thus obtained are useful for assigning category to a data point. Therefore, supervised classification algorithms may be executed now for building a suitable classifier. The classifier may be based on KNeighbors classifier, Random Forest or Decision Tree classifier. The application of PCA is useful in reducing the components used for clustering, further helping in the classification step of supervised learning.

References

[1] Binkhonain, Manal, and Liping Zhao. "A review of machine learning algorithms for identification and classification of non-functional requirements." *Expert Systems with Applications (2019).*

[2] Tong, Simon, and Daphne Koller. "Support vector machine active learning with applications to text classification." *Journal of Machine Learning Research* 2, no. Nov (2001): 45-66.

[3] Nitze, I., U. Schulthess, and H. Asche. "Comparison of machine learning algorithms random forest, artificial neural network and support vector machine to maximum likelihood for supervised crop type classification." *Proceedings of the 4th GEOBIA,* Rio de Janeiro, Brazil 79 (2012): 3540.

[4] Somvanshi, Madan, Pranjali Chavan, Shital Tambade, and S. V. Shinde. "A review of machine learning techniques using decision tree and support vector machine." In: *2016 International Conference on Computing Communication Control and Automation (ICCUBEA),* pp. 1-7. IEEE, 2016.

[5] Rebentrost, Patrick, Masoud Mohseni, and Seth Lloyd. "Quantum support vector machine for big data classification." *Physical Review Letters* 113, no. 13 (2014): 130503.

[6] Crisci, Carolina, Badih Ghattas, and Ghattas Perera. "A review of supervised machine learning algorithms and their applications to ecological data." *Ecological Modelling* 240 (2012): 113-122.

[7] Kotsiantis, Sotiris B., I. Zaharakis, and P. Pintelas. "Supervised machine learning: A review of classification techniques." *Emerging Artificial Intelligence Applications in computer engineering* 160, no. 1 (2007): 3-24.

[8] Belavagi, Manjula C., and Balachandra Muniyal. "Performance evaluation of supervised machine learning algorithms for intrusion detection." *Procedia Computer Science* 89 (2016): 117-123.

[9] Ozay, Mete, Inaki Esnaola, Fatos Tunay Yarman Vural, Sanjeev R. Kulkarni, and H. Vincent Poor. "Machine learning methods for attack detection in the smart grid." *IEEE Transactions on Neural Networks and Learning Systems* 27, no. 8 (2015): 1773-1786.

[10] C. Jiang, H. Zhang, Y. Ren, Z. Han, K. C. Chen and L. Hanzo, "Machine learning paradigms for next-generation wireless networks," In: *IEEE Wireless Communications*, vol. 24, no. 2, pp. 98-105, April 2017, doi: 10.1109/MWC.2016. 150035 6WC.

[11] G. Goovaerts, S. Padhy, B. Vandenberk, C. Varon, R. Willems and S. Van Huffel, "A machine-learning approach for detection and quantification of QRS fragmentation," In: *IEEE Journal of Biomedical and Health Informatics*, vol. 23, no. 5, pp. 1980-1989, Sept. 2019, doi: 10.1109/JBHI.2018.2878492.

[12] L. Liu, P. Wang, J. Lin and L. Liu, "Intrusion detection of imbalanced network traffic based on machine learning and deep learning," In: *IEEE Access*, vol. 9, pp. 7550-7563, 2021, doi: 10.1109/ACCESS.2020.3048198.

[13] H. Zhang, Y. Guo and D. Zanotto, "Accurate ambulatory gait analysis in walking and running using machine learning models," In: *IEEE Transactions on Neural*

Systems and Rehabilitation Engineering, vol. 28, no. 1, pp. 191-202, Jan. 2020, doi: 10.1109/TNSRE.2019.2958679.

[14] T. Bao, B. N. Klatt, S. L. Whitney, K. H. Sienko and J. Wiens, "Automatically evaluating balance: A machine learning approach," In: *IEEE Transactions on Neural Systems and Rehabilitation Engineering*, vol. 27, no. 2, pp. 179-186, Feb. 2019, doi: 10.1109/TNSRE.2019.2891000.

[15] C. Di, B. Zhang, Q. Liang, S. Li and Y. Guo, "Learning automata-based access class barring scheme for massive random access in machine-to-machine communications," In: *IEEE Internet of Things Journal*, vol. 6, no. 4, pp. 6007- 6017, Aug. 2019, doi: 10.1109/JIOT.2018.2867937.

[16] Asadulaev, I. Kuznetsov, G. Stein and A. Filchenkov, "Exploring and exploiting conditioning of reinforcement learning agents," In: *IEEE Access,* vol. 8, pp. 211951-211960, 2020, doi: 10.1109/ACCESS.2020.3037276.

[17] X. Lü, L. Meng, C. Chen and P. Wang, "Fuzzy removing redundancy restricted Boltzmann machine: Improving learning speed and classification accuracy," In: *IEEE Transactions on Fuzzy Systems*, vol. 28, no. 10, pp. 2495-2509, Oct. 2020, doi: 10.1109/TFUZZ.2019.2940415.

[18] J. Zhang, Z. Yin and R. Wang, "Pattern classification of instantaneous cognitive task-load through GMM clustering, Laplacian eigenmap, and ensemble SVMs," In: *IEEE/ACM Transactions on Computational Biology and Bioinformatics*, vol. 14, no. 4, pp. 947-965, 1 July-Aug. 2017, doi: 10.1109/TCBB.2016.2561927.

Chapter 8

Research Challenges, Opportunities and Future Directions in Applying Big Data Technology in the Healthcare Sector

Ram Singh[1,*], PhD, Rohit Bansal[2], PhD and Vinay Pal Singh[1], PhD

[1]School of Business,
Quantum University Roorkee,
Uttarakhand, India
[2]Department of Management,
Vaish Engineering College, Rohtak, India

Abstract

The idea of "Big Data" is mainstream in an assortment of spaces; Big data in medical services is performing well. As individuals of the present day and age, we definitely know that a vast amount of information is immense and not effectively reasonable. Closely related to other innovations, big data is playing a critical role in opening new doors of potential outcomes. Clinical information is touchy and can cause extreme issues whenever it is not controlled. Information science in medical care can secure this information and concentrate on numerous significant highlights to bring progressive changes. New advancements in AI, image processing, and data mining procedures are also available to find examples and create representable visuals in medical services using big data. The motivation behind this survey was to summarise the highlights, applications, examination approaches, and difficulties of big data in medical services. Large data in medical care has its own highlights, like heterogeneity, deficiency, idealness, life span, security, and possession.

* Corresponding Author's Email: ramsinghcommerce@gmail.com.

In: Blockchain Technology Based Big Data for Healthcare
Editors: Basetty Mallikarjuna, Niranjanamurthy M, Sheng-Lung Peng et al.
ISBN: 978-1-68507-968-0

These highlights present a series of challenges for data storage, mining, and sharing in order to advance health-related research. To manage these difficulties, investigation approaches zeroing in on big data in medical care should be created and laws and guidelines for utilising big data in medical care should be instituted. From a patient's point of view, the utilisation of big data investigation could achieve further developed treatment and lower costs. Patients, governments, clinics, and research institutions could all benefit from big data in medical services.

Keywords: public health, cloud computing, big data, medical applications, electronic health records (EHRs)

Introduction

The expression "Big Data" isn't new to the world, yet its definition is continually advancing. Different endeavors to characterize enormous amounts of information portray it basically as an assortment of information components whose size, speed, type, and intricacy require the quest for, reception of, and creation of new equipment and programming systems to effectively store, investigate, and envision the information [1]. The necessity for a great deal of information is likewise being filled by a shift away from biased clinical choices and toward proof based medication.

The volume of information in the medical services industry is expanding at a stunning rate. One of the principal models in information investigation is healthcare, where three V's of information (Velocity, Variety, and Volume) are a natural component of the information it produces [2]. Big information has been characterized as information that is a lot of huge and compound information to be examined and commonplace enough to be overseen by customary processing procedures and strategies. Verifiably, the medical services industry has produced a volume's measure of information for record keeping, different lawful consistencies, and for patient consideration [3]. Huge medical care information alludes to compounded datasets that, notwithstanding their enormous size, make them recognize qualities that both work with and entangle the way toward removing significant information about a discernible wonder. Large medical service data frequently includes heterogeneous, multi-phantom, fragmented, and uncertain perceptions (for example, analysis, socioeconomics, treatment and infection counteraction, and physical and mental impediments) gleaned from various sources utilising inconsistent examining.

Big Data

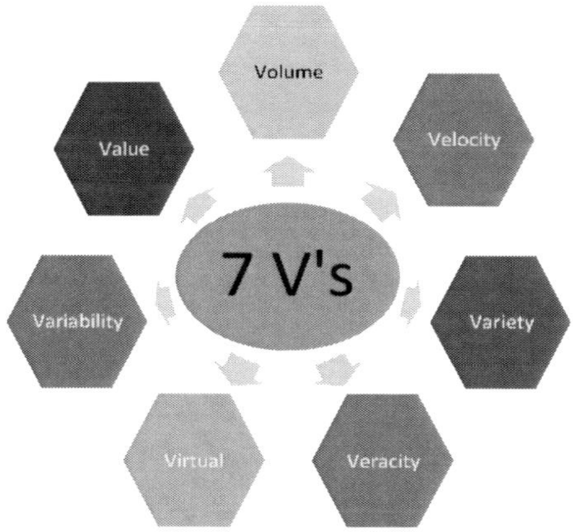

Figure 1. 7 V's of big data.

Big data in medicine refers to digital health information sets, which are thus complex and massive data sets that are impossible to manage using traditional PC software. They cannot be easily managed with common or conventional resources and methods [15]. Healthcare analytics refers to the organized way to use data related to health and develop insights through applying various statistical, predictive, contextual, and other techniques to drive fact based decisions for planning, organizing resources, and controlling the pitfalls in the healthcare industry. As compared to different sectors, it is determined that the availability of massive records within the healthcare industry is extensive and is projected to develop exponentially in the near future. In advanced countries, massive records are collected, saved, and shared via the means of healthcare provider companies and are associated with diverse patient services [4]. The growing power of big data is promising new possibilities to recognize and forecast contexts or issues within the healthcare segment. The amount of information associated with healthcare has explosively increased with the improvement of the internet. It isn't always simply accrued in healthcare provider settings, but additionally in cyber virtual space, along with conventional and cellular internet [5]. Information and the communiqué era are the principal driving forces of voluminous and massive information to be controlled and analyzed. This massive amount of information, consisting of text, audio, video, or some other virtual medium, may be analyzed to offer new and beneficial information [6]. After a long time of technological foot-dragger, the sphere of medication has started to acclimatize to today's virtual statistics age [8].

Healthcare Data

This is where the utility of big data analytics in healthcare transforms from a nice-to-have to a must-have. This sort of information can be specifically labeled as "structured," "semi-structured" or "unstructured" data sets [12]. This type of data set can be defined as below:

Administrative Data and Electronic Health Records

Medical care organizations can collect information about which of their services are being used and how those services are being paid for, and this information is frequently gathered on a personal level, based on claims, patient encounters, or enrollment in wellness programmes [16]. Administrative facts can assist medical agencies in advance by being aware of the matchless wishes of the populations they serve and nicely distributing resources. "Electronic Health Records (EHRs)" incorporate a patient's whole medical history, along with beyond diagnoses, remedies, and outcomes [28]. This information is created and stored in the present via the centre of doctors, nurses, and directors. Clinicians can use EHRs to more acutely deal with individual patients, while different experts and businesses may also use them to calculate percentage statistics, ensuring they have a complete picture of a patient's desires.

Clinical Data and Insurance Claims Data

Some fitness corporations, which include nursing homes, are required to file standardized medical statistics. This form of statistics can be utilized by Medicare or through regulatory corporations to evaluate desires and make modifications to useful resource allocation. It can also permit a facility-unique overall performance assessment. Health corporations can also have a look at statistics and tendencies in coverage claims statistics, which give a window into the forms of offerings their sufferers, are seeking [10]. These statistics may be utilized in some ways, along with the identification of overused or expensive remedies that would be phased out in favour of something more efficient.

Patient Surveys

Medical services partnerships might be proactive in reviewing their patients, asking them roughly which areas in their consideration region had been superb or inadmissible [17]. These measurements can be more subjective than quantitative, but they could still offer clinicians and chief's opportunities for improvement. This is fundamental for homegrown wellness and for following rehashed conditions. Social Determinants of Health (SDoH) and genomic measurements can likewise offer a fuller image of the patient's medical care status.

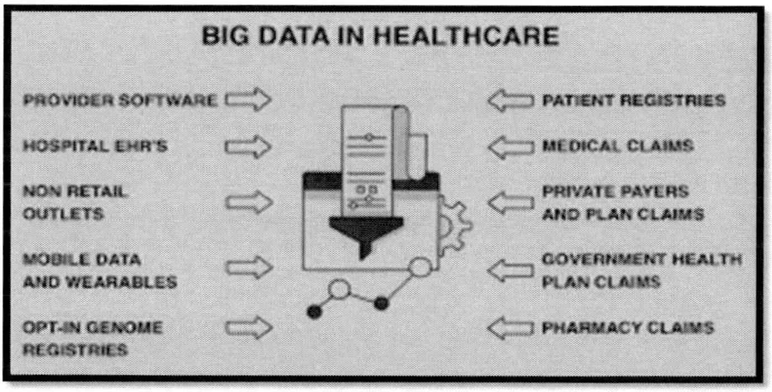

Figure 2. Big data in healthcare.

Role of Data Analytics in Healthcare Sector

"Big Data" is changing the globe at a higher level. Indeed, it is right! This information is changing some businesses. We should peruse exhaustively one of the ventures that is the "Medical Services Industry." The medical services industry is one of the greatest and most muddled divisions in the current age of society [18]. There is a reliable interest in more prevalent and more useful help for patients. Subsequently, the medical care industry is experiencing a disturbance. Over the most recent couple of years, the medical care industry has seen huge advances in the proportion of information accumulated.

Recover Patient Healthcare

The important data obtained from massive statistical analytics provides greater scientific insights to a wide range of healthcare practitioners. These modern-day analytics improve patient care in the healthcare system by allowing clinicians to prescribe more potent therapies and make more logical decisions, removing any therapeutic uncertainty [19, 20].

Anticipate High Risk Patients Rapidly and Efficiently

Predictive analytics, when considering population-extensive statistics for a specific location, in particular, pinpoints which sections of the patients are at higher risk for sickness and recommends early intervention to protect them. This type of prediction is especially appropriate for depictions of people with an appreciation for positive continual sicknesses [19]. Predictive analytics is drawn through aggregating statistics which are associated with a range of things, which incorporate a patient's scientific history, demographic location statistics, socio-financial profile statistics, a patient's co morbidities present within the location, etc.

Easy to Diagnose Patients with EHRs (Electronic Health Records)

This is the commonly used application that permits effective patient diagnostics with each affected person having their own "Electronic Health Records (EHRs)." This EHR consists of demographics, clinical history, hypersensitive reactions of sufferers, and a diagnostic look at the effects of modern and former ailments together with different details. These EH facts are shared through secure statistics arrangements and are easily accessible to doctors and other healthcare professionals. They can get entry to those documents and the non-public statistics can't be changed. However, the diagnostics and remedy may be up to date via the docs [9]. The EHRs can also cause notifications alerting the sufferers about their approaching doctor's visits or diagnostic visits or even songs on their prescriptions.

Reduction in Overall Costs

Analytics are beneficial for figuring out how much an affected person costs. This allows for value reductions. In addition, we can also use them to pick patients' styles outside of healthcare institutions. During this, we will help them by setting up healthy conduct and reducing their desires for assistance. Predictive analytics allows us to estimate character affected person charges and maximize healthcare performance fairly by cautiously planning treatment.

Assess Medical Practitioner Performance

We've left the conventional healthcare technique that makes a specialty to some extent to a cutting-edge value-based technique. Patients can now, without any trouble, rate their physicians via an on-line method. They can go away with great remarks that describe their experience [14]. Furthermore, we've got access to robust, digitalized databases concerning the patient's effects and exercise patterns. All in all, we are able to feed our information analytics software programme with all the data it desires to investigate the practitioners' overall performance in real-time.

Delivering Additional Insights into Affected Person's Cohorts

By analyzing healthcare data, it gains a better understanding of the patient cohorts who are most at risk for various illnesses, allowing for the capture of a few proactive prevention measures. Surprisingly, this type of analytics can be successfully used to raise awareness and cautiously encourage patients to take responsibility for their own happiness. By means of bringing over the medical statistics together, it allows us to bring out greater effectiveness in the patient remedy plans, which guarantees higher patient outcomes [21].

Help to Facilitate Superior Healthcare with Health Devices

Today, a lot of customers' fitness products are offered, like Fitbit, Apple Watch, etc. which maintain a track record on the bodily activity levels of the users. The statistics thus gathered through several gadgets used by users are transferred to cloud servers, which are categorically being utilized by physicians to realize the general fitness and might even therefore plan for an individual's health programmes [13]. Consumer data is analyzed which may be accessed by physicians to realize approximately their physical hobby degrees, and the data can be used to realize approximately precise fitness-associated trends.

Big Data-Driven Healthcare Architectural Framework

A building structure is a fundamental necessity for any expert disclosure method. At the point when it's set up for enormous records investigation in medical care records, at that point it's far too obligatory for a right assessment and idea age. A reasonable rendition presents the clues throughout the total assessment method, from medical care records acquisition to the inordinate phase of records assessment. A sure-to-understand structure is introduced underneath. For excellent research, a simple and uncomplicated structure is required. In clinical philosophy, the theoretical foundation for massive records assessment experience is very similar to that of a regular health examination, and the execution of planning is the most important capacity. In common wellbeing assessment projects, the evaluation may be finished with an undertaking understanding contraption set up on a free structure that joins a PC. Since a massive record, by definition, is a titanic in which getting ready is squashed down and executed all through more than one centre point, allotted taking care of has existed for a significant length of time [22].

What is incredibly new is its use in concentrating particularly enormous records units as clinical benefit providers strike into their tremendous records stores to benefit wisdom for choosing better-learned and wellbeing related decisions. Additionally, open reserve structures which consolidate Hadoop/Map Reduce, to be had in the cloud, have accepted the use of gigantic data assessment in clinical benefits. Regardless of whether the various estimations and models are comparable, the client interfaces of traditional examination equipment and those used for large scale testing are absolutely remarkable. Traditional health examination equipment has improved and become clearer, whereas large truth-factor devices are extremely perplexing, programming-genuine, and necessitate a wide range of capabilities. The data in healthcare comes from two major sources via *internal* and *external* sources [11].

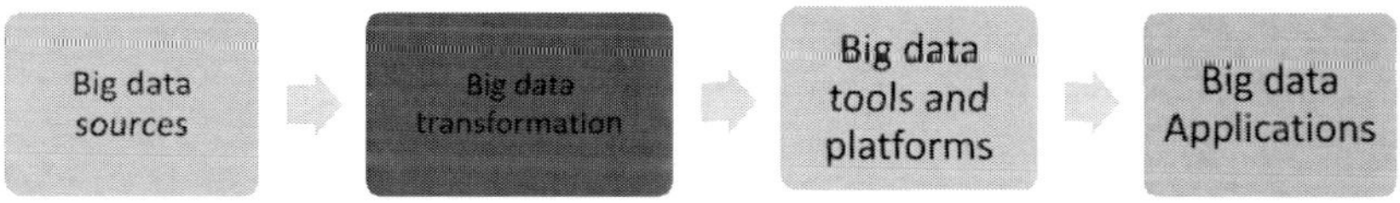

Figure 3. Conceptual architecture of big data analytics.

One of the potential outcomes is a helpful designated building strategy mixed with internet providers. Another critical methodology is information warehousing, wherein information from various sources is assembled and made accessible for handling through which significant data has to be extricated because of the non-accessibility of information in continuously changing circumstances. It relies upon the accessible information to determine whether the information is in a fitting configuration that can be used as a crude contribution to the enormous information investigation.

The other theoretical factor in the medical services system is that various determinations are made identified with the records entered approach, administered plan, gadget decision and investigation models. Finally, in the correct way, the 4 ordinary bundles of monstrous records investigation in medical services are displayed in Fig 3. This includes questions, patient reports, OLAP, and record mining. Representation is a general subject all through the 4 bundles. To draw information from such regions, current science, applied mathematics, and financial aspects, a wide scope of systems and innovations have been progressed and redone to total, control, inspect, and picture gigantic records in medical care.

The most impressive stage for huge reality examination is the open-source information giving stage, Hadoop (Apache stage), at first used for such conventional capacities as totaling net pursuit files [19]. It has a place in the gathering "NoSQL" advances, others comprised of Couch DB and Mongo DB, created to blend realities precisely. Hadoop has the ability to handle exceptionally huge amounts of realities explicitly through dispensing parcelled information units to different workers (hubs), all of which address particular segments of the bigger issue after which they coordinate for the final product. Hadoop can serve double duty as a reality coordinator and an examination gadget. It gives a fantastic arrangement of offices, allowing organizations to outfit the realities that have been, as of recent, difficult to control and investigate. Hadoop, in particular, makes it possible to methodology extremely large volumes of realities with various frameworks or no shape by any stretch of the imagination. However, Hadoop might be difficult to introduce, arrange, and direct, and individuals with Hadoop abilities aren't effectively accessible. Moreover, therefore, it appears organizations aren't really equipped to assess Hadoop completely.

Different Tools Used in Big Data Analytics in Healthcare Data

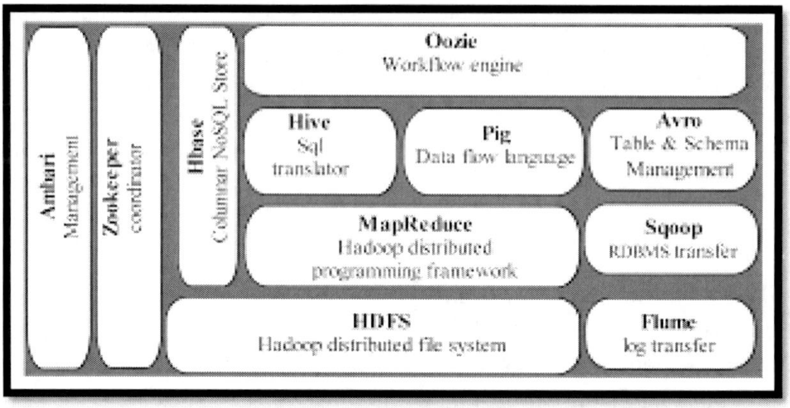

Figure 4. Tools used in big data analytics.

Apart of Hadoop, variety of various systems and equipment are used in massive facts analytics in medical care data. Among them, the ones which can be regularly used are in brief added below:

- *Social Media:* Social communication data from various social websites like face books, Twitter and LinkedIn, various informative blogs. It includes health plans websites.
- *M2M data:* Machine to machine Data from meters, remote sensors and other vital signal devices.
- *Big Data Transaction:* Structured and Unstructured formats of healthcare claims are increasingly available [22].
- *Biometric Data:* Pulse reading, X-ray images, finger prints, blood pressure reports, and all the required information are accessible in "crude" configuration and wish to be advanced or changed, at which point different choices are promptly accessible.
- *MapReduce:* MapReduce is a very important part of the Apache Hadoop software programme framework. It plays two crucial roles: mapper and reducer. In its primary role, it filters and parcels workouts

to different nodes within the cluster or map, and its secondary role is to systematize and decrease the effects of every node in a steady solution to a query.

- *Oozie:* To handle Hadoop jobs, Apache Oozie is a server based workflow scheduling system that is defined as a set of manipulable glide and movement nodes in a directed acyclic graph. The primary gain of Oozie is its capability to release workflows as a way to develop because the cluster grows [23].
- *HBase:* HBase is an open-source, non relational, dispensed database model. This may be described as a column-orientated database control machine that sits on top of HDFS and makes use of a non-SQL approach. One of the prime advantages is its linear and modular scalability. One major disadvantage of HBase is the lack of exception management.
- *Avro:* Avro facilitates data series services, versioning, and version control, a few extra capabilities and features. The best advantage to using Avro is its smallest size. "Avro works with the trading of large amounts of information between programmes written in any language. With the serialisation administration, projects can proficiently serialize information into documents or into messages." The information stockpile is smaller and more productive. Avro stores both the information definition and the information together in one message or record. Its disadvantages consist of being a sort of schema-based device and requiring a schema for reading and writing information [24].
- *Mahout:* Mahout is a venture that forgiving the coder a ready-to-use structure for doing fact-mining jobs on huge volumes of facts. Mahout shall we programmes to investigate large amounts of data correctly and quickly.
- *Apache Zookeeper:* It is an open-access source project under the mentorship of the Apache Software Foundation. Zookeeper offers a centralized delivery service to maintain and configure information, provide a set of services, and supply disbursed synchronization. Synchronization provides a bunch of servers that are used by data analytics to manage parallel processes across big clusters. High scalability is its main objective, and the biggest disadvantage is the limited support of cross-clusters.

- *Apache Cassandra:* It is an open source database trusted by hundreds of agencies for scalability and high availability performance without any compromise for better efficiency. Its cloud infrastructure makes it an appropriate platform for mission-vital data.

Advantages of Big Data in the Healthcare Sector

Higher Quality Care

Since big data draws from different sources, including past trained professional and pharmacy visits, electronic media, and other outer sources, it can create a more complete picture of a patient. Using standard graphs filled by labourers with clinical record planning on the web, experts just moved toward a confined proportion of patient information, similar to several diagrams and some near and dear information. With the gigantic proportion of data now open, clinical consideration providers can see what really makes an individual tick and use that information to give better quality thought. If a patient loves to go skiing, as shown on her online media accounts, an expert can connect with her over that or use that information to recognise what could be causing a redundant leg issue. Similarly, an expert may have the choice to see covered up explanations behind a clinical issue that wouldn't be made clear with basic prosperity information [33].

Early Intervention

The overall goal of tremendous data in clinical benefits is to use perceptive examination to find and resolve clinical issues before they become greater issues. Colossal data absolutely increases the capability of the entire communication.

For example, a patient who is seeing an expert about endeavouring to shed pounds could be prescribed medicine to address raised cholesterol. If that patient posts by means of online media about changes in their everyday presence that cause pressure, the huge data computation could analyse that information and pennant the patient as being at risk of a respiratory disappointment. The expert would then have the option of changing the treatment to reduce the risk of a coronary event, effectively killing the problem before it became dangerous [18]. Giant data can also be linked to DNA records to determine whether a patient is at risk of a disease that runs in their family line.

Fraud Detection

Deception, or patients submitting sham cases to be paid, is a causing issue in the clinical consideration and security spaces [33]."Colossal data is useful in combating this since it can get to a massive proportion of data to find inconsistencies in submitted cases and flag possibly bogus cases for extra thought. Using its undeniable level of estimations, tremendous data can channel through a large number of reports to find bungles considerably more quickly than any gathering of individuals could. Government health care coverage has saved more than $1 billion over the last two years by using gigantic data to check patient cases."

Predictive Analytics in Healthcare

Everyone is a patient at one time or the other and all need extraordinary clinical thought. We acknowledge experts are clinically trained professionals and what they decide for us is ideal. Yet have you ever figured out how inconvenient it would have been for them to examine the patient's entire history and make fitting decisions for their meds? Judicious examination prompts the patient's prosperity and quality of thought. It keeps experts informed about the patient's clinical annals and predicts results for the future [12].

For example, the examination devices would have the choice to expect which patient is at risk for what disease, so to make decisions in a like manner to chip away at lenient prosperity. Farsighted computations using particular programming lingo can be made to expect the prosperity of a patient as time goes on. Optum Labs gathered data from more than 30 million patients to make an informational index for farsighted assessment gadgets that will additionally foster clinical consideration structures, according to a US study shared.

Big Data Can Help Cure Cancer

"Threatening developments" are flighty ailments where, for example, a lone tumour can have billions of cells. Hearing this, we feel that it might be cared for best at clinical facilities and not in PC rooms. Clinical experts can now use data examination to see the recovery speeds of harmful developments in patients, which specific therapy to use, and the best drugs that will have the highest rates of treatment for that particular ailment. To make this successful, patient's data bases from different prosperity associations ought to be linked up to recall patient's data. For example, a patient's tumour tests can be broken down with their other treatment records, which, accordingly will help experts with passing on the treatment in a similar way. Finding such examples will likely produce better results. This approach isn't just limited to serious health threats, it can be used for various other diseases as well. This is another example in which tremendous data assessment is influencing clinical consideration. With the usage of state-of-the-art tremendous data examination, clinical consideration providers can help with chipping away at open minded outcomes, while cutting down costs at the same time. On the off chance that you are a startup aficionado in this space, these are some middle areas where new organizations can be publicised [25].

Challenges for Applying Big Data in Healthcare

As an example, compared to various ventures, the slow rhythm of advancement shows requesting circumstances which may be exact to wellness care in forcing and applying "monstrous realities" devices. To address these constraints, various policies for introducing data analytics must be developed. Prosperity structures today make use of stacks of data from different sources, for instance, research focus tests, clinical notes, patient reports, etc. The authentic test is the best approach to assemble, take apart, and direct such monstrous information to predict the outcomes and make likely decisions. "Clinical data today is spread across different sources addressed by different clinical centres and divisions; consequently, there is a necessity for the improvement of new establishments that can join all of the data from such sources" [26].

Privacy

Likely the most grounded negative aspect related to enormous data is the shortfall in security, especially concerning in-depth clinical records. To be effective and get the broad understanding of a patient, gigantic data should be moved to encompass everything, including private records and online media posts. As demonstrated by various tremendous data-trained professionals, though, this advancement comprises absolute security of a patient's private information. Since this method, in essence, will allow experts to screen a patient's information from essentially wherever, it leaves their records at constant risk. Despite the there being existing laws related to the security of clinical records, most of those laws don't hold any critical bearing on huge data sharing. Various subject matter experts and clinical consideration providers acknowledge that overhauls to the current security rules are relied upon to guarantee patients' safety while at this point outfitting agents with enough data to make a fruitful assessment.

Replacing Doctors

While a couple of gatherings see the ability to predict future clinical issues as certain, the vast majority of data similarly addresses the risk of overriding trained professionals. Huge data basically isn't at the point yet where it will be used exclusively, and it unquestionably misses the mark on the individual piece of a human trained professional. A couple of experts fear that the advancement of immense data may really disrupt trained professionals and leave patients going to development for answers rather than using an approved trained professional. There's no avoiding the enormous data on clinical benefits, especially as more associations and providers develop their inclinations nearby. Regardless, as technology advances, the drawbacks must be considered in order to create a capable and acceptable experience for patients and subject matter experts.

Ethical and Legal Issues

The utilisation of data in medical services presents a new upright and lawful impediment in light of the non-public nature of the records encased. Moral and lawful issues comprise the opportunity to think twice about, private independence, notwithstanding results on open call for straightforwardness, acceptance, and value while utilising big data [21].

Lack of Infrastructure

The absence of appropriate foundations for information storage emerged as a critical specialised and infrastructural issue that could jeopardise Big-Data-driven medical care. Another issue in a massive information investigation is the heterogeneity of realities. The enormous length and particularly heterogeneous nature of enormous realities in medical care makes it extraordinarily, significantly less useful by utilising conventional innovation. Typically, select clinical focuses (clinics, drug stores, and individual facilities) use an elite programming system and reality sheet that makes information correlation, examination, movement, and sharing extremely difficult.

Future for Big Data in Healthcare

Nowadays, various biomedical and medical services and hardware, such as genomics, cell biometric sensors, and phone applications, generate massive amounts of data. For example, the assessment of such data can offer further experience in procedural, clinical, specialized, and various types of improvements in medical care. After a profound assessment of those medical service methodologies, it appears that the all-out ability of patient-specific clinical uniqueness or customised therapy is in progress. The aggregated, gigantic data assessment of EHRs, EMRs, and distinctive clinical data is continually helping build a higher prognostic structure in the medical services industry. The businesses that provide transporters for medical care examinations and clinical changes are bringing us closer to a better and more amazing outcome. Normal goals for those organizations include lowering the cost of research, creating incredible Clinical Decision Support (CDS) structures, granting frameworks for higher cure strategies, and sorting out and preventing misrepresentation associated with massive data sets. However, almost all of them are confronting testing circumstances involving government inconveniences like how non-public data is dealt with, shared, and put away protected.

The mixed pools of data from medical care organizations and biomedical specialists have resulted in a higher standpoint, assurance, and cure of various sicknesses. This has also helped in developing a higher and better customised medical care structure [22]. Present day medical services brotherhood has discovered the capacity of monstrous data and thus has applied huge data investigation in medical care and clinical practices. These days, everything from supercomputers to quantum PC frameworks is helping with extricating critical realities from gigantic data sets in drastically diminished timeframes. Analysts are diving into biomedical monster data rather than its difficulties, with excessive expectations of separating new information that may improve the common distinction of medical care administrations. The shift to fused data and environmental factors is a renowned obstacle to survival. Adequately intriguing, the idea of huge data sets depends intently on having more current realities. The additional experiences one can take from these realities might set expectations for forthcoming occasions. It is legitimately projected, through various reliable counselling partnerships and wellness care enterprises that the gigantic data medical services commercial centre is ready to be created at a dramatic rate [24].

In any case, we have seen a variety of examinations used in a short period of time that have demonstrated impressive effects in decision making and general medical care industry execution. The dramatic blast of clinical data from various areas has constrained computational experts to design progressive methodologies to research and decipher such a goliath amount of data in a given time period. The coordination of computational designs for sign preparing from each examination and clinical experts has been hit by a blast. The high amount of clinical data accumulated all through heterogeneous frameworks has set a task for data researchers for wary joining and execution. As a result, it is proposed that insurgency in medical care is also required to support all things considered bioinformatics, wellness informatics, and research in order to sell customised and incredible therapies [27]. Besides, new procedures and innovation should be implemented to perceive the construction of information, intricacy (measurements and quality), and amount of data to infer huge realities. The best possibility of monstrous data lies in its endless potential outcomes. Transmission and integration of colossal data from clinical tests into a sedate bundle for perplexing human ailments, including most malignant growths and neuro messes, we agree that massive data will supplement and support the overall pipeline of medical services, rather than replace skilled labor, issue skill experts, and learned people.

Conclusion

Clinical assessment that consolidates big data will contribute to a more critical degree of human prosperity at a broader and more significant level. This section primarily presents the associated concepts of clinical big data, the establishment, and the major applications, as well as familiarizes with a couple of key clinical big data advancements. Prosperity data is fundamental for the improvement of clinical benefits at the global, regional, neighborhood, institutional, and particular patient level. While this is correct, it should be noted that the quality and exactness of the information conveyed by health information will have a significant impact on the nature of care and the effect of bits of knowledge conveyed by health information. Past digitization, the maximum capacity of this information has yet to be acknowledged in business. In addition, we summarise and think about the odds and hardships associated with the examination of immense clinical data. When in doubt, the rhythmic movement research on clinical data isn't yet capable; there are various issues that ought to be settled. To abuse the critical models contained in the gigantic data sets, big data accumulation, mining, assessment, and related capacity are principal. These advancements and capabilities will support research on the clinical benefits of big data and will further serve a wide range of clinical applications such as general wellbeing, clinical thought, and clinical security, among others.

References

[1] Abenstein, J. P., & Tompkins, W. J. (1982). A new data-reduction algorithm for real-time ECG analysis. *IEEE Transactions on Biomedical Engineering,* 29(1), 43–48.

[2] Abernethy, A. P., Wheeler, J. L., & Bull, J. (2011). Development of a health information technology-based data system in community-based hospice and palliative care. *American Journal of Preventive Medicine,* 40(5, Suppl 2), S217–S224.

[3] Agrawal, R., Imieliński, T., & Swami, A. (1993, May). Mining association rules between sets of items in large databases. In B. Peter, & J. Sunshil(Eds.), *Proceeding of the ACM SIGMOD Conference on Management of Data*(pp.207-216).

[4] Alyass, A., Turcotte, M., &Meyre, D. (2015). From big data analysis to personalized medicine for all: Challenges and opportunities. *BMC Medical Genomics,* 8(1), 33.

[5] Anderson, J. E., & Chang, D. C. (2015). Using electronic health records for surgical quality improvement in the era of big data. *Jama Surgery,* 150(1), 24-29.

[6] Antonie, M. L., Zaïane, O. R., & Coman, A. (2001). Application of data mining techniques for medical image classification. *Proceedings of the Second International Conference on Multimedia Data Mining,* 94-101. doi:10.1.1.23.9742

[7] Asante-Korang, A., & Jacobs, J. P. (2016). Big Data and paediatric cardiovascular disease in the era of transparency in healthcare. *Cardiology in the Young,* 26(8), 1597–1602.

[8] Asri, H., Mousannif, H., Al Moatassime, H., & Noel, T. (2015, June). Big data in healthcare: challenges and opportunities. *Proceedings of 2015 International Conference on Cloud Computing Technologies and Applications*, Marrakech, Morocco.

[9] Augustine, D. P. (2014). Leveraging big data analytics and Hadoop in developing India's healthcare services. *International Journal of Computers and Applications,* 89(16), 44–50.

[10] Austin, C., & Kusumoto, F. (2016). The application of Big Data in medicine: current implications and future directions. *Journal of Interventional Cardiac Electrophysiology,* 47(1), 51-59.

[11] Azar, A. T., &Hassanien, A. E. (2015). Dimensionality reduction of medical big data using neural-fuzzy classifier. *Soft Computing,* 19(4), 1115–1127.

[12] Backonja, U., Kim, K., Casper, G. R., Patton, T., Ramly, E., & Brennan, P. F. (2012, June). Observations of daily living: putting the "personal" in personal health records. *NI 2012: 11th International Congress on Nursing Informatics,* Montreal, Canada.

[13] Bagayoko, C. O., Dufour, J. C., Chaacho, S., Bouhaddou, O., &Fieschi, M. (2010). Open source challenges for hospital information system (HIS) in developing countries: A pilot project in Mali. *BMC Medical Informatics and Decision Making,* 10(22), 1-13.

[14] Bates, D. W., Saria, S., Ohno-Machado, L., Shah, A., & Escobar, G. (2014). Big data in health care: using analytics to identify and manage high-risk and high-cost patients. *Health Affairs,* 33(7), 1123-1131.

[15] Galetsi, P., &Katsaliaki, K. (2020). A review of the literature on big data analytics in healthcare. *Journal of the Operational Research Society,* 71(10), 1511-1529.

[16] Gubbi, J., Buyya, R., Marusic, S., &Palaniswami, M. (2013). Internet of Things (IoT): A vision, architectural elements, and future directions. *Future Generation Computer Systems,* 29(7), 1645-1660.

[17] Jacofsky, D. J. (2017). The myths of 'big data' in health care. *The Bone & Joint Journal,* 99(12), 1571-1576.

[18] Kamble, S. S., Gunasekaran, A., Goswami, M., & Manda, J. (2018). A systematic perspective on the applications of big data analytics in healthcare management. *International Journal of Healthcare Management.*

[19] Kumar, S., & Singh, M. (2018). Big data analytics for healthcare industry: impact, applications, and tools. *Big Data Mining and Analytics,* 2(1), 48-57.

[20] Mallikarjuna, B. (2020c). Feedback-based resource utilization for smart home automation in fog assistance IoT-based cloud. *International Journal of Fog Computing* (IJFC), 3(1), 41-63.

[21] Mallikarjuna, B., Addanke, S., & Anusha, D. J. (2022a). An improved deep learning algorithm for diabetes prediction. In *Handbook of Research on Advances in Data Analytics and Complex Communication Networks* (pp. 103-119). IGI Global.

[22] Mallikarjuna, B., Addanke, S., & Sabharwal, M. (2022c). An improved model for house price/land price prediction using deep learning. In *Handbook of Research on Advances in Data Analytics and Complex Communication Networks* (pp. 76-87). IGI Global.

[23] Mallikarjuna, B., Anusha, D. J., & Sabharwal, M. (2022b). An effective video surveillance system by using CNN for COVID-19. In *Handbook of Research on Advances in Data Analytics and Complex Communication Networks* (pp. 88-102). IGI Global.

[24] Mallikarjuna, B., Kiranmayee, D., Saritha, V., & Krishna, P. V. (2021b, June). Development of efficient E-health records using IoT and Blockchain technology. In *ICC 2021-IEEE International Conference on Communications* (pp. 1-7). IEEE.

[25] Mallikarjuna, B., Sathish, K., Krishna, P. V., & Viswanathan, R. (2020a). The effective SVM-based binary prediction of ground water table. *Evolutionary Intelligence*, 1-9.

[26] Mallikarjuna, B., Shrivastava, G., & Sharma, M. (2021a). Blockchain technology: A DNN token-based approach in healthcare and COVID-19 to generate extracted data. *Expert Systems,* e12778.

[27] McAfee, A., Brynjolfsson, E., Davenport, T. H., Patil, D. J., & Barton, D. (2012). Big data: the management revolution. *Harvard Business Review,* 90(10), 60-68.

[28] Raghupathi, W., &Raghupathi, V. (2014). Big data analytics in healthcare: promise and potential. *Health Information Science and Systems,* 2(1), 1-10.

[29] Razzak, M. I., Naz, S., & Zaib, A. (2018). Deep learning for medical image processing: Overview, challenges and the future. *Classification in BioApps,* 323-350.

[30] Reisman, M. (2017). EHRs: the challenge of making electronic data usable and interoperable. *Pharmacy and Therapeutics,* 42(9), 572.

[31] Tsai, C. W., Lai, C. F., Chao, H. C., & Vasilakos, A. V. (2015). Big data analytics: a survey. *Journal of Big Data,* 2(1), 1-32.

[32] Vayena, E., Dzenowagis, J., Brownstein, J. S., & Sheikh, A. (2018). Policy implications of big data in the health sector. *Bulletin of the World Health Organization,* 96(1), 66.

[33] Ward, M. J., Marsolo, K. A., & Froehle, C. M. (2014). Applications of business analytics in healthcare. *Business Horizons*, 57(5), 571-582.

About the Editors

Dr. Basetty Mallikarjuna

Dr. Basetty Mallikarjuna currently works at the School of Computing Science & Engineering at Galgotias University in Uttar Pradesh, India. He obtained his Ph.D degree from Bharathiar University in the year 2018, a Mater Engineering Degree at VIT University in 2009, and received a Bachelor of Technology in Computer Science and Engineering from JNTU University Hyderabad in 2006. He is the program chairman at B.Tech CSE-IBM in the School of Computer Science & Engineering.

With nineteen years of professional experience, Dr. Mallikarjuna has published over 60 research papers in various national and international conferences, and well-reputed international journals He is a member of several societies such as IEEE, IEI, ISTE, and CSI. Dr. Mallikarjuna's research areas focus on cloud computing, Internet of Things, green computing, Blockchain and health care applications.

For more information:
https://vidwan.inflibnet.ac.in/profile/214080
https://scholar.google.co.in/citations?user=mTRZix0AAAAJ&hl=en
https://publons.com/researcher/2062077/basetty-mallikarjuna/

Dr. Niranjanamurthy M

Dr. Niranjanamurthy M is an Assistant Professor(S) in the Department of Computer Applications at M S Ramaiah Institute of Technology in Bangalore, Karnataka. His degrees include a Ph.D. in Computer Science (2016), MPhil-Computer Science (2009), a Masters in Computer Applications from Visvesvaraiah Technological University (2007), and a BCA from Kuvempu University in 2004, ranking 5th in the university. He has 12 years of teaching experience and 2 years of industry experience as a software engineer.

Dr. Niranjanamurthy M published 15 books with international publishers like Scholars Press (Germany), CRC Press (USA), WILEY-SP (USA), Springer, (Netherland), DE Gruyter (Germany). He was a series editor in Taylor and Francis (USA), Nova Science Publishers (USA) and Wiley-SP (USA). Dr. Niranjanamurthy M has published over 80 research papers in various national and international conferences and reputed international journals. He filed 25 patents and had 5 granted. Currently, he is guiding four Ph.D. research scholars in the area of Data Science, Edge Computing, ML, and Networking. Dr. Niranjanamurthy M is working as a reviewer in 22 international journals. His awards include Best Research Journal Reviewer (twice received), the Young Researcher Award in Computer Science Engineering (2018, 2019, 2020, 2021), the Patent Award from KSCST Karnataka in 2021, and was listed in AD World Scientist and University Rankings in 2021 and 2022. Dr. Niranjanamurthy M worked as a national/international Ph.D. examiner. He has conducted various national level workshops and lectures, technical talks, and conducted national and international conferences.

Dr. Niranjanamurthy M is a member of various societies such as IAENG, IEEE, and INSC, among others. He is an advisory board member of the industries Deepiotics Indore Madya Pradesh and MN Envirotech Bangalore. His area of interests include data science, ML, augmented and virtual reality, edge computing, e-Commerce and m-Commerce related to industry internal tool enhancement, software testing, software engineering, web services, cloud computing, and Google Scholar.

For more information:
https://scholar.google.co.in/citations?user=NnIivp8AAAAJ&hl=en
https://www.amazon.in/s?i=stripbooks&rh=p_27%3AM.+Niranjanamurthy&ref=dp_byline_sr_book_1

Dr. Sheng-Lung Peng

Dr. Sheng-Lung Peng PhD is a professor in the Department of Creative Technologies and Product Design at the National Taipei University of Business in Taipei City, Taiwan. He received a Doctor of Philosophy in Computer Science from National Tsing Hua University in 1999. His Doctoral Thesis was entitled, "A Study of Graph Searching on Special Graphs" and his advisors were Chuan Yi Tang and Ming-Tat Ko. Dr. Peng received a Master of Science in Computer Science and Information Engineering from National ChungCheng University in 1992. His Master's Thesis was entitled, "Efficient Algorithms for Domatic Partition Problem on Interval Graphs and their Extensions." Dr. Peng earned his Bachelor of Science degree in Mathematics from the National Tsing Hua University in 1988. Dr. Peng has published more than 100 research articles and over 35 books.

For more information:
https://ntub.academia.edu/ShengLungPeng
https://dblp.org/pid/30/1658.html
https://www.researchgate.net/profile/Sheng-Lung-Peng
https://ntub.academia.edu/ShengLungPeng/CurriculumVitae
https://publons.com/researcher/1415597/sheng-lung-peng/

Mrs. Amulya M P

Amulya M P, (Ph.D – Computer Science and Engineering) received her Master's degree in Computer Science and Engineering from PES College of Engineering (Affilated with the Visvesvaraiah Technological University in Karnataka), in Mandya in 2014. She received her Bachelors of Engineering degree in Computer Science and Engineering from the BGS Institute of Technology, Mandya in the year 2012.

Presently, Mrs. Amulya M P is working as an Assistant Professor in the Department of Computer Science and Engineering in the BGS Institute of Technology and has published many articles in national and international journals. She has filed 3 patents in the area of computer science and applications. Mrs. Amulya M P is an editor for Wiley-SP in the USA. She's a member of various societies such as IAENG, IEEE, ISTE, CSTA, among others. Her area of interests include distributed computing, data science, big data, cloud computing, and Blockchain technology.

For more information:
https://acu.irins.org/profile/119708
https://www.scopus.com/authid/detail.uri?authorId=57210603109

Index